Freedom Is Not Enough

FREEDOM
IS NOT ENOUGH

The MOYNIHAN REPORT and
AMERICA'S STRUGGLE over BLACK
FAMILY LIFE—from LBJ to OBAMA

JAMES T. PATTERSON

BASIC
BOOKS

A MEMBER OF THE PERSEUS BOOKS GROUP
New York

Books published by Basic Books are available at special discounts for bulk purchases in
the United States by corporations, institutions, and other organizations. For more
information, please contact the Special Markets Department at the Perseus Books Group,
2300 Chestnut Street, Suite 200, Philadelphia, PA 19103, or call (800) 810-4145, ext. 5000,
or e-mail special.markets@perseusbooks.com.

Designed by Timm Bryson

Library of Congress Cataloging-in-Publication Data
Patterson, James T.
   Freedom is not enough : the Moynihan report and America's struggle over black
family life—from LBJ to Obama / James T. Patterson.
      p. cm.
   Includes index.
   ISBN 978–0-465–01357–9 (alk. paper)
   1. Moynihan, Daniel P. (Daniel Patrick), 1927–2003—Political and social views. 2.
African American poor families—Government policy. 3. African American families—
Social conditions—20th century. 4. United States—Social conditions—20th century. I.
Title.
   E185.86.P33 2010
   305.896'073—dc22
   2009047048

10 9 8 7 6 5 4 3 2

To Gareth Davies, Steve Gillon, and John Dittmer,
good friends and fine historians

CONTENTS

Preface: "To Fulfill These Rights," Spring 1965   ix

ONE The Pluck of the Irish   1

TWO The Case for National Action   21

THREE The Report   47

FOUR "The Moment Lost"   65

FIVE Families, Welfare, and Race, 1966–1968   87

SIX Moynihan, Nixon, and the Family Assistance Plan   109

SEVEN Unproductive Dialogue, 1971–1983   129

EIGHT Combating the Silence, 1984–1994   145

NINE Welfare Reform, Slavery, and Jeremiads   167

TEN Families in the Early 2000s   187

ELEVEN From Cosby to Obama   203

Acknowledgments 217

A Note on the Sources 219

Notes 225

Index 241

PREFACE

"To Fulfill These Rights," Spring 1965

On June 4, 1965, President Lyndon B. Johnson delivered a commencement address at Howard University in which he outlined to a throng of some 5,000 people the most far-reaching civil rights agenda in modern U.S. history. Pointing proudly to recent legislation, notably to the historic act of 1964 that attacked racial segregation and discrimination and to a voting rights bill then moving successfully through Congress, he hailed the freedom these historic measures would guarantee black people in the United States.

But "freedom," the president insisted, "is not enough." Federal protections of legal and civil rights were only a first step toward ensuring equal justice for blacks:

> You do not wipe away the scars of centuries by saying: Now you are free to go where you want, do as you desire, and choose the leaders you please. You do not take a person who, for years, has been hobbled by chains and liberate him, bring him up to the starting line of a race and then say, "You are free to compete with all the others," and still justly believe that you have been completely fair.
>
> Thus it is not enough just to open the gates of opportunity. All our citizens must have the ability to walk through those gates.
>
> This is the next and more profound stage of the battle for civil rights. We seek not just freedom but opportunity—not just legal equity but human ability—not just equality as a right and a theory but equality as a fact and as a result.

Johnson then turned to the serious racial problems at hand. After hailing the impressive achievements of middle-class black Americans, he dwelt at length on the social and economic ills—"deep, corrosive, obstinate"—that afflicted what he called "the great majority." Blacks were still "another nation," a people damaged by a "cultural tradition" that had been "twisted and battered by endless years of hatred and hopelessness." "Perhaps most important," the president emphasized, is the "breakdown of the Negro family structure" that flowed from "centuries of oppression and persecution of the Negro man." The family, he exclaimed, "is the cornerstone of our society. More than any other force it shapes the attitudes, the hopes, the ambitions, and the values of the child. When the family collapses it is the children that are usually damaged. When it happens on a massive scale the community itself is crippled."[1]

What was to be done? Anxious to take charge of the civil rights movement, Johnson called for what in effect was affirmative action, to be secured via large-scale socioeconomic programs. A chief goal of his administration, he promised, was to fight for policies to improve black employment, health care, housing, education, and for "social programs better designed to hold families together." He closed by saying that he would convene a White House conference in the fall featuring "scholars, and experts, and outstanding Negro leaders—men of both races—and officials of government at every level." The theme and title of the conference would be "To Fulfill These Rights."

Some reporters who commented on the president's thirty-minute speech wondered if policymakers could devise the programs—or secure the funds—to wage the massively complex and expensive struggle required to promote equality of results. Johnson's escalation of the war in Vietnam, they added, threatened to divide the nation and swallow up funding for domestic programs. Conservatives, however, posed the largest obstacles to enactment of Johnson's goals. Any major governmental effort to combat poverty and the related behavioral ills of black Americans, they believed, would mire Washington in a costly and futile effort to change the culture of "undeserving" people. Then and later, many conservatives would fight hard against ambitious liberal economic programs that claimed to attack the deeply set family problems of lower-class black Americans.

Johnson's listeners, however, responded jubilantly to his remarks, swarming about him (and alarming Secret Service men) to shake his hand after he finished. Liberals, delighted that he planned to address racial tensions in the North as well as in the South, hailed his egalitarian message. Civil rights leaders, including A. Philip Randolph, head of the Brotherhood of Sleeping Car Porters, and Whitney Young, head of the National Urban League, telegraphed their congratulations. Martin Luther King Jr. declared, "Never before has a president articulated the depths and dimensions [of the problems] more eloquently and profoundly." Johnson himself later said—and rightly so—that this was the greatest civil rights speech he had ever given.

There was ample reason for high hopes, because liberalism was cresting at an extraordinarily high tide in early 1965. After winning the presidential election of 1964 with what remains the highest percentage of popular votes (61.1) in modern U.S. history, Johnson understandably believed the people had given him a mandate for change. "Hell," he had exclaimed, "we're the richest country in the world, the most powerful. We can do it all!" Lighting the White House Christmas tree in December, he announced, "These are the most hopeful times since Christ was born."

LBJ's optimism was infectious at the time. *Time* magazine, naming him Man of the Year for 1964, predicted in January 1965 that the United States, which was enjoying great prosperity, was "On the Fringe of a Golden Era." Polls showed that Americans were developing grand expectations about the capacity of government to promote progress. The civil rights movement, though exhibiting signs of division, climbed to the peak of its inspirational power during demonstrations for voting rights in Selma, Alabama. When white authorities reacted with violence in Selma, LBJ gave a prime-time, televised speech to Congress in March that he closed by emphasizing, "And . . . we . . . shall . . . overcome."

Taking full advantage of these propitious times, LBJ was relentless as well as brilliant in driving Democratic majorities on Capitol Hill toward enactment of his highly ambitious Great Society agenda. By June 1965, Congress had passed the Elementary and Secondary Education Act, which for the first time in U.S. history provided substantial federal funding for public schooling. Its key provision, calling for compensatory education, was the core of his broader War on Poverty, which had been set into motion in 1964. Congress was also well on its way that June toward enacting other liberal landmarks, such as the voting rights bill and Medicare and Medicaid. By October, Congress had approved an enormous bundle of liberal legislation, including long-overdue reform of discriminatory immigration law, additional funding for the War on Poverty, a higher education act, clean air and water acts, establishment of the Department of Housing and Urban Development, and creation of the National Endowment for the Arts and the National Endowment for the Humanities. No Congress in modern U.S. history has been more productive.

Neither then nor in later years, however, did the United States come close to securing the egalitarian racial goals Johnson outlined in his speech at Howard. A consequential source of this failure, which had become painfully obvious by late 1965, was clear: the tortuous trail of misunderstandings, misrepresentations, and destructive controversies that followed release that summer of the so-called Moynihan Report. Titled *The Negro Family: The Case for National Action*, the seventy-eight-page report, which painted a dismal portrait of lower-class black family life in the inner cities, rested in part on research and statistics compiled by the Policy Planning and Research staff of the U.S. Department of Labor. Its author was Daniel Patrick "Pat" Moynihan, a thirty-eight-year-old politician-academic who initiated the research and who completed the report in March 1965—three months before Johnson's address at Howard—while serving as an assistant secretary of labor.

Moynihan was a liberal, and he aimed his report at top administration officials in the hope that they would thereby understand the most powerful forces—especially unemployment and poverty—devastating many lower-class black families. Unlike the Howard address, which was couched in moral language, the report was cool in tone. It was diagnostic, not prescriptive, and it offered no specific policy recommendations. Still, *The Negro Family* obviously aimed to start a serious conversation among policymakers and to prod government officials into devising far-reaching socioeconomic reforms. Moynihan, moreover, was a gregarious, ambitious, and persistent fellow who had crafted good connections with influential presidential aides.

He also had a talent for dramatic phrasemaking that caught the eyes of readers. Secretary of Labor W. Willard Wirtz, forwarding a summary of the report to the president in May, described an accompanying Moynihan memo as "nine pages of dynamite about the Negro situation." Excited White House officials said to Moynihan, "Pat, I think you've got it." Johnson, apprised of the report, then asked Moynihan to help draft his speech at Howard University. After completing a draft on June 1, Moynihan and presidential speechwriter Richard Goodwin worked into the early morning hours of June 4 to put together a finished version.[2]

This is how the woes of lower-class, inner-city black families, then and later a key concern of Moynihan's, found a prominent place in Johnson's widely hailed address about the "next and more profound stage of the battle for civil rights" in the United States.

In his speech, Johnson did not mention Moynihan. Indeed, only a few government officials had then seen the report, which had been written and printed as an in-house document, not as a manifesto for public consumption. Nowhere did it identify the name of its author. The report soon leaked, however, and news stories about it (and its author) began appearing in mid-July, whereupon it became known as the Moynihan Report. The White House then arranged for copies to be printed so that they might be ready for sale in mid-August.

Before the report was released publicly, however, the most fearsome urban violence in U.S. history broke out in the predominantly black area of Watts in Los Angeles. Starting on August 11, it lasted five days before the National Guard restored order. Thirty-four people were killed, and more than 1,000 were injured. It was a disaster for the morally powerful, interracial, nonviolent civil rights movement King and many others had succeeded in shaping into a luminous force for racial justice. Many white Americans, appalled by the rioting, began to reconsider their views of black people—not as cruelly segregated, long-suffering southerners, but as violent, out-of-control ghetto dwellers, many of whom lived in the North. Johnson despaired, "I'm giving them boom times and more good legislation than anyone else did, and what do they do—attack and sneer. Could FDR do better? Could anybody do better? What do they want?"

The Watts Riot, which surprised many civil rights leaders as well as Johnson, led reporters and others to scramble in search of the key sources of black urban unrest. In the process, they rushed to get their hands on copies of the Moynihan Report, which news accounts—hyping its influence within the government—often referred to as secret. As of early September, by which time the report had been released on request, stories about it began to proliferate, and demand for it exploded.[3] Some of these stories correctly connected the report to Johnson's subsequent speech at Howard, but others (including many that depended upon media accounts, not on the report itself) concluded inaccurately that it represented the administration's explanation for the breakdown of order in Los Angeles.

Further misunderstandings and misrepresentations ensued. Although some of these early stories reported correctly that the Moynihan Report pointed to the rise of a black middle class, others insinuated that its author had lumped all black families together, thereby leaving the impression that all were badly damaged. A number of stories also recognized that Moynihan, a committed liberal, had identified white racism and high unemployment rates as the primary sources of the instability of lower-class black families; the causes of their plight, he emphasized, were primarily economic, not cultural, in nature. But many other news stories and commentators zeroed in on boldfaced headlines and passages in his report that painted a devastating portrait of family disorganization. Moynihan dwelt on statistics—the report featured a great many graphs and tables—showing "startling increases in welfare dependency," "matriarchy," and "illegitimacy ratios" among blacks. These ratios, he wrote, were eight times higher than among whites. Fond of dramatic language, he wrote that lower-class black families were caught in a "tangle of pathology" that had its roots in North American slavery and that had perhaps "begun to feed on itself." Passages such as these, framing highly sensitive issues in near-apocalyptic terms, seemed to suggest that deep-seated historical forces had all but irreparably savaged black culture.

As it happened, Moynihan had resigned from government service in July to run in the Democratic primary for the presidency of the City Council of New York. But as of September, his identity as author of the report having been exposed, he was facing increasingly irate criticisms from militant civil rights leaders, many of whom had been shaken by Watts and were beginning to adopt what later became known as Black Power strategies of protest. A number of women, too, resented his not altogether flattering descriptions of black "matriarchy." Stung by Moynihan's grim portrait, angry African American spokespeople charged that he had smeared black culture and "blamed the victim." As Christopher Foreman, a professor of social policy, later lamented, these leaders were in no mood to "hear some Irishman's embarrassing prattle about 'Negro family structure,' however plainly sympathetic and data laden."

In December, James Farmer, head of the Congress of Racial Equality (CORE), denounced the report as a "massive cop-out for the white conscience." He added, "We are sick unto death of being analyzed, mesmerized, bought, sold, and slobbered over, while the same evils that are the ingredients of our oppression go unattended."[4]

So it was that during the summer and fall of 1965, a pivotal time in modern U.S. political history, the exuberant liberal mood of the spring dissipated. The civil rights movement, which had been so inspiring during the struggles in Selma, was breaking apart. Johnson, shaken by the rioting, was disengaging from his egalitarian call at Howard. And events abroad were absorbing the president's attention. On June 7, only three days after his speech at Howard, he had received a cable from General William Westmoreland, his commander in Vietnam, calling for massive military escalation. Johnson publicly announced a policy of escalation in late July. Thereafter, there was no turning back. As casualties began to soar, antiwar protests mounted. Polls revealed that Americans were losing faith in their government. Liberalism, so strong in the spring, fell on the defensive, never again in the twentieth century to regain the political power it had enjoyed in early 1965. As Moynihan later pointed out, LBJ's address at Howard was his "last peacetime speech."

For these reasons, and to distance himself from the hail of criticism battering *The Negro Family*, LBJ downsized his promised White House conference to a planning session that finally took place in November. Deliberately underplaying the importance of sensitive family issues, the session accomplished nothing. And Moynihan, a messenger of inconvenient tidings, remained a very large target of criticism. Then and forever after, in an otherwise successful and visible career as an author, professor at Harvard, high-level official in the Nixon and Ford administrations, and (starting in 1977) four-term Democratic senator from New York, the most celebrated intellectual in U.S. politics had to dodge negative fallout from his report.

Later chapters of this book follow Moynihan's ideological odyssey as he continued to promote public interest in helping solve lower-class black family problems. His thinking culminated in social welfare legislation as well as in eighteen books, many of which offer shrewd and provocative commentary about the relationship between scholarship and public policy, and about the forces that have helped to revolutionize family life in the United States—and many other industrialized nations—since 1965. Until relatively recently, however, many liberals and civil rights leaders, fearing to be attacked as he had been, continued to avoid talking about many black family issues. As Foreman observed in 1999, "Social policy thinkers and researchers have been making up for considerable lost time as a result."

But this is not a biography. These pages focus on the efforts by Moynihan and others to cope with the revolutionary developments that have worsened the plight of inner-city black families over the years—and on the countermoves by a variety of groups, mostly conservative in temperament, that have stymied liberal initiatives to better the situation. Indeed, many of Moynihan's alarms in 1965 were prophetic. Out-of-wedlock black births in the United States, shown by Moynihan to be 23.6 percent of all babies born to black families in 1963, jumped to 72 percent by 2007. Millions of these babies, growing up in female-headed families, have suffered from poverty and a host of social and behavioral ills. Ratios of nonmarital births among whites and Latinos, too, have escalated over the years. In 2007, a record-high 39.7 percent of all babies in the United States were born out of wedlock.

On Father's Day of 2008, Barack Obama, whose father had left his mother, publicly lamented the meteoric rise in the numbers of fatherless black families. He exclaimed, "I know the toll it took on me, not having a father in the house. . . . So I resolved many years ago that it was my obligation to break the cycle—that if I could be anything in life, I would be a good father to my children." "Too many black fathers," he declared, "have abandoned their responsibilities, acting like boys instead of men." Heartened by Obama's remarks, some reformers now dare to believe that something like the national action of which Moynihan dreamed might someday come to pass.

Effective approaches to dealing with lower-class black family miseries remain elusive, however, in part because of the enduring sensitivity of the issues. Even now, it remains easy to be charged, as Moynihan was, with blaming the victim. Indeed, the Rev. Jesse Jackson accused Obama of "talking down to black people." Liberal reformers, moreover, continue to struggle for answers that will receive political support. So it is that the trail of misunderstandings remains treacherous. The stubbornness of historically rooted racial antagonisms, the apparently inexorable cultural and economic trends that have al-

tered sexual behavior and family structure, and the burdens that have continued to afflict the poor—all have conspired to dim the dreams of Moynihan,
LBJ, and other advocates of racial "equality as a fact and a result" in the
United States. Freedom, as Johnson had recognized at Howard, has not been
enough.

CHAPTER 1

The Pluck of the Irish

After Daniel Patrick Moynihan became a controversial public figure in 1965, interviewers for major publications wrote a great many stories about his early life and career. The *New York Times Sunday Magazine* carried five features on him between 1965 and 1979. *Time* magazine had him on its cover twice during this time. After 1976, many interviewers gushed that he was the only man in American history to have served in cabinet or subcabinet positions in four successive presidential administrations—under Kennedy, Johnson, Nixon, and Ford—before winning a seat in the U.S. Senate in 1976.

Although Moynihan did not like to talk much about his youth, he volunteered enough information that the interviewers could put together an inspirational though not always wholly accurate story. In their telling it was a classic tale of a bright and engaging young man who had overcome poverty and family disruption and achieved the American Dream. Recalling his boyhood in Depression-era New York City, Moynihan described the hard times that he, his mother, his younger brother, and his sister had to endure after his father, John, a gambler and alcoholic, abandoned them in 1937. Pat, as he was called, was then ten years old. Hard-pressed, he added, the family moved from tenement to tenement to take advantage of landlords who offered a free first month's rent. What little money they had came mostly from wages that his mother Margaret earned as a low-paid nurse and as an English teacher at the Woman's House of Detention in the city, along with (he later said) public assistance. Trying to help, he set up as a shoeshine boy in Times Square. "We lived in practically every slum neighborhood in Manhattan," he told the *Times* in 1966, "in Hell's Kitchen, in all the worst parts of the Upper West Side, and even in Harlem." To a later interviewer he said, "I grew up in Hell's Kitchen. My father was a drunk. I know what this life is like."[1]

According to this version of the story, Moynihan still had to scramble even after the worst stretches abated. Because the family moved about, he attended a number of different schools—Catholic parochial schools in the early grades—before entering Benjamin Franklin High School as a junior, from which he graduated as class valedictorian in 1943 at the age of sixteen. Located on 116th Street in East Harlem, it was a fairly good school that had a heavily Italian American (and, secondarily, black) student body. In addition to shining shoes, at various times in these years he worked as a stock boy at Gimbels Department Store, sold newspapers in a bar, and labored as a stevedore on the Hudson River docks, where—the story went—he heard in 1943 that he might be able to take an entrance exam for the City College of New York (CCNY). The *Times* reporter in 1966 quoted Moynihan as saying that he walked into the exam with his "longshoreman's loading hook sticking out of my back pocket. I wasn't going to be mistaken for any sissy kid."[2]

This was a turning point. Pat, as he was called, passed the exam and spent an academic year at CCNY, working part-time on the docks, before enrolling in the Navy's wartime V-12 officer training program in July 1944. This took him to Middlebury College in Vermont, and then to Tufts University outside of Boston, where he was enrolled in ROTC and received his first degree in 1946, an AB in Naval Science. Commissioned as an ensign, he was assigned in June 1946 to a repair ship in Norfolk, Virginia, and then as a communications and gunnery officer on a ship in the Caribbean. In early 1947, he returned to civilian life, intending to rely upon the GI Bill to resume his studies at Tufts. (In later years, he often cited the GI Bill as an enlightened example of governmental activism.) Some of the time, however, Pat had to assist his mother, who had borrowed money to acquire a lease on a saloon (thereby naming it Moynihan's Bar) on West 42nd Street in New York City. This was in the Hell's Kitchen area, a tough, predominantly Irish American neighborhood near Times Square.

Writers who later looked into Moynihan's early years confirmed much of what was portrayed in the inspirational narratives of his formative years that appeared in publications like *Time* and the *New York Times*. His family did plunge into poverty after his father abandoned them. Indeed, though Moynihan learned that his father had moved to California—and remarried—he never saw him again. It was also true that Pat had shined shoes in Times Square and worked at the docks. More than most prominent public figures in the United States, he had struggled through hard times. Having seen close up the problems of people in families living precariously, he identified with them.

Some of these inspirational accounts, however, have also fashioned an image that Moynihan did not reject of a young man who had arisen, as if a character out of a Horatio Alger novel, entirely out of rags to respectability and fame. The truth is more nuanced.

When Pat was born in March 1927, it was not in the slums of New York City but in Tulsa, Oklahoma, where his father, John, a second-generation Irish American Catholic from Bluffton, Indiana, who had briefly attended Notre Dame, was employed as a newspaper reporter. Six months later, John was hired as an advertising copywriter in Manhattan, and the family lived briefly in Greenwich Village before relocating to various suburban homes in the greater New York City area. Patrick's mother, Margaret, who had grown up in a middle-class family (her father was a successful attorney in Jeffersonville, Indiana), had received training as a nurse. Pat and his brother Mike had happy early childhood summer stays at their paternal grandfather's farm in Bluffton. Though his father's flight pitched him into the dismal world of Manhattan tenements, Pat's middle-class background had given him memories and aspirations that differed greatly from those of other shoeshine boys—some of them blacks—he encountered in Times Square. Although his father was indeed a drunk, Pat never lived in Hell's Kitchen as a boy.

The toughest economic times for the family ended in summer 1940, three years after his father had decamped, when Pat's mother married an older man, Henry Stapelfield, and moved with her children to his fourteen-room house in rural Kitchawan, in Westchester County. The marriage did not last, breaking up in spring 1941—a few months before his mother gave birth to another son, Tommy Stapelfield. Taking Tommy with her, she moved her family yet again, first to stay with a sister in Indiana and then to West 92nd Street, at which point Pat, aged fourteen, started at Benjamin Franklin High. By this time, the Great Depression was finally ending, and New York City began to enjoy a boom. Margaret found a good job as chief nurse in a war production plant, and moved again, this time to rent a large apartment in a converted mansion in Queens. When the war was over, by which time Pat had joined the navy, she acquired the lease on the bar in Hell's Kitchen.

Though Pat had to return periodically to New York to help at the bar, he finished his undergraduate coursework at Tufts, and graduated cum laude in June 1948. He then entered the Fletcher School of Law and Diplomacy at Tufts, where he received his master's degree in June 1949. After failing a Foreign Service exam that summer, he started work for a doctorate in international relations at Fletcher in the fall, only to find himself again helping his mother behind the bar for a time in early 1950. Still, he managed to win a Fulbright award to attend the London School of Economics and Political Science (LSE) to pursue research for a thesis on the International Labour Organisation (ILO). Money from the GI Bill, which would continue to finance his studies, further ensured that he would manage comfortably in Britain. When his mother sold her interest in the saloon, he was freed at last from his chores behind the bar. After attending a summer session at Harvard, he sailed for England in September 1950.

Because LSE did not require him to take exams, Moynihan had considerable freedom in setting his schedule. He was an omnivorous and retentive reader, moreover, and through his studies and personal contacts he learned a good deal about British and European history, political philosophy, and socioeconomic public policies. In later years, he repeatedly advocated some of these policies, notably family allowances, which served to cushion people (especially mothers and children) against the economic vicissitudes of life.

Moynihan was also a sociable young man who enjoyed convivial and bibulous conversation about all manner of subjects, especially political philosophy and history. He moved gracefully about London, cultivating the social and intellectual companionship of U.S. journalists, Labour Party politicians, and blue-collar union members. Sander Vanocur, an American who later became a well-known television news reporter, was among the many friends and fellow students who joined him at pub-crawling, concerts, and the theater.

Thoroughly enjoying himself, Moynihan picked up some of the mannerisms and speech of the English upper classes—traits he displayed (sometimes, it seemed, deliberately) throughout his long career, and that Tim Russert, who served as a senatorial aide in the late 1970s and early 1980s before becoming a well-known television news reporter, loved to parody. He also developed a taste for fine cheeses, wines, and well-cut clothing. Later he had a Saville Row tailor fashion some of his clothes.

In no hurry to return to the United States, Moynihan managed to find work as a budget assistant at an American air base near London, and thereby to remain abroad for two more years, during which time he traveled extensively in England and on the European continent. By the time he returned to the United States in September 1953, at age twenty-six, he had virtually remodeled himself into a worldly, confident, and ambitious young man. He had made very little progress on his doctoral dissertation. It was not until 1961 that he finally received his PhD for a thesis titled "The U.S. and the I.L.O. 1889–1934."

Many people who knew Moynihan in the 1950s and early 1960s found him an unusually bright and charming fellow. By then he had become a sturdily built young man who at six feet five inches towered over most people. One interviewer described him as an "amiable, gregarious, drink-loving, skillful-teller-of-funny-stories, Brendan Behan type of Irishman" who "almost always had a smile on his ruddy map-of-County-Kerry-face." Another journalist wrote that acquaintances regarded him as the "jolliest, humblest, most self-effacing, wittiest, most whimsical fellow they ever met—a bouncing encyclopedia of arcane historical fact, literary reference, and political lore." There is no doubt that these personal characteristics—as well as a penchant for Olympic-class flattery—helped him acquire a great many friends and admirers who proved useful to him as he navigated the labyrinthine byways of academe and politics.

Though it is never easy to draw a straight line connecting youthful experiences to later beliefs, it is possible that the trials of Pat's early years heightened his sense of vulnerability. The wrenching times he had experienced in New York may also have made him prone to worry that something apocalyptic would render the nation incapable of getting through crises. Moynihan's writing betrays a fondness for overwrought language, as in his report in 1965, and in his especially anguished predictions of doom during the rise of Black Power and urban rioting in the late 1960s.

Seeking socioeconomic stability, Moynihan devoted a good deal of energy during his career to the strengthening of institutions such as families and communities. Afraid that overambitious government bureaucracies might intrude on families and neighborhoods (and identifying with ethnic and religious minorities), he was more sympathetic to urban political machines than were many liberal reformers in the postwar years. For similar reasons, his writings frequently warned of the unforeseen consequences that well-meaning but hastily thought-through government policies might cause.

Still, Moynihan was hardly insecure. Although some people who knew him thought he could be thin-skinned, he struck most observers as supremely self-confident, especially when it came to arguing about ideas, which he did with considerable enthusiasm and skill. It was evident, moreover, that Moynihan's early and varied experiences honed his street smarts: emerging from adolescence with large ambitions, he was always a remarkably energetic, resourceful, and opportunistic man—skilled indeed at the game of politics and at bringing attention to himself. It is equally obvious that living in a fatherless family sharpened his sensitivity to the plight of the poor, especially single mothers and their children.[3]

His travails as a boy also left him with very mixed feelings about life on welfare. Though he thought that public assistance programs were absolutely necessary, he often complained that the U.S. welfare system was ill designed, poorly funded, and stigmatizing, and argued that it badly needed reform. Interviewed in the 1990s, he described people on welfare as "recipients," "paupers," and "failed persons," not as "clients."[4] Dramatizing his experiences, he explained to an interviewer, "I've lived much of my life in a jungle of broken families, watching them tear out each other's minds, watching them feast on each other's hearts."

Moynihan's reservations about hastily assembled government programs became especially obvious in the mid- and late 1960s when he repeatedly pointed out flaws in Johnson's highly touted War on Poverty. As an Irish Catholic from polyglot New York City, he was especially mindful of the enduring power of religious, ethnic, and racial identifications; the powerful cultural attachments of people, he believed, must always be considered before reformers jumped in to better their world. And the center must hold. For a time during the turbulent late 1960s and early 1970s, when it appeared to him that political polarization was tearing the country apart, he cast his lot with neoconservatives who lashed out at the ideas and activities of what they called the irresponsible liberal Left.

But Moynihan, like most Irish Catholics of his generation, grew up in Democratic circles. Though he often displayed the mannerisms of an English gentleman, he continued to connect well with people from the blue-collar world, and throughout his later career he insisted on calling himself a Democrat and a liberal. He was an early member of Americans for Democratic Action, a liberal, anticommunist organization that blossomed in the late 1940s, and a supporter of President Truman over the Progressive Henry Wallace during the election of 1948. Though he came to know various socialists and Marxists while at CCNY—and especially while at LSE—he did not share their enthusiasms. Carefully crafted liberal reforms, he thought, could best smooth over the wrinkles of capitalism. He had no sympathy with Americans on the left who criticized the anti-Soviet policies that Britain and the United States fashioned in the early cold war years.

Above all, Moynihan in the 1950s and early 1960s was a staunch liberal in the mold of FDR and Truman. With the optimism of youth, he was a can-do believer in the capacity of government—aided by social science—to design, administer, and (especially) evaluate effective domestic policies. All manner of later experiences in politics were to test this youthful faith.

On the voyage home from Britain in 1953, Moynihan met a Democratic Party activist who asked him what he planned to do when he reached the United States. Moynihan replied that he had no idea, whereupon the activist offered to introduce him to the man who was running the mayoral campaign of Robert Wagner Jr. in New York City. Within days of his arrival in the city, Moynihan was working as a volunteer on the campaign. After the election, which Wagner won, Moynihan took a paying job with the International Rescue Committee, a private organization located in the city that tried to help refugees, before jumping again into the political world in late 1954. This was when a friend from the Wagner campaign asked him to work for Averell Harriman, an aristocratic and prestigious former diplomat who was running as a Democrat for the governorship of New York.

This decision was significant to Patrick's life and useful in many ways. It enabled him to meet a bright and attractive young woman, Elizabeth "Liz" Brennan, who was also working for Harriman. When Harriman won the election, both moved to Albany, the state capital. Within a few months—in May

1955—they were married in a Catholic church in her mother's hometown of Cohasset, Massachusetts. Moynihan remained on Harriman's staff for four years, during which he assumed increasingly important duties as a speechwriter and administrator. Between 1956 and 1960, Liz had three children with Pat—Timothy Patrick, Maura Russell, and John McCloskey. Liz was an energetic, politically keen woman who, among many other activities—later she became an authority concerning Mogul architecture and landscaping—deftly managed Moynihan's senatorial campaigns.

When Harriman lost his race for reelection in 1958—to Republican candidate Nelson Rockefeller—Moynihan was again in need of a job. This time it was Harriman who came to the rescue, commissioning him to write the history of his administration and paying his salary as director of the New York State Government Research Project at Syracuse University. While living with his family there in a large, run-down house on campus, Moynihan also became an assistant professor of government at the Maxwell Graduate School of Citizenship and Public Affairs at the university. He finished his PhD thesis, thereby receiving his doctoral degree in early 1961. Working away at the history of the Harriman administration, he also completed a 500-page typescript. (Harriman, however, appears to have regarded it as insufficiently laudatory, and it was never published.)

During these two years Moynihan first ventured into a wider world that was to engage him off and on for the remainder of his life: writing. His first important essay, "Epidemic on the Highways," appeared in the *Reporter*, a liberal magazine, in April 1959. Solidly researched, it criticized the automobile industry for failing to improve the safety of cars, and urged tougher regulation by the government. As it happened, the article appeared nineteen days after a young man named Ralph Nader had published a similar critique of the industry in the *Nation*. (Admiring Nader's work, Moynihan later put him on the payroll as a consultant on auto safety at the Labor Department. There, Nader worked feverishly on a manuscript that in late 1965 resulted in publication of his nationally acclaimed indictment of U.S. automakers, *Unsafe at Any Speed*.)

Encouraged by Irving Kristol, the *Reporter*'s discerning editor, Moynihan wrote other articles for the magazine—among them a piece on the passion for highway building at a time when U.S. cities needed better mass transit, an essay on the Irish in the political history of New York, and (after he had left Syracuse) an essay on organized crime. Blessed with the ability to type out first drafts that needed little revision, he also published articles in other magazines. These efforts, like many in later years, revealed his ability to weave broad reading, an investigator's quest for facts, a reporter's eye for detail, and a lively prose style into authoritative work.

The essays, moreover, impressed not only Kristol but also Douglass Cater, the *Reporter*'s Washington, D.C., editor, who was later to serve on President Johnson's staff as an adviser on domestic policy, and Meg Greenfield, who was then working as a researcher for the magazine and who rose to become editorial page editor for the *Washington Post* as well as a good friend of the Moynihans. Through Kristol, Moynihan also made contact with sociologist Nathan Glazer, who was writing a book about ethnicity in New York City. Handling by himself four chapters on Jews, Negroes, Puerto Ricans, and Italians, Glazer persuaded Moynihan to contribute what became a chapter (the longest in the book) on the Irish. Moynihan also wrote much of the book's conclusion, "Beyond the Melting Pot," completing his work in March 1962, and became coauthor of the book with Glazer. Published in 1963, *Beyond the Melting Pot* was a widely praised addition to ethnic studies, thereby endowing Moynihan with very useful scholarly credentials.

In their book, Glazer and Moynihan challenged a view of the experiences of ethnic groups that had long been influential: that the descendants of immigrants assimilated fairly quickly into U.S. culture. Having known firsthand the power of ethnic, racial, and religious ties in the city of their youth, Moynihan and Glazer emphasized instead the continuities—of values, faiths, family structure, and the like—that characterized immigrant communities across generations. The chapters also made clear that there was no single immigration experience—ethnic groups, often clinging to Old World traditions, responded in varying ways in the process of becoming American.

Beyond the Melting Pot was not especially flattering to the ethnic groups under consideration. Glazer's chapter on blacks, for instance, included a four-page section featuring grim statistics about out-of-wedlock pregnancy and female-headed families. Moreover, the book (anticipating a view Moynihan later highlighted in his famous report) stressed the enduring power of ethnic and racial cultures. "The melting pot," the authors concluded, "did not happen. At least not in New York and *mutatis mutandis*, in those parts of America which resemble New York." On the contrary, the authors concluded, "religion and race define the next stage in the evolution of the American peoples." "The principal ethnic groups of New York City will be seen maintaining a distinct identity, albeit a changing one, from one generation to the next."

Nothing Moynihan undertook at Syracuse—or in his writing—did more to change his life than the election of John F. Kennedy to the presidency in 1960. Although Moynihan was not a Kennedy insider, he had been chosen as an alternate delegate from New York to the Democratic Party's national convention in Los Angeles. Later in 1960, he gave some speeches on JFK's behalf, and he eagerly hoped that a Democrat and a Catholic might reach the White House. At the time, however, he was also trying to finish his thesis and the book on the Harriman administration, and it appears that he met the candidate only briefly in a hotel lobby.

But Pat (like Liz) was ready to move on from Syracuse and to serve the New Frontiersmen in Washington, and he searched eagerly for a post. Though early explorations were fruitless, a word from his old friend Sandy Vanocur enabled him to strike gold. Kennedy's choice for secretary of the Labor Department, Arthur Goldberg, asked Vanocur, who was then with NBC in Washington, for suggestions of people who might serve in his department. Vanocur, who knew that Moynihan's thesis concerned the International Labour Organisation, arranged a meeting between Moynihan and Goldberg's undersecretary, W. Willard Wirtz. The meeting went well, and Wirtz asked Moynihan to join the department as a special assistant to the secretary.[5]

So it was, as often during Moynihan's career, that an admiring and well-placed friend helped the enterprising young Democrat move onward and upward in life. In July 1961, he moved his family to the capital and started work. *Time* later wrote that at the age of thirty-four he was the youngest subcabinet official in Washington. As a statement, that was a little overblown—Moynihan was an obscure low-level appointee. But in an administration that attracted a host of youthful intellectuals and reformers, that was still saying a good deal.

For most of the next four years, Moynihan was very happy in Washington. Settling after a while in a farmhouse on the expansive estate of Joseph Davies in the northwest part of the city, he and Liz enjoyed a lively social life that included a circle of political figures, writers, and journalists, among them Meg Greenfield, Mary McGrory, a reporter for the *Washington Post*, and the Vanocurs, who lived nearby. His salary, rising to $20,000 a year following a promotion to assistant secretary in early 1963, enabled him to feel financially secure for the first time in his life, and in 1965 to buy a 200-acre working farm with a pond in Pindars Corners, some eighty miles west of Albany. For most of the rest of his life this was a summer refuge where he could get away and write—banging away on a Corona typewriter in an abandoned, sunlit schoolhouse a little way uphill from the house.

His work at the Labor Department was a little less satisfying at times. Though Democrats controlled Congress, a loose but effective bipartisan coalition of conservatives blocked most of the administration's modest domestic initiatives. President Kennedy, moreover, was far more interested in foreign affairs than in matters closer to home. Still, Pat deeply admired JFK. When he heard of Kennedy's assassination, he barged out of his office to speak before the TV cameras. In what became a widely shown television spot, he said, "I guess there's no point in being Irish if you don't know the world will break your heart some day." Mary McGrory later phoned him, observing, "We'll never laugh again." "No, Mary," he replied. "We'll laugh again, but we'll never be young again."

Staying on at the Labor Department during the Johnson administration, Moynihan continued to be an enterprising, can-do appointee. His broad interests included traffic safety, unemployment, federal aid to education, crime, food costs, and minimum wage coverage. From the beginning of his tenure, he took it upon himself to become involved in architectural reform, especially the promotion of well-designed, attractive public buildings and their environs. He urged especially upgrading the area around and along Pennsylvania Avenue, which was then a drab and run-down street. In early 1965, when Johnson named him to a temporary commission on Pennsylvania Avenue, efforts to improve the area began to intensify, and Moynihan, who remained deeply concerned with architectural matters for the rest of his life (living in an apartment overlooking Pennsylvania Avenue during his last ten years as senator), could take considerable credit for the redevelopment of the area.[6]

In September 1962, the Senate confirmed Labor Secretary Goldberg as Kennedy's nominee for a position on the Supreme Court, whereupon Wirtz ascended to the top spot at the Department of Labor. Shortly thereafter, in early 1963, Moynihan acquired a more impressive title, assistant secretary of labor for policy planning and research. Wirtz assigned him few administrative chores, thereby affording him considerable freedom to think broadly about domestic issues, to take advantage of the skilled civil servants on his four- to five-person staff and at the Bureau of Labor Statistics, and to produce reports on public concerns that attracted his interest. Nicholas Lemann, a journalist who later wrote about Moynihan's work in those years, remarked without exaggeration that he used this freedom creatively, "practically inventing the role of the social welfare intellectual in government." Moynihan's "extraordinary radar," Lemann added, enabled him to pick things out of government reports and scholarly journals and "to dramatize his findings in a way that would get the attention of high government officials."[7]

In the summer of 1963, Moynihan chanced upon an announcement by Lewis Hershey, director of the Selective Service System. It stated that large numbers of the young men called up for the military draft had failed the mental test, physical test, or both. Already concerned, as were others in the Labor Department, about unemployment, Moynihan pressed to investigate this situation. Responding in late September, President Kennedy established the Task Force on Manpower Conservation, and Moynihan, taking charge of it, set to work. After naming Paul Barton, a trusted member of his staff, to lead the research, Moynihan drove the group to produce a report. "He worked me to death," Barton observed later.[8]

Within three months Moynihan and the staff had completed their work, and their statistically laden report of thirty-five pages (along with fifty-one pages of appendices) was released on New Year's Day of 1964. Moynihan, knowing his history, titled it *One-Third of a Nation*, thereby echoing the phrase FDR had made famous in 1937 in his second inaugural address: "I see one-third of a nation ill-housed, ill-clad, ill-nourished." The department's report emphasized that one-third of all young men then turning eighteen would be rejected if they were examined for induction into the armed services. Of those men who failed, about one-half would be rejected for medical reasons. The others would fail through inability to qualify on the mental test, which meant that they had acquired no more than the equivalent of a seventh-grade education. The report predicted that men flunking the tests, especially those who suffered from educational disadvantages, would likely fall into a "lifetime of recurrent unemployment unless their skills are sufficiently upgraded." Among the report's recommendations, set in motion by presidential order and carried out in 1964 and 1965, was one that called for the Department of Defense and the Selective Service System to examine all men on their eighteenth birthday to enable officials to spot their problems.[9]

Moynihan's politically resonant title (along with his talent for getting friendly journalists to write about his work) helped *One-Third of a Nation* receive a fair amount of public attention. Though his findings did not surprise experts—large percentages of young men in the United States had always failed such tests—the hard-hitting report was nonetheless distressing to people who read it. Moreover, its considerable array of statistics made clear that family problems accounted for many of the recent failures. About half of the young men who were failing the mental tests, the report noted, came from families with six or more children, almost a third from families broken by divorce or separation, and a fifth from families that had been on public assistance within the previous five years. According to the report, a "major proportion" of the young men who failed the mental test "are the products of poverty. They have inherited their situation from their parents, and unless the cycle is broken, they will almost certainly transmit it to their families."

Moynihan persisted in drawing attention to these problems, dashing off memoranda to Wirtz and others over the next year and a half. Many of these focused on the special problems of blacks—some 56 percent flunked the mental exam in 1964. Writing White House aide and close friend Harry McPherson in July 1965 (his last memo as a Labor Department official), Pat argued—not for the first time—that government should "quietly adjust" the mental test so as "to compensate for the general difficulty of Negroes (and Southerners generally) to handle such questions." It should also start a "hard, steady Manpower Development Training Program and Job Corps program to qualify men for the Armed Forces." He emphasized, "*The single most important and dramatic instance of the exclusion of Negro Americans from employment opportunities is that of the Armed Forces.*" If blacks were able to enter the services in proportion to their share of population (11.8 percent), he added, 100,000 fewer would be unemployed. "*Above all things the down-and-out Negro boy needs to be inducted into the male American society.*"[10]

Chief among Moynihan's duties in early 1964 was the question of what to do about poverty. In late 1963, Kennedy had decided to tackle the issue, which the government had largely ignored since the Great Depression. Though the economy was improving by 1964, poverty as measured in official statistics still remained serious, afflicting 18 percent of the population, roughly 33 million people. Before Kennedy had a chance to develop legislation, however, he was assassinated. LBJ, who had headed the Texas branch of the New Deal's National Youth Administration (NYA), which provided job and education programs for young people, jumped at the chance to carry forth Kennedy's initiative. In his state of the union address in January 1964, Johnson declared his goal of fighting a war on poverty. Moynihan then became a key Labor Department representative in a multidepartmental effort that plunged into round-the-clock meetings to launch the war.

Though LBJ did not draw up a blueprint, he had strong preferences. Like FDR, who had declared that "continued dependence upon relief induces a spiritual and moral disintegration fundamentally destructive to the human spirit," LBJ did not wish to expand the dole, much less to rely on the Aid to Families with Dependent Children (AFDC) program, the nation's chief source of public assistance to women and children in poverty. Instead, LBJ aimed to help people, especially young people, help themselves, so that they might leave the welfare rolls. The War on Poverty, he thought, should be a hand up, not a handout. It should open doors to opportunity, not establish governmentally guaranteed floors under income.

As Moynihan worked on plans for the War on Poverty, he was excited by the chance to put into practice his faith in the capacity of expert social scientists to fashion public policy. As he was to point out in his essay "The Professionalization of Reform," published as the lead article of the first issue of *The Public Interest* in the fall of 1965, government funding of social science research in 1964 was small, at around $500 to $600 million per year—only 10 percent or so of the money available for research in the biological and physical sciences. Exhibiting his fondness for sweeping observations about social change, Moynihan went on to emphasize that the "professionalization of the middle classes," the "exponential growth of knowledge," and the "econometric revolution" that had led to the growth of Keynesian economic thinking offered all manner of possibilities for the expansion of expertise in governmental planning. The economic policies of the Kennedy administration, he wrote, represented "perhaps the most impressive demonstration of the capacity of organized intelligence to forecast and direct events that has yet occurred in American government of the present era."[11]

Moynihan shared Johnson's ambivalence about AFDC. It was indeed a poorly funded, politically embattled program that fell far short of covering all needy mothers and their children, and that in most states provided aid only to impoverished female-headed families—many of them black. A great many low-income two-parent families, no matter their extent of need, were ineligible for the assistance. For this reason, Moynihan and others wondered if the program, in effect penalizing marriage, offered perverse incentives. In a speech in February, he asserted that welfare "rotted the poor."

At this time, Moynihan did not press for governmentally guaranteed programs of income maintenance for people living in poverty. Approaches such as these were widely discussed only later, especially during the early years of the Nixon administration.[12] Instead, influenced by European-style social planning and Catholic social welfare philosophy (which placed family well-being at the core of the good society), he favored enactment of family allowances that would be given to *all* families with children.[13] Such a system could operate without means tests, without stigma to recipients, and without cumbersome bureaucratic management. As he recognized, however, a reasonably generous family allowance system would be an extraordinarily expensive proposition. Conservatives were especially cool toward the idea, which they said (citing the goal of such programs in some European countries) would invite poor people to have more children. Washington's antipoverty warriors in 1964 scarcely considered the idea.

Moynihan looked, therefore, for other ways of sustaining male heads of poor families. This could not be achieved, he insisted, via job training or education programs alone, which were aimed mainly at young people. The key, he believed, was large-scale provision of public jobs. "The only way out of poverty for a man is employment," he declared in February 1964. Again and again in late 1964 and early 1965 he whipped off memoranda to Wirtz and others proposing ways in which the government might help black men—not only by opening up military service but also by reestablishing twice-a-day mail delivery. This would add many thousands of postal jobs—civil service work that many black men might be expected to get.[14]

Moynihan believed that other programs must also be aimed at providing work for blacks, whose joblessness was unique. In 1964, their unemployment rate (9.6 percent) was more than twice the rate for whites (4.5 percent). Many black men, discouraged, had dropped out of the labor force entirely.

His solution—relatively bold for the time—was to urge the administration to confront the need for "unequal treatment for the Negro." Writing Wirtz in April 1964, he stated, "We cannot avoid it." Prominent black leaders such as Martin Luther King Jr. and National Urban League executive director Whitney Young, he pointed out, were already demanding such an approach. "The Negroes," he added, "are asking for unequal treatment. More seriously, it may be that without unequal treatment in the immediate future there is no way for them to achieve anything like equal status in the long run." Moynihan expected Johnson to balk at what in fact was a call for affirmative action to benefit blacks. But he pressed on. "Obviously," he observed, "this is filled with political peril, but I suspect we may have to face it anyway."[15]

While he was advocating these advanced ideas in Washington, Moynihan also took time to urge them upon scholars attending a conference in Boston in May 1964 concerned with black Americans. Sponsored by the American Academy of Arts and Sciences, it attracted many of the nation's preeminent social scientists. They included sociologists Daniel Bell, Talcott Parsons, and Robert Merton, anthropologist Clifford Geertz, and psychiatrist Erik Erikson. Moynihan advised the scholars, "If you were ever to have anything like an equal Negro community, you are for the next thirty years going to have to give them unequal treatment. I think the possibilities of thus legitimizing such treatment might have some relevance to public policy right now." He stressed the issue of jobs. "The biggest question," he asked, "is will the Negro community itself get pulled apart by the problem of employment? It would seem to us to be absolutely devastating, and they are not Negro problems, but their differential effect on the Negro is potentially disastrous."

The needs of black families, Moynihan told the conferees, were especially large. "The problem of the Negro family," he warned the scholars, "is practically the property of the American government. I mean we spend most of our money on this, in health, in welfare, and on employment, and yet we know nothing about it, or not much about it, and one of the reasons is that we are not supposed to know anything about it."

Referring to statistics concerning Harlem, Moynihan underscored the sensitivity of such matters:

> It's none of your business that 40 percent of the kids are illegitimate and don't, for heaven's sake, try to get it published, you can't. And if it is getting worse, that's even less of your business. All you're expected

to do is keep on supplying welfare, and if we could, for heaven's sake, find something besides the inheritance from slavery, which sort of leaves you there—that's it, that's it—but if there is something that is new, if it's getting worse because of reasons that are new, then there is a possibility of public policy reacting to it.[16]

In early May, he sent Wirtz yet another memo, alerting him to "the major and sometimes wrenching changes in our way of doing things that will be required if we are going to bring them [blacks] in as full-fledged members of the larger community." He worried that the War on Poverty would simply "pension the Negroes off" through welfare: "Nothing would be more terrible, if it should come to pass. We will have created an entire subculture of dependency, alienation, and despair. We have already done as much to whole sections of Appalachia, as I understand it, as also to the Indian reservations. It is in truth the way that we cope with this kind of problem. As against giving the men proper jobs and a respectable place in their community and family."

Wirtz, a strong liberal, needed no persuading from Moynihan concerning the need for large-scale employment programs. He, too, hectored the administration, suggesting that funds for a jobs initiative could be found by raising cigarette taxes. But Johnson, recalling that opponents during the 1930s had branded government job programs as wasteful make-work, recognized also that promising initiatives of that sort would likely cost billions of dollars. Refusing to consider tax increases, he was deaf to the pleas from the Labor Department. As early as March, the planners, headed by Kennedy brother-in-law Sargent Shriver, emerged with a bundle of hastily assembled ideas that Johnson sent on to Capitol Hill. Congress then struggled to fashion them into a law that LBJ signed in August. A new bureaucracy, the Office of Economic Opportunity (OEO), would coordinate the war.

As this title indicated, and as Johnson had desired, the focus of the new struggle against poverty was on advancing individual opportunity, not on the expansion of welfare. Doors to opportunity, mainly to help young people, would be widened through government funding of training and education programs, such as the Job Corps and Volunteers in Service to America (VISTA). The law also called for community action programs (CAPs) that would involve the "maximum feasible participation" of the poor. These would direct many efforts, such as Head Start, to help children and young people.

Though Moynihan offered loyal support to what his party and president had accomplished, he was disappointed. As he had feared, the law was sold as a color-blind measure to help all people. It did not provide what Moynihan had been seeking, "unequal treatment for the Negro." Nor did it include his department's key proposal of large-scale funding for governmental employment programs to help adult men—and thereby to sustain two-parent families. What Shriver and his people had come up with, he later complained, was "not a choice among policies so much as a collection of them."[17]

After Moynihan left the administration in July 1965, he became an outspoken critic of the OEO, which by then was encountering a host of problems. A number of liberals complained that it was inadequately funded; it was not a war but a skirmish that raised false expectations and disillusioned the poor. Others assailed it as an administrative mess. Powerful Democratic mayors such as Richard Daley of Chicago fumed that radical activists—blacks as well as whites—had managed to interpret the ill-defined idea of "maximum feasible participation" of the poor so as to take command of the community action programs, thereby exploiting them for their own benefit and depriving city halls of funds and political advantage. In an extreme example, the Blackstone Rangers, a violent gang, received community action funds in the Windy City.

Moynihan, joining the chorus of complainers, wrote many articles about the War on Poverty over the next few years. He highlighted two points. The first repeated the arguments he had made in 1964: a struggle against poverty must above all feature public employment programs, mainly for men. Without decent income for the male breadwinner, many families would fall apart. The second emphasized that the "professionalization of reform," which had seemed so promising during the economic policies of the Kennedy years, had misfired when aimed at poverty. Moynihan complained especially that "intellectual leaders of the social welfare profession"—people who failed to understand that the poor needed money most of all—had overtaken the planning process and inserted the notion of community action into the legislation. In so doing, he added, the intellectuals had tended to downplay the economic needs of poor people, driven the war into political hot water, and sunk all chances of winning it. A historic opportunity to combat poverty, promising because of the political strength of liberals at the time, had been frittered away.

The involvement of Moynihan in the skirmish against poverty in 1964 had yet another long-term consequence: it led a number of scholars to charge in later years that he held a cultural view of the problem. This charge was true to a small extent. Sensitive to the forces of race, religion, and ethnicity, Moynihan worried greatly about the deep-set nature of some of the behaviors—such as out-of-wedlock parenting—that damaged the lives of poor black people. In this way he followed in the footsteps of many earlier observers of the poor. In 1961, anthropologist Oscar Lewis had written *The Children of Sanchez* (1961), a much-discussed book about the "culture of poverty" that engulfed the poor in Mexico City, causing a "way of life which is passed down from generation to generation." In 1962, Michael Harrington published *The Other America*, an impassioned overview of poverty that conveyed a similar message: the poor in the United States were also an "other," trapped in a "culture that is radically different from the one that dominates the society." Harrington added, "The most important analytic point . . . is the fact that poverty in America forms a culture, a way of life and feeling, that makes it a whole." A best-seller, *The Other America* helped cause a national rediscovery of poverty. Harrington's ideas were among the varied influences that motivated JFK to take on the issue.

In portraying the poor as perpetuating a culture of poverty, however, Harrington did not mean to argue that their plight was inbred or they could not be helped. On the contrary, he was a democratic socialist who employed vivid descriptions of the miseries of the poor—as many other social reformers had done—to generate public outrage. *The Other America* was above all an urgent call for a "comprehensive assault on poverty" by government. Moynihan was in no sense a radical. But he had been a drinking companion of Harrington in New York City, and he understood that his friend had to exaggerate to be heard.

Like Harrington, Moynihan was a reformer who believed that poor people had to receive substantial governmental help. This did not mean that he dismissed the power of cultural forces—in *Beyond the Melting Pot* he had stressed their durability. He worried that racist and economic pressures had driven many poor Americans, especially blacks, so far into the depths that they were in great danger of passing on a host of dysfunctional behaviors to future generations. But as *The Negro Family* would stress, he also believed that unemployment was the major source of instability within poor families, and that government could and should act to improve their chances in life. This was a liberal and structural view of poverty to which he adhered during a host of controversies that engaged him over the years.

CHAPTER 2

The Case for National Action

W orried about racial problems that had sparked rioting in Harlem and other cities during the summer of 1964, Moynihan became convinced that government had to act boldly and quickly to counter the poverty and related ills harming black Americans. The historic Civil Rights Act signed into law earlier in the year, he mused in November, had at last guaranteed legal rights for black people, but "it's not going to make any difference in their lives." With these concerns in mind, he sat down to compose a twelve-page, single-spaced memorandum to Labor Secretary Wirtz.

It is clear from this memo that Moynihan had by that time decided to write a report about inner-city black problems—the report he would later title *The Negro Family: The Case for National Action*. The memo called for family allowances as well as for "funds for birth control clinics through the poverty program," reflecting his belief that large families were "the major source of individual poverty in the United States." He emphasized, however, the need for governmental employment programs. "It is my hunch," he explained to Wirtz, "that the American public is ready to face up to the proposition that unemployment is destroying the Negro family structure." This was a clear indication that he was eager to focus on *family* issues in black communities. Such a focus, he added, would raise "the possibility of enlisting the support of conservative groups for quite radical social programs."[1]

Exactly why Moynihan decided to undertake this report remains subject to debate. Journalist Nicholas Lemann offered one highly unflattering speculation in his book *The Promised Land*, published in 1991, that many people who followed Moynihan's career readily believed. Lemann wrote that Moynihan "needed to be known as an original thinker" and had a "thirst for more attention than intellectuals were accustomed to getting." A report on the black family "was the kind of major statement that could establish his place in the first rank of American intellectuals."

Lemann also portrayed Moynihan as an ambitious political operator who was then involved in "complex career machinations that a stunning new report might serve." For one thing, Moynihan was looking for a way to repair his standing with the president, who had become furious upon learning that he had done some campaigning for Robert F. Kennedy, LBJ's hated political enemy, during Kennedy's successful run for a Senate seat from New York in 1964. For another, Moynihan was thinking about running for political office in New York City in 1965: "Being known as the author of a great liberal call to arms," Lemann wrote, "might help his chances there."[2]

Moynihan, needless to say, had a different explanation for his determination to write a report. By late 1964, he recalled, he had become concerned about what he considered the unwarranted optimism of administration officials about the future of civil rights. "I felt I had to write a paper about the Negro family," he added, "to explain to the fellows how there was a problem more difficult than they knew and also to explain some of the issues of unemployment and housing in terms that would be new enough and shocking enough that they would say, 'Well, we can't let this sort of thing go on. We've got to do something about it.'"

It was also evident that Moynihan hoped to help the Johnson administration, which was worrying about the mounting militancy of black leaders, to take charge of the direction of civil rights activity in the future. As he put it later, it was his (and Richard Goodwin's) idea, in writing the speech LBJ was to deliver at Howard in June, to enable the administration "*to deliberately leap frog the civil rights movement*—to get out in front so far that you would avoid chasing it because you would never catch up to it."

How can we reconcile these differing explanations for Moynihan's decision to write a report? Lemann was correct in describing him as a man who hoped to gain greater recognition within intellectual circles. As of 1965 Moynihan had published several well-received articles on subjects ranging from auto safety to crime, along with the highly regarded academic book on ethnicity he and Nathan Glazer had published in 1963. But he was untrained in sociological or anthropological methods, and he hardly rated as a star in scholarly circles. At that time, as in later years, many people envied the cultural radar that enabled him to pinpoint and dramatize contemporary issues. Associates and staffers also marveled at his fund of knowledge, which, reflecting wide reading, was extraordinary. This, along with an unusually strong memory, allowed him to more than hold his own in debates with adversaries as well as to weave the writings of leading historians, social scientists, and political philosophers into his smoothly composed articles. As an essayist concerning political and social ideas he was widely admired, and as an intellectual entrepreneur, he had few if any equals. But these skills, considerable though they were, did not mark him as an original scholar.

Lemann was also correct in viewing Moynihan as a politically ambitious character with a gift for self-promotion. In 1984 historian Allen Matusow described him as having a "penchant for ambitious hypotheses, and a talent for cultivating the right political connections." Among these connections were influential journalists and presidential aides whom he would ask into his office for a drink or two. A special ally was his friend Harry McPherson. In April 1965, Moynihan went to visit him in the hospital, where he was recuperating from surgery. McPherson recalled that Moynihan was "carrying a bottle of Scotch in one hand and a copy of his secret report in the other." He added, "For the next four hours we talked and read and drank." McPherson, who greatly admired Moynihan, was clearly important in channeling his friend's ideas toward top officials.[3]

It was also true that by early 1965 Moynihan was seriously contemplating a run for political office in New York City—some news stories mentioned him as a possible candidate for mayor. Knowing that LBJ distrusted him, he had grounds for trying to impress him and to patch up the relationship. Indeed, Moynihan ultimately did run for office, leaving the Johnson administration in mid-July to seek the position of president of the New York City Council. Still later, Moynihan displayed great agility—critics considered him a chameleon—in maneuvering for high political office in Republican circles as well as in the Democratic electoral politics of New York.

It remains doubtful, however, that personal ambitions, either for intellectual recognition or for political advancement, played the major role in Moynihan's decision to write a report on black family life. The product of a broken home, he empathized with the plight of poor and fatherless children, whose life chances, he recognized, were likely to be savaged. In a number of ways—for example, in *One-Third of a Nation*, in his participation in scholarly studies on the status of black Americans, and in his insistence during the battles for the War on Poverty on advancing social and economic equality for blacks—he had already shown that what he identified as the uniquely desperate situation of lower-class black families seriously engaged him. It always would.

Wasting no time in December 1964, Moynihan began to seek advice concerning lower-class black family life from knowledgeable people. Among his contacts were Kenneth Clark, a psychologist who was completing a book (*Dark Ghetto*) about inner-city ills; Hylan Lewis, a Howard University sociologist; and Herbert Hill, labor secretary of the National Association for the Advancement of Colored People (NAACP). He also appears to have talked to Bill Moyers, a top Johnson aide, about putting together the report.

Moynihan took the first decisive step toward research in late December. Paul Barton, who became the key staffer behind the effort, remembers in his unpublished history of the report that Moynihan took him aside at Christmastime and directed him to begin research. "We have to do something," he said. "We have to be different." The work, which was sensitive, was to be conducted in secret. "We were going to write a report on the Negro family," Barton recalls, "and we were going to do it quickly."[4]

Barton started the research on New Year's Day 1965. He and Moynihan's executive assistant, Ellen Broderick, labored intensely until mid-February, amassing data and meeting regularly with their boss. It was evident from the start, however, where Moynihan was headed. In an outline he prepared in January, he began by emphasizing that the first phase of the civil rights revolution had been completed, and that there was now a period of "maximum danger and opportunity." Worrying that the gulf would widen between black expectations and results, he wrote, "*Thesis:* the principal effect of exploitation, discrimination, poverty, and unemployment on the Negro community has been a profound weakening of Negro family structure." He added, "The process has reached the point where the problem is feeding on itself—the situation is getting *worse* not better."[5]

Moynihan's outline revealed that he had little faith in existing federal policies concerning low-income black families. On the contrary, it argued, many of these families were "crumbling." From the start he fired off a series of memoranda aimed at alerting key government officials to this situation. On January 21 he sent a four-page memo to Moyers explaining that the deteriorating stature and authority of the black male had created a "pathological matriarchal situation which is beginning to feed on itself." It is the "condition of the Negro family," he added, "where the cycle of poverty and despair . . . is transferred from one generation to the next." On January 26 he wrote Arthur Goldberg, his former boss at the Labor Department, of his fears about crime. "I hold with a small but convincing body of research that suggests the weakness of the Negro family structure, in particular the large number of Negro youths who are raised in matriarchal families without fathers, predisposes the males to acts of violence in their early years of manhood."[6]

In early February, he wrote yet another lengthy memo, this time to Wirtz. It made a point that he would often repeat in the months to come—that "freedom" for black people was "not enough." Blacks, having gained liberty as a result of the Civil Rights Act, must also receive equality. As he put it, "The demand [by blacks] for economic equality is not now the demand for equal opportunities for the equally qualified: it is the demand for equality of economic *results. . . . The principal challenge of the next phase of the Negro revolution is to make certain that equality of results will now follow.*"[7]

A key research finding in early 1965 strengthened Moynihan's sense that the troubles of many low-income black families were rapidly increasing. Barton had collected considerable data concerning the rapid growth of welfare take-up, especially by blacks, and uncovered a disturbing new relationship between nonwhite male unemployment rates and new cases of Aid to Families with Dependent Children (AFDC). Although the fact that the nonwhite unemployment rate had declined slightly during the economic growth of the early 1960s was "encouraging," the clear correlation between lower nonwhite male joblessness and fewer family breakups had begun to weaken. Barton recalled, "What was really disturbing was that this long-term relationship had reversed in the prior two years. For the first time, rates of family breakup and new welfare cases continued to *rise* as the unemployment rate *fell.*" On statistical charts, therefore, the trend lines of these two measures—one decreasing, the other increasing—had crisscrossed. As Moynihan remembered it, this discovery—which his friend James Q. Wilson, a sociologist, memorably called "Moynihan's scissors"—was stunning. "The numbers went blooey on me," Moynihan said. It seemed that something deeper than economic hardship alone was damaging lower-class nonwhite families and causing the situation to "feed upon itself."[8]

In later interviews Moynihan elaborated further on his interpretation of this discovery—one that led him to emphasize in his report the damage that was increasingly afflicting lower-class black families and that thereby helped enmesh him in furious controversy. "We had just begun President Johnson's proposal to abolish poverty," he explained. "I suddenly found myself thinking," he added, "my God, something's happening independently of those large economic things. . . . The problem of [black] family breakup was becoming independent. . . . Things that previously could retard it or accelerate it were losing that influence, it was just exploding on its own. It had reached a critical mass, perhaps. That's an image from physics. But it's independent. The reaction takes place."

Though the research by Barton and others was valuable, it by no means provided all the ideas that were to appear in the report. On the contrary, Moynihan, an inveterate reader, also drew upon a considerable body of historical and sociological research into black family life as well as upon the views of a number of civil rights leaders. The final report was his bold and in many ways impressive attempt to combine these two strands of information—scholarly and activist—into a call for governmental action.

Even as late as 1965, any serious scholarly discussion concerning black family life had to return to the writings of the most distinguished black U.S. social scientist and historian: W. E. B. Du Bois. Born in 1868, Du Bois was the first black American to receive (in 1896) a PhD from Harvard University, after which he became an extraordinarily productive scholar as well as a ceaselessly persistent activist. He was a founder in 1909 of the NAACP. He died in Ghana at the age of ninety-five on the eve of the March on Washington in August 1963, at which Martin Luther King Jr. gave his "I Have a Dream" speech.

Some of Du Bois's earliest research, as expressed first and most impressively in *The Philadelphia Negro: A Social Study* (1899), pioneered sociological investigations into black urban life in the United States. Moynihan had read Du Bois's book, though he did not cite it in his report. As he recognized, it strongly influenced the later scholars upon whose writings he relied. Du Bois made clear that sharp class cleavages divided the black residents of Philadelphia, at that time the U.S. city with the largest black population. Some families, Du Bois had concluded, were managing reasonably well. Indeed, given the short transition since slavery, the black family was "a more successful institution than we had a right to expect." Du Bois focused, however, on the city's Seventh Ward, where 9,675 of the city's 40,000 black residents were crowded together. This, in Du Bois's words, was the "bane of respectable Philadelphia," an area where crime was widespread and where "dangerous people with multiple problems"—what he called the "submerged tenth" of the black populace—set the tone.[9]

The two greatest hindrances bedeviling black Philadelphians, Du Bois emphasized, were economic: "the low wages of men and the high rents." After identifying the racist sources of these encumbrances, Du Bois dwelt on their social and familial effects. Young people, he argued, encountered the "difficulty of earning income enough to afford to marry." The result was unstable unions that had "ill effects on the sexual morality of city Negroes." Women had to work, leaving children "without guidance or restraint"—a development that was "disastrous to manners and morals." A "large number of families," he added, "are centres of irregular sexual intercourse."

Du Bois also highlighted the disastrous legacy of slavery and of postemancipation developments, such as sharecropping in the rural South. Here he stopped short of saying slavery had wiped out all traces of African culture in the United States: African survival, he wrote, could be seen in the black church. But in his era, black family life was troubled. "Among the masses of the Negro people in America," he wrote, "the monogamatic home is comparatively a new institution." Instead, "cohabitation of a more or less permanent character is a direct offshoot of the plantation life and is practiced considerably." In the Seventh Ward, he estimated, between 10 and 25 percent of black unions were of this character. Du Bois stressed that the "widespread and early breaking up of family life" as well as the "astoundingly large number of deserted wives" had deep roots in "the "lax moral habits of the slave regime."

In *The Negro American Family*, an edited study that appeared in 1908 and examined trends in the South, Du Bois repeated these arguments. He continued to bewail the "economic condition of the Negro," which was "influencing the sexual morals of the race." He added, "Without doubt the point where the Negro American is furthest behind modern civilization is in his sexual mores."

Citing what he admitted were imprecise statistics, he wrote that the percentage of black children born to unmarried women in Washington, D.C., ranged between 18.8 in 1879 and a high of 27.6 in various years between 1889 and 1899 before dropping a little to between 21 and 25 percent between 1904 and 1908. White children born out of wedlock, by contrast, numbered around 2 percent.[10]

Du Bois concluded by deploring again the legacy of slavery. Its "essential features in America," he wrote, were "1. No legal marriage; 2. No legal family; 3. No legal control over children." The book concluded: "Sexual immorality is probably the greatest single plague spot among Negro Americans, and its greatest cause is slavery and the present utter disregard of a black woman's virtue and self-respect, both in law court and custom in the South."

For many years, no scholar concerned with the black family in the United States came close to rivaling Du Bois, whose research dominated the field. By the 1930s and 1940s, however, a new generation of able social scientists, both black and white, had emerged to study U.S. race relations. They painted a picture of economic and racial discrimination even more dismal than the findings of Du Bois. Charles Johnson, a black scholar, made important studies of life among rural blacks in the South, notably *Shadow of the Plantation* (1934), which among other things traced the impact of slavery and sharecropping on black families. Other black scholars—Horace Cayton, St. Clair Drake, and Allison Davis—focused on the troubles that afflicted black families following urbanization. John Dollard, a white psychologist and social scientist who wrote about race relations in the city and in the small-town South, wrote in 1937 of the "anger and self-loathing" of lower-class black men. In a book about black children titled *Children of Bondage* (1940), Dollard and Davis estimated that one-third of black births in Natchez, Mississippi, in 1938 had been illegitimate.

These and other scholars in the 1930s and 1940s largely agreed that most black families differed substantially—generally in unsettling ways—from most white families. In 1939, Hortense Powdermaker, a white anthropologist, published a book called *After Freedom*, on "Cottonville" (Indianola), Mississippi, in which she wrote, "The typical Negro family throughout the South is matriarchal and elastic [extended], in striking contrast to the more rigid and patriarchal family organization of occidental white culture." E. W. Burgess, a leading white sociologist, also declared in 1939 that "an unorganized and disorganized family life" was the "chief handicap" of black Americans. Gunnar Myrdal, the Swedish economist who published an influential study of U.S. race relations in 1944, *An American Dilemma*, reached the same conclusion. Slavery, he wrote, had caused great "instability" in black families. Sizable migrations since 1910 of blacks from the South to the city had led to widespread "disorganization" and "demoralization" of black family life.

No author in these and later years had a greater influence on the study of black families—or on Moynihan—than E. Franklin Frazier. Born in 1894, Frazier had been educated in the black schools of segregated Baltimore before attending Howard University, from which he was graduated in 1916. He taught briefly at the Tuskegee Institute and at Fisk University, and earned his PhD in sociology from the University of Chicago in 1931. At that time the University of Chicago was by far the most important U.S. center for sociological studies—the work of these scholars became known as the "Chicago School" of thought. Burgess, a mentor of Frazier's, was a professor at Chicago, and Johnson and Dollard had been students there. Much of the work emanating from the university, focusing on the processes and effects of urbanization, emphasized that rural folk migrating to the cities encountered bewildering and disorganizing experiences. Frazier, publishing *The Negro Family in Chicago* in 1932, quickly entered the ranks of scholars in this field of study. Two years later he joined the faculty at Howard, where his publications earned him widespread recognition. In 1948 he became the first black scholar to serve as president of the American Sociological Society (later renamed American Sociological Association [ASA]).

Compared to some of his academic peers, Frazier held fairly radical political views concerning solutions to the conditions of black family life. FDR's New Deal, he thought, was nothing more than "half-hearted reformism." The NAACP, relying on a "traditional strategy of civil libertarianism and moral appeals to elite whites," was ineffective. Blacks, he advised, should form interracial labor unions with white workers and fight together for economic justice.

Frazier also believed in the power of assimilation over time. Like others who were part of the Chicago School of sociology, he thought this occurred in stages. Rural black people who migrated to the city were naturally battered and disorganized by their experiences in a new environment, to the extent that they shed their older "peasant culture," but in time they could expect to find work and to adopt the values of white U.S. culture. Many black people, Frazier wrote, had already entered the ranks of what he called the "industrial proletariat." Small numbers had even succeeded in securing white-collar employment.

Frazier enunciated this cautiously hopeful view in his magnum opus, *The Negro Family in the United States*, an ambitious and comprehensive account of black families past and present that appeared in 1939 to great acclaim, winning the Anisfield Prize for the most significant work published in the field of race relations. Following Du Bois, whose work he greatly admired, Frazier emphasized the brutality of slavery, which had ripped up the African roots of black people, emasculated black men, and created a female-dominated family form he called a "matriarchate." Frazier, however, also pointed out that there were various kinds of black families. After emancipation, some black men managed to acquire property and education, thereby succeeding in forming stable families and playing important roles as breadwinners and role models for their children. A chapter titled "The Downfall of the Matriarchate" described this encouraging development.

But for the most part, Frazier remained glum, emphasizing instead the catastrophic impact of slavery on the subsequent family organization of the majority of black people. "Probably never before in history," he wrote, "has a people been so nearly completely stripped of its social heritage as the Negroes who were brought to America." In case readers did not get his point, he titled two of his chapters "The Matriarchate" and "Granny: The Guardian of the Generations." Most blacks after emancipation, he argued, had formed their own "folk culture" in which the "maternal family organization, a heritage from slavery, has continued on a fairly broad scale." Out-of-wedlock births were widespread. Fifteen of his book's seventy-two tables of statistics measured various aspects of "illegitimacy" among black families, a development that had also troubled Du Bois. In a chapter titled "Outlawed Motherhood," Frazier warned that statistics were not altogether reliable, but nonetheless estimated that the proportion of black births out of wedlock, amounting to 20 percent in the 1930s, was five to ten times higher than that among whites. This problem, he wrote, was most serious among the poor and among "the naïve and ignorant folk who are newcomers to the city."

Frazier frequently reiterated this message, which greatly influenced later writers, including Moynihan. In a section titled "In the City of Destruction," Frazier dwelt on the disastrous effects of the migration of millions of southern black people to cities in the twentieth century. In his widely cited conclusion,

"Retrospect and Prospect," he wrote that urbanization since 1900 had "torn the Negro loose from his cultural moorings" and "brought the most momentous changes in the family life of the Negro since Emancipation." The "disintegrating forces of the city," he added, stranded black migrants in "deteriorated slum areas from which practically all institutional life has disappeared." These forces also caused the "dissolution of the rural folkways and mores" of black people and created a "tide of family disorganization."

In closing his book, Frazier wrote cautiously about possibilities for interracial integration in the future. There were "evidences at present," he wrote, that "Negroes and whites in the same occupational classes are being drawn into closer association than in the past" and that "intermarriage in the future will bring about a fundamental type of assimilation." But he also reiterated his far gloomier message:

> It appears that the family which evolved within the isolated world of the Negro folk will become increasingly disorganized. Modern means of communication will break down the isolation of the world of the black folk, and, as long as the bankrupt system of southern agriculture exists, Negro families will continue to seek a living in the towns and the cities of the country. They will crowd the slum areas of southern cities or make their way to northern cities where their family life will become disrupted and their poverty will force them to depend upon charity.[11]

Frazier's book deeply affected Myrdal, whose 1,400-page *An American Dilemma* remained the most widely cited analysis of U.S. race relations between 1944 and 1965. This work concentrated on the "dilemma" faced by white Americans, who struggled to resolve the contradiction between their ideals concerning democracy and equality and the reality of racism. Myrdal's predictions, based on the expectation that democratic ideals would win out in the end, were guardedly optimistic. But the book also included a 300-page section titled "The Negro Community" (written by one of Myrdal's assistants) that closely followed Frazier's book.[12]

Indeed, Myrdal relied on Frazier's expertise when developing his argument, soliciting from him a couple of essays to guide his writing. He also asked him to serve as a reader on the final draft of "The Negro Community.".This draft was if anything more grim than Frazier's own conclusions, referring—in words that obviously influenced Moynihan—to "The Negro Community as a Pathological Form of an American Community." Slavery and white racism, Myrdal maintained, had established black culture as "a distorted development, or a pathological condition, of the general American culture." Though a few scholars who read the draft criticized the negativity of this perspective, it survived in the book as published. Not only Frazier but also Du Bois read this section before publication and approved of it.[13]

Even as civil rights activism in the United States mounted in the 1940s and 1950s, sociologists did not do much to advance scholarly work on black family life. No studies approached the authority of Frazier's or Myrdal's. Insofar as Moynihan's later efforts were concerned, this was an unfortunate development—it meant that in 1965 he had to rely heavily on sociological findings that were more than twenty years old. But these were also years when the academic field of psychology blossomed as never before and when sweeping psychological interpretations gained emphasis in social science and in the culture at large. One of these was the idea in Myrdal's landmark book that black culture, having been savaged during the uniquely barbarous years of enslavement, had become "pathological."

Many other social scientists in these decades adopted psychological language to buttress their findings about various deprived groups in U.S. culture. Among them, in 1963, were Nathan Glazer and Moynihan in *Beyond the Melting Pot*. In his otherwise bleak chapter on blacks, Glazer offered a few guardedly optimistic predictions. New York City, he wrote, "will very likely in the end be an integrated city—or rather something even better, a city where people find homes and neighborhoods according to income and taste." But he also included disturbing statistics, observing that one-fourth of black households in New York City were female-headed compared with fewer than one-tenth of white households, and that the proportion of births out of wedlock among blacks was fourteen to fifteen times higher than that among whites. Glazer reminded readers that the majority of black families were *not* broken. But, echoing Du Bois and Frazier, he wrote that "the experience of slavery left as its most serious heritage a steady weakness in the Negro family."

The incidence of family problems among blacks, Glazer continued, was "enormous," increasing the likelihood of "psychological difficulties" among the males. His most memorable passage—one liberal critics later cited repeatedly to highlight his emphasis on cultural damage—stated: "It is not possible for Negroes to view themselves as other ethnic groups viewed themselves because—and this is the key to much in the Negro world—the Negro is only an American, and nothing else. He has no values and no culture to guard and protect."[14]

In 1963, Glazer wrote a mostly favorable introduction to the paperback edition of a book that, more than any other notable publication in that era, applied psychological theories to the historical study of black people in the United States—and that also clearly impressed Moynihan. This volume, by historian Stanley Elkins, was *Slavery: A Problem in American Institutional and Intellectual Life*. Elkins's new and, in some ways, unprecedented interpretation followed—but moved beyond—the recent historical work that had endeavored to show that slavery in the U.S. South, far from having been a relatively benign institution featuring magnolia blossoms, mint juleps, and benevolent masters, had been inexpressibly brutal. *Slavery*, a comparative history, maintained that the institution had been more savage in the United States than in other areas of the Western Hemisphere. It featured the "absolute power" of masters who had created a "closed system." This had eradicated African cultural traditions and had led to "a cruelly logical reduction of the African to a piece of mere property."

To cinch his point, Elkins relied on the findings of sociologists, psychologists, and anthropologists and on the research of child psychiatrist Bruno Bettelheim, who had argued that the totalitarian cruelty enforced in Nazi concentration camps had infantilized many of the inmates. Slaves in the United States, Elkins wrote, having been cruelly deprived of a culture of their own, similarly reverted to "infantile regression" and survived in a "truly childlike situation." The slave boy was a "Sambo," "docile but irresponsible, loyal but lazy, humble but chronically given to lying and stealing; his behavior was full of infantile silliness and his talk inflated with childish exaggeration."

This infantile condition was nowhere more clear, Elkins insisted, than in the family life of slaves. Like Du Bois, Frazier, and others, Elkins stressed that slavery allowed black marriage no standing in law and that slave parents had no way to prevent their children from being sold away. Adult male slaves, known only as "boy," lost "even the honorific attributes of fatherhood." Indeed, "father, among slaves, was 'unknown,' a husband without the rights of his bed." Slave women were treated as concubines. "Motherhood was clothed in the scant dignity of the breeding function."[15]

Having absorbed the ideas of all these scholars, including Elkins, Moynihan was preparing his report in early 1965 when yet another psychologically informed book appeared: Kenneth Clark's *Dark Ghetto*. Clark was a graduate of Howard and of Columbia University, where he had earned a PhD in psychology in 1940. During the preparation of Myrdal's *An American Dilemma* he had served as a research associate for the author (who reciprocated by writing a foreword to Clark's book in 1965). Clark had then become a professor of psychology at the College of the City of New York (CCNY). In 1954 Clark had earned fame in civil rights circles when U.S. Chief Justice Earl Warren cited his research arguing that racial segregation in the schools psychologically damaged black children. The Court's unanimous decision against state-mandated public school segregation, *Brown v. Board of Education*, was a milestone in the civil rights movement as well as a sign that psychological approaches to the study of racism had arrived on a significant stage.

Clark had also joined the social scientists—and Moynihan—to write essays on the "Negro American" for a special issue of *Daedalus*, the scholarly journal of the American Academy of Arts and Sciences. In the early 1960s, he was the guiding force behind Harlem Youth Opportunities Unlimited (HARYOU), which had received modest funding from President Kennedy's Committee on Juvenile Delinquency and Youth Crime. Established in 1961, this was the Kennedy administration's first venture into policymaking concerned with urban problems. *Dark Ghetto*, Clark explained, stemmed from his work with HARYOU as well as from his having lived for more than forty years in Harlem; it was a "summation of my personal and lifelong experiences and observations as a prisoner of the ghetto."

Clark did not portray black Americans as infantile or without hope. Many black people, he wrote, displayed "surprising human resilience." In Harlem, for instance, they had rioted in 1964 to protest racist indignities such as badly paid jobs, dilapidated housing, ill-financed schools, and inadequate health care. Racial protests had also broken out in other U.S. cities that summer. The Civil Rights Act of 1964, Clark explained, had been too little, too late for inner-city blacks, who suffered especially from economic woes. "The dark ghettos," he emphasized, "are social, political, educational, and—above all—economic ghettos." Economic deprivation had provoked a rising militancy among upwardly mobile youths who were "demanding a higher standard of living than their families had."

But Clark, like Frazier, Myrdal, Elkins, and Glazer, also maintained that economic distress had caused grievous psychological harm as well as what he called a "Culture of Cultural Deprivation." Moreover, the harm had deep historical roots. Writing of the damage slavery had inflicted on black people, especially men, he emphasized that the male slave had been "systematically used as a stud." Slavery had fostered the rise of a "Negro Matriarchy," which along with the "continued post-slavery relegation of the Negro male to menial and subservient status, has made the female the dominant person in the Negro family." After citing statistics concerning family breakup (these showed that roughly 50 percent of black children in Harlem lived with only one parent and that one-fourth of these children were on welfare, he pointed to the high prevalence of childbearing by blacks out of wedlock. A "distorted masculine image" that led black men to flaunt their maleness helped to inflate such high numbers. More generally, he added, "Negroes have come to believe in their own inferiority." Their doubts have "become the seeds of a pernicious self- and group-hatred, the Negro's complex and pernicious prejudice against himself." Hence the "preoccupation with hair straighteners, skin bleaches, and the like."

Dark Ghetto traced this psychological legacy to its roots in the past. Indeed, one of Clark's earlier reports had coined the phrase "tangle of pathology" to describe lower-class black life in the inner city. In *Dark Ghetto* this emphasis was most apparent in chapters titled "The Psychology of the Ghetto" and "The Pathology of the Ghetto." Clark wrote that "the dark ghetto is institutionalized pathology; it is chronic, self-perpetuating pathology." Moreover, "the pathologies of the ghetto commonly perpetuate themselves through cumulation, ugliness, deterioration, and isolation and strengthen the Negro's sense of worthlessness giving testimony to his impotence."[16]

All of these writers deeply influenced Pat Moynihan, who frequently cited them, especially Frazier, in his famous report. He closed his preface by quoting Myrdal's opinion that whites could still improve race relations. "America is free," Myrdal had said, "to choose whether the Negro shall remain her liability or become her opportunity." Moynihan was also excited by Elkins's book. In the final report, he cited Glazer's introduction to it at length. Obviously indebted to Clark as well, Moynihan cited a HARYOU report of 1964 four times and titled his longest chapter "The Tangle of Pathology."

Later critics punched holes in Moynihan's reliance upon these writers, whose scholarship had encountered a number of serious obstacles. Firsthand historical sources (as from plantations) were hard to access, and demographic data from the past were incomplete. It was difficult if not impossible to document the mysterious processes of intergenerational transmission of cultural traits. Moreover, Moynihan's use of some of these sources was controversial. Elkins, some critics claimed, exaggerated the long-range psychological and cultural damage caused by slavery in the United States. Moynihan's reliance on him, historian Peter Novick observed later, resulted in "the most hyperbolic passage in a document not generally given to understatement."[17]

Frazier, critics of Moynihan added, had held out hope that blacks in time would integrate into the economic mainstream; the abject state into which they had fallen during the Depression-haunted 1930s might be temporary. But Moynihan, they said, nonetheless selected the most pessimistic passages from Frazier to argue that blacks, unless helped, were in danger of falling into an irremediably disorganized state. Other critics simply thought that Frazier's magnum opus had been too gloomy. One hypersuspicious critic wondered if Moynihan or his staff had made a "calculated effort" to "find a well-known black scholar to legitimate the Moynihan-Johnson viewpoint."

It is easy to see, however, why Moynihan cited the writers he did. Elkins's book, to be sure, had already whipped up controversy: had Moynihan consulted seriously with black militants, he might have decided not to mention it. But a number of prominent black authors during the early 1960s, writing ever more bitterly about the impact of slavery on black Americans, had adopted nearly the same catastrophic view as Elkins's. James Baldwin, for instance, wrote in 1961 that the American Negro slave "is unique among the black men of the world in that his past was taken from him, almost literally, in one blow."[18] Moreover, the publications of Du Bois, Frazier (who had died in 1962), and Myrdal—all of whom shared this grim view—were very highly regarded. Glazer was a respected sociologist, Clark a psychologist of note.

Anyone who hoped to employ the expertise of scholars in order to prepare a report on the black family would necessarily have turned to their writings, which stressed two points: blacks suffered from economic exploitation, and slavery had disastrous long-range cultural effects.

The argument that blacks were deeply submerged economically was beyond doubt. Moreover, although some of the statistics used by Du Bois, Frazier, and others concerning children born out of wedlock were inexact, Moynihan was on solid ground in believing that these numbers had always been considerably higher among blacks, especially low-income blacks, than among whites of comparable income levels. He was also correct to stress that the proportion of black births that were nonmarital (though a little lower, according to U.S. Census numbers, than Frazier and others had estimated) had increased since 1940—especially since 1960. Official statistics indicated that 2 percent of births to white women had been nonmarital in 1940, a percentage that remained stable in 1950 and 1960 before rising to 4 percent in 1965. By contrast, the proportion among blacks had been 17 percent in 1940, increasing to 18 percent in 1950 and 22 percent in 1960—and more rapidly to 25 percent in 1965.[19]

These scholars' emphasis on the damage slavery had caused to lower-class black family life, however, remained contested. If a group suffers from centuries of abuse and subjection, does it mean, as Elkins supposed, that its culture is likely to be shattered, or that it can be left in such a psychologically weakened condition that it passes on that miserable and pathetic situation to its children, who in turn pass it on to theirs? Scholars who wrote with alarm about an intergenerational "culture of poverty" tended to think so, and to offer similarly pessimistic perspectives and predictions.

But it can also be argued that racial oppression—even if rooted in so powerful an institution as slavery—likely affects individual people in varying ways. Some ex-slaves (like property-owning blacks in the late nineteenth century) and their descendants (like some who joined the "industrial proletariat" in the 1930s) may have shown greater resourcefulness than others. Overcoming long odds, they may have secured reasonably stable employment, formed two-parent families, and imparted mainstream values to later generations. Indeed, as Moynihan pointed out, many African Americans were moving into the middle classes. Moreover, only 22 percent of black births as late as 1960 were nonmarital. If cultural transmission dating from slavery had been truly overwhelming, creating thereby a black "matriarchy," would not black families have become far more fragile by that time?

May it not also be the case that developments in the structural environment of communities—the availability of decent employment, housing, and schools—are the primary sources of changes in any group's cultural traits? After all, it was obvious that female-headed families—and the economic and behavioral ills often associated with such families—were far more prevalent among the black inner-city poor than among the black middle classes. If economic burdens were the major cause of family disorganization, as many liberals then and later insisted, well-targeted reform of structural conditions could make a difference. The vicious cycle of poverty and related problems, not puncture-proof, might then slow down. As sociologist Lee Rainwater later put it to Moynihan, "culture can by and large not be changed directly, or at least is inordinately difficult to change." But culture was not immutable. "If one can change the situation to which it [the culture] is an adaptation," he added, "then one can count on the people themselves to gradually change their culture."[20]

Although scholarship influenced Moynihan's thinking in 1965, the demands of various black civil rights leaders also played a significant role in the development of his arguments. These demands escalated rapidly in the early 1960s. Up until 1963, most civil rights leaders, notably Martin Luther King Jr., had practiced a strategy of protest that featured nonviolent direct action and interracial cooperation. Condemning the Jim Crow system of segregation as immoral, they appealed to the consciences of white people. These appeals enabled civil rights activists in the South—brave and Christlike targets of racism and violence—to hold the moral high ground. Aided further by the counterproductive viciousness of many southern law enforcement officials, they gained the support of sympathetic whites who believed in what Myrdal had called the "American creed" of equality of opportunity. Among these sympathizers as of mid-1963 was President Kennedy. Calling for civil rights legislation, he intoned, "We are confronted primarily with a moral issue. It is as old as the scriptures and is as clear as the American Constitution."

Even then, however, King's nonviolent interracial efforts, which were focused on the South, had seemed to arouse relatively little overt enthusiasm among blacks in the cities of the North and West. Many inner-city blacks were members of the working poor—patriotic, church-going, blue-collar Americans who cherished the virtues of hard work and self-reliance. Many others, however, were crowded into poverty-stricken ghettos and struggling to find living-wage employment. Millions of blacks, inspired by rising rights consciousness, were becoming increasingly proud and impatient. The demonstrations that broke out in Harlem and other central cities in 1964 attested to their restlessness.

By late 1964, civil rights leaders seeking to apprehend the feelings of the inner-city masses began to worry that urban rioting might break out on a larger scale. As they struggled to keep up with the mounting unrest in cities, they increased their demands for major governmental assaults on poverty, de facto segregation, and other racist practices in the North. Some whites, too, demanded reforms to improve the ghettos. Myrdal had already drawn attention to the terrible conditions of black inner-city areas, publishing *Challenge to Affluence* in 1962, in which he deplored the "emergence of an American 'under-class' of unemployed and largely unemployable and underemployed."

Malcolm X also rose to prominence, especially after 1963. As a black nationalist, he rejected the interracial cooperation strategies of leaders such as King. Stressing (as Elkins had) that slavery had ravaged U.S. black culture, he also spoke often about the disorganization of black families. Blacks, he declared, must take charge of their own lives. "Get off the welfare," he exclaimed. "Get off that compensation line. Be a man. Earn what you need for your family." Though Malcolm X toned down the racialism of his message before he was assassinated in February 1965, it was clear that his rage at white oppression resonated with many black people, especially those who lived in the ghettos. Relatively few blacks joined either the Nation of Islam or Malcolm X's spin-off Organization of Afro-American Unity, but huge numbers were tiring of nonviolent strategies. Soon they would be demanding Black Power.

Bayard Rustin, a prominent black activist and theoretician, rejected Malcolm X's black nationalism, advocating instead massive governmental programs to promote social and economic equality for poor whites as well as blacks. As a key organizer of the March on Washington of 1963, he had named the effort "A March for *Jobs* and Freedom." Though King stole the show with his "I Have a Dream" speech, Rustin continued to press for what he and veteran black civil rights leader A. Philip Randolph were to label a Freedom Budget. In 1965, they called upon the U.S. government to appropriate $100 billion—a sum that was almost as large as the entire federal budget in that year—to use in a fight for economic justice. In an article Rustin wrote for *Commentary* in February 1965, "From Protest to Politics: The Future of the Civil Rights Movement," he argued that the struggle for civil rights was becoming a large-scale social movement and that Washington must move to confront the unique and disastrous plight of the black poor.

Whitney Young, executive director of the National Urban League, outlined in 1964 a similar (though politically more realistic) program in *To Be Equal*. The title conveyed its message: blacks needed not only legal rights but also socioeconomic justice in order to achieve equal citizenship. Like Rustin, he laid out a program—a "domestic Marshall Plan" of $20 billion in public and private aid—to rescue black people in the cities. Citing Michael Harrington's *The Other America*, Young demonstrated that black unemployment and school dropout rates had become far higher than those of whites and that black family income in the cities, relative to that of whites, had been slipping since 1952. As a result, the economic situation had led to "disaster," "a study in inhumanity."

Young also sought to repair the disorganization of black families, which he believed had deep historical roots. Slavery, he wrote, had promoted "promiscuous breeding." Even after emancipation, the "Negro male was emasculated economically" and "the composition of the Negro family continued to be such that the father, if identified, had no established role, and the Negro male, his manhood weakened, suffered economically and psychologically." Blacks lived in a "matriarchal society" perpetuated by a poorly designed welfare system that managed only to keep female-headed households barely afloat. In addition to better housing, schools, and jobs, blacks needed family planning information, publicly supported day-care centers, and better-trained social workers.[21]

No writer better described the rapidly rising militancy of urban black people than Charles Silberman, a white editor at *Fortune* magazine who published a well-received book about race relations, *Crisis in Black and White*, in mid-1964. Liberal whites, he wrote, had come at last to appreciate the need for measures (notably the Civil Rights Act of 1964) to combat legal inequality. But they were blind to the frightful socioeconomic condition of the ghettos and to the mounting pride and bitterness among the black masses. "The tragedy of race relations in the United States," he declared, "is that there is no American Dilemma." Whites, he argued, must go beyond guaranteeing civil rights to advance social and economic equality for black people. Without major action, the "crisis in black and white" would explode.

To make his case, Silberman followed in the footsteps of the many other scholars and activists who had described the oppression and discrimination—structural forces—that had caused "disorganization of the family," which in turn had long-term cultural consequences. "The difficulty Negro men experience in finding decent jobs," he wrote, "is central to the perpetuation of matriarchy and the weakness of family relationships." The root cause of this situation was slavery, which "had emasculated the Negro males, had made them shiftless and irresponsible and promiscuous," and by negating their role as husband and father, forced them to become "totally dependent on the will of another." After emancipation, Silberman continued, there had been more of the same: "With no history of stable families, no knowledge even of what stability might mean, huge numbers of Negro men took to the roads as soon as freedom was proclaimed. . . . Thus there developed a pattern of drifting from place to place and job to job and woman to woman that has persisted (in lesser degree, of course) to the present day."[22]

While preparing his report, Moynihan did not consult the most militant civil rights leaders, and he did not cite Silberman. But his first chapter was titled "The Negro American Revolution," which featured a "demand for equality." He wrote, "The Negro revolution, like the industrial upheaval of the 1930s, is a movement for equality as well as for liberty." Citing Rustin's article and (later in the report) Young's book, Moynihan made it abundantly clear that he was aware of the rising impatience of black people in the North, that blacks faced awesome structural obstacles, and that decisive governmental action, especially in the area of family policy, was essential if these obstacles were ever to be overcome.

Moynihan on occasion referred to a Negro "subculture," but, believing structural barriers were the major enemy, he did not dwell on cultural issues. Like Young, he favored "national action" that would in effect become a form of affirmative action. Like Young, Silberman, and the many other writers from the strands of opinion that he consulted—scholarly as well as activist—he agreed that the matriarchal family structure of Negro society had powerful historical roots and that it "reinforces itself over the generations." Because this structure was different from that of whites, it was disadvantageous in the predominantly patriarchal U.S. society and a major part of a "tangle of pathology" that harmed black people. As he soon wrote in the report, "At the heart of the deterioration of the fabric of Negro society is the deterioration of the Negro family. It is the fundamental source of the weakness of the Negro community at the present time."

The words "deterioration," "fundamental," and "weakness"—favorites of Moynihan's—made clear his essential message that many American blacks, brutalized by centuries of oppression, needed massive help. The freedom they were at last conferred by the Civil Rights and Voting Rights acts of 1964 and 1965 was simply not enough.

With these ideas in mind, Moynihan and Barton sat down in mid-February 1965 to produce what Barton later called a "writer's outline." As Barton remembered, Moynihan then "pounded [the report] out of his typewriter," completing his labors within a few weeks. It was to be an internal report for the eyes of top government officials, not a public document. Barton emphasized, "He had conceived the Report and directed work on it; now he wrote it, word for word. It truly was the Moynihan Report—but it was a government report with no names on the cover."[23]

Moynihan's final draft went to the basement of the Labor Department, where on March 15 the publications office printed 100 copies, 99 of which went into a safe. They were marked "For Official Use Only." Wirtz, shown a copy, recalled the "almost physical excitement of reading it." Getting the report printed, Moynihan believed, would help it to receive more attention from top officials than would a typewritten paper. Barton also recalls thinking that the work "had been done in an extraordinarily short time. *And no reviewers had been used, and no one else, to my knowledge, had even read the Report.*"

After the report had been printed, Moynihan moved quickly to bring it to the attention of top administration officials. Wirtz, aiding him, sent a copy of it to Moyers on March 23, adding, "Bill, this is the Moynihan report I called you about. I think it warrants *very serious* consideration. There are *no* other copies in circulation." Moynihan later said that Moyers "read it [the report] and got very interested in it." On May 3, Moynihan wrote a memo summarizing his main arguments, and on May 4, Wirtz relayed it to the White House. Wirtz added the excited comment, "the attached Memorandum is nine pages of dynamite about the Negro situation." He added, "I agree with Pat's analysis and concur in his recommendations."[24]

Highlighting many of the major arguments of his report, *The Negro Family: The Case for National Action*, Moynihan's memorandum of May 3 reveals the strength of his personal feelings about the need of children to have the presence of two parents. It is hard to read it without believing that memories of his own childhood heightened his desire to bring about changes in inner-city black family life.[25]

The memo began by declaring, as Moynihan had done earlier, that the civil rights movement was then "entering a second stage, and a new crisis." The first stage had focused on securing rights "traditionally associated with *Liberty*"— the right to vote, to assemble, to petition, "to move about in public places," and to "compete for jobs and other rewards of the marketplace." The second stage for progress in civil rights featured demands for "the democratic ideal of *Equality*"—for "equally good education, equally good housing, equally good jobs." This argument echoed those Moynihan had made in early 1964 when urging a poverty program to address the special problems of blacks. "Equal *opportunity* for Negroes," he now repeated, "does not produce equal *results*—because the *Negroes today are a grievously injured people who in fair and equal competition will by and large lose out.*"

"How come?" Moynihan asked. His answer: "*the master problem is that the Negro family structure is crumbling.*" "Everyone knows from personal experience," he went on to say, how fundamental family structure is. He then stroked Johnson: "You were born poor. You were brought up poor. Yet you came of age full of ambition, energy, and ability. Because your mother and father gave it to you. The richest inheritance any child can have is a stable, loving, disciplined family life."

As evidence that Johnson should comprehend, Moynihan explained that one-fourth of all Negro children born in the United States in 1964 had been "illegitimate," that 36 percent of black children were living with one or both parents missing, and that "56 percent of Negro youth, sooner or later on, receive Aid to Families with Dependent Children payments. . . . As against 8 percent of whites." "*Probably not much more than a third of Negro youth reach*

18 having lived all their lives with both parents." He concluded, again underlining his message, "*Without exception every statistical measure of Negro family stability has gotten worse, not better, over the past fifteen years.*"

Moynihan went on to say, "Many people think that the color problem is insoluble." "Nonsense," he retorted. To prove his point he stressed that Japanese and Chinese Americans had faced "the worst kind of racial discrimination and mistreatment." But they had become "a prosperous middle-class group." How? "One of the reasons that it was possible . . . is that the Japanese and Chinese have probably the most close-knit family structure of any group in America."

Moynihan closed by suggesting how the government might deal with the many and interconnected needs of blacks. A "working party" should "review every relevant program of the Federal government to determine whether it is helping to strengthen the Negro family or simply perpetrating its weaknesses." For example, he added, the United States was "practically the only industrial democracy in the world that does not have a system of family allowances for families with *fathers present*, but we have a vast Federal system [of welfare] to support families with *fathers absent.*"

Still, he had more policies than family allowances in mind. As in 1964, he advocated a large-scale public employment program for black men "even if we have to displace some females" so that "every able-bodied Negro male is working," and a housing effort to enable blacks to live in the suburbs. He added that "Negro youth must be given a greater opportunity to serve in the Armed Forces," and that dissemination of birth control information was needed to help "bring the Negro birth rate back into line with that of whites and cut down the rate of illegitimacy." Returning to the necessity of helping *men* find work, he said, "More can be done about redesigning jobs that are thought to be women's jobs and turning them into men's jobs: his type of job is declining, while the jobs open to the Negro female are expanding."

Whether Johnson ever read Moynihan's report or memos is unclear—Moynihan did not know, and LBJ's aides said later that he had not done so. But Moynihan soon tried again to arouse presidential attention, directing yet another memo on the subject to Moyers on May 19. "*Ways must be found,*" he wrote, "*to free the Negro male at every social level to assume responsibility up to the limit of his talent.*" A day later, he wrote McPherson about the need to promote *equality* for blacks. "It seems to me that if there was one thing for which Lyndon Johnson was put on earth," he added, "it is to make it possible for this to happen."[26]

Somehow, the barrage of memoranda finally reached their target. In late May, Moynihan and LBJ's chief speechwriter, Richard Goodwin, were asked to rush ahead with a speech on civil rights that the president was scheduled to give at Howard University's commencement on June 4. By June 1, Moynihan completed a draft of an address titled "To Fulfill These Rights."[27]

While Moynihan and Goodwin were at the White House crafting the final version of the speech during the night of June 3 and early morning of June 4, Moynihan telephoned Barton and asked him to list ten areas, backed by statistics, in which blacks had made progress, and ten in which they had lost ground. With the aid of a researcher from the Bureau of Labor Statistics, Barton supplied the information. (Later, reading the speech, Barton discovered that only the losing-ground statistics had been included.) Moynihan also asked him whether everything in the report was absolutely correct. "Both our jobs," he said, "might depend on it." Barton replied that the report indicated that there were no differences between the races in terms of intelligence, but that he, Barton, was not sure that science had established that. "Well," Moynihan shrugged, "we won't worry about that one."[28]

As Moynihan had urged in his memo to Wirtz in December 1964, the Howard speech announced the "next and more profound stage of the battle for civil rights," one the government, not civil rights leaders, would lead. It also called for the establishment of "equality as a fact and as a result" for black Americans. Had its goals been implemented, it would indeed have engaged the government—and the American people—in a new and far more ambitious quest for racial justice.

CHAPTER 3

The Report

M oynihan's report did not bear his name. Its spare title page carried the date March 1965 and the words "Office of Policy Planning and Research, United States Department of Labor." The text that followed was short, but it was clearly organized, boldly stated, and statistically rich. After a one-page preface, its text of fifty-three pages contained forty-one tables and graphs, as well as sixty-one footnotes, thirty-eight of which cited books, articles, HARYOU findings, and government reports published between 1963 and 1965. Twelve of the notes referred readers to sources that had appeared in December 1964 or afterward—testimony to Moynihan's efforts to include up-to-date information. An appendix of twenty-two additional tables followed the text and notes. As Paul Barton observed later, it was remarkable that the report, which was completed with extraordinary speed (in less than three months) contained "no significant errors."

The preface began with this dramatic point: "The United States is approaching a new crisis in race relations." The nation, Moynihan continued, had made considerable strides since the *Brown v. Board of Education* decision of 1954, notably by passing the Civil Rights Act of 1964, through which "the demand of Negro Americans for full recognition of their civil rights was finally met." But "a new period is beginning," in which "the expectations of the Negro Americans will go beyond civil rights. Being Americans, they will now expect that in the near future equal opportunities for them as a group will produce roughly equal results as compared with other groups."

Moynihan went on, "This is not going to happen. Nor will it happen for generations to come unless a new and special effort is made." In six short paragraphs Moynihan gave two reasons for this prognosis. The first, set forth in a memorable phrase, was that "the racist virus in the American bloodstream still afflicts us: Negroes will encounter serious personal prejudice for at least another generation." The second—a key to the argument of the report as a whole— was that "three centuries of sometimes unimaginable mistreatment have taken their toll on the Negro people. The harsh fact is that as a group, at the present time, in terms of ability to win out in the competitions of American life, they are not equal to most of those groups with which they will be competing." Moreover, he added, "In these terms the circumstances of the Negro American community in recent years has probably been getting *worse, not better.*"[1]

The "fundamental problem," Moynihan then wrote,

> is that of family structure. The evidence—not final, but powerfully persuasive—is that the Negro family in the urban ghettos is crumbling. A middle-class group has managed to save itself, but for vast numbers of the unskilled, poorly educated city working class the fabric of conventional social relationships has all but disintegrated. There are indications that the situation may have been arrested in the past few years, but the general post-war trend is unmistakable. So long as this situation persists, the cycle of poverty and disadvantage will continue to repeat itself.

Closing his preface, Moynihan repeated his argument that the nation confronted a "new kind of problem." He added, "Measures that have worked in the past, or would work for most groups in the present, will not work here. A national effort is required that will give a unity of purpose to the many activities of the Federal government in this area, directed to a new kind of national goal: the establishment of a stable Negro family structure."

The preface made it clear that Moynihan was primarily describing a subset of low-income families in "urban ghettos," not the considerably larger numbers of blacks who lived in the countryside or in relatively stable working-class or middle-class neighborhoods.[2] This emphasis, which reflected his ecological approach to social problems, necessarily imposed a gloomy tone on the report. Nonetheless, it should have been evident that Moynihan was making an effort not to generalize too much or to dump all blacks into the same foundering boat. A "middle-class group," he reminded readers, "has managed to save itself." "There are indications that the situation may have been arrested in the past few years." "Given equal opportunities," children of intact middle-class families "will perform as well [as] or better than their white peers." Black girls tended to do better in school and in the workforce than black men. At one point he stated, "Individually, Negro Americans reach the highest peaks of achievement."

Readers of the preface would also have realized that Moynihan was preaching an aggressively liberal message. He did not blame blacks living in ghettos for having fallen into the depths: the source of their troubles was "three centuries of sometimes unimaginable mistreatment." For this reason they were different from "other ethnic and religious and regional groups." Bitter at their treatment, they were not going to tolerate it any longer. A national effort by the federal government must be mounted to combat the new crisis in race relations and to help black people achieve "equal results" as well as "equal opportunities."

Even a reader unfamiliar with these issues would likely have come away from the preface with several other impressions. It was clear that Moynihan, eschewing dry academic prose, had a fondness for dramatic language, memorable images, and italicized and boldfaced type. A "racist virus" still afflicted the "American bloodstream." Matters were getting "*worse, not better.*" Black families in the ghettos were "crumbling." The "cycle of poverty and disadvantage will continue to repeat itself." Attention-grabbing language and images such as these, which also appeared in the chapters that followed, were hardly unique in writings about ghetto life: Clark's *Dark Ghetto* was full of them. In general, however, Moynihan's writing conveyed the grim message that lower-class blacks in the cities were trapped by strong systemic forces. Unless these could be challenged, things could only get worse.

Five chapters followed the preface, the first of which, "The Negro American Revolution," briefly recounted recent events in the civil rights movement as well as the contributions of the Kennedy and Johnson administrations to improve race relations. But programs enacted in the "first phase of the Negro revolution—Manpower Retraining, Job Training, Community Action, and the like—only make opportunities available. They cannot insure the outcome." Blacks, Moynihan emphasized, were now engaged in a "demand for equality." Quoting recent *Commentary* essays by Bayard Rustin and Nathan Glazer to bolster his case, he emphasized a key argument of his report: "The principal challenge of the next phase of the Negro revolution is to make certain that equality of results will now follow." An ominous warning followed: "If we do not, there will be no social peace in the United States for generations."

At the start of the second chapter, "The Negro American Family," Moynihan sharpened the already urgent tone of his writing, declaring that the "deterioration of the Negro family" is "at the heart of the deterioration of the fabric of Negro society." As in his preface, he stressed that this deterioration stemmed from "three centuries of exploitation." He then emphasized, "There is one truly great discontinuity in family structure in the United States at the present time: that between the white world in general and that of the Negro American." He concluded,

> **The white family has achieved a high degree of stability and is maintaining that stability.**
>
> **By contrast, the family structure of lower class Negroes is highly unstable, and in many urban centers is approaching complete breakdown.**

As if recognizing that he might appear to be overgeneralizing, Moynihan again reminded readers that "the Negro community is in fact dividing between a stable middle-class group that is steadily growing stronger and more successful, and an increasingly disorganized and disadvantaged lower-class group." But he went on to note that the "emergence and increasing visibility of a Negro middle class may beguile the nation into supposing that the circumstances of the remainder of the Negro community are equally prosperous, whereas just the opposite is true at the present, and is likely to continue so." He added, "The lumping of all Negroes together in one statistical measurement very probably conceals the extent of the disorganization among the lower-class group."

Moynihan then asked readers to remember that many of the statistics in the report "refer only to a specific point in time. . . . They do not measure the experience of individuals over time." The average monthly unemployment rate for black males in 1964, he pointed out, was recorded at 9 percent. "But *during* 1964, some 29 percent of Negro males were unemployed at one time or another." He added, "If 36 percent of Negro children are living in broken homes *at any specific moment*, it is likely that a far higher proportion of Negro children find themselves in that situation *at one time or another* in their lives."

Having alerted his readers to the ways statistics can be misunderstood, Moynihan crammed the rest of the chapter with graphs and tables—ten in nine pages. Many boldfaced and capitalized headings summarized their findings:

Nearly a Quarter of Urban Negro Marriages Are Dissolved
Nearly One-Quarter of Negro Births Are Now Illegitimate
THE NONWHITE ILLEGITIMACY IS 8 TIMES THE WHITE
    RATIO[3]
ALMOST ONE FOURTH OF NONWHITE FAMILIES ARE
    HEADED BY A WOMAN

Text accompanying the statistics highlighted three facts: black family disorganization, as defined by measures such as these, was far more prevalent than that of whites; trends among blacks were rapidly getting worse, not better; and the behavioral ills of blacks in large urban ghettos were considerably more frightening than those elsewhere. The proportion of white births out of wedlock, for instance, had risen from 2 percent in 1940 to 3.07 percent in 1963. By contrast, the proportion for blacks during these years had jumped from 16.8 to 23.6 percent (thereby remaining roughly eight times that among whites). In central Harlem, 43 percent of live births to nonwhite women were nonmarital in 1963. In many other cities—for example, Chicago, Cincinnati, St. Louis, Memphis, and Washington, D.C.—the proportion of nonwhite births out of wedlock had risen substantially between 1950 and 1963, from around 20 percent in 1950 to 30 percent or more in 1963. "The percent of nonwhite families headed by a female was more than double the percent for whites. Fatherless nonwhite families increased by nearly 17 percent between 1950 and 1960, but held constant for white families." Moynihan added, "Only a minority of Negro children reach the age of 18 having lived all their lives with both their parents."

With a boldfaced heading announcing "The Breakdown of the Negro Family Has Led to a Startling Increase in Welfare Dependency," Moynihan introduced statistics that especially alarmed him. A total of 14 percent of nonwhite children, he wrote, were receiving AFDC assistance compared with 2 percent of white children. Eight percent of white children got such assistance at some time in their lives, compared with 56 percent of nonwhites. Deploring the inadequacy of the program, he added, "Let it be noted, however, that out of a total of 1.8 million nonwhite illegitimate children in the nation in 1961, 1.3 million were *not* receiving aid under the AFDC program, although a substantial number have, or will, receive aid at some time in their lives."

"Again," the report emphasized, "the situation may be worsening." Moynihan explained that AFDC had been intended mainly to provide care for needy widows and orphans. In 1935, only one-third of the families covered were families in which the father had deserted. "Today it is two-thirds." The Department of Health, Education, and Welfare (HEW), he said, estimated that between two-thirds and three-fourths of the 50 percent increase from 1948 to 1955 in the number of absent-father families receiving AFDC could be explained by an increase in broken homes in the population. Moynihan concluded: "The steady expansion of this welfare program, as of public assistance programs in general, can be taken as a measure of the steady disintegration of the Negro family structure over the past generation in the United States."

In chapter 3, "The Roots of the Problem," Moynihan turned to the causes of these unhappy developments. Enter the grim statistics and explanations of Frazier, Glazer, and Elkins concerning slavery, the dominance of women in slave families in the United States, and the appearance of the Sambo personality. He quickly narrated the miseries of Reconstruction and of the late nineteenth century, when "Jim Crow made its appearance" and when "keeping the Negro 'in his place' can be translated as keeping the Negro male in his place: the female was not a threat to anyone." These historical developments were covered quickly, in two and a half pages. But, coming as they did at the start of the chapter, it was easy to see that he considered them powerful sources of present-day problems. Moynihan colorfully explained that these events "worked against the emergence of a strong father figure. The very essence of the male animal, from the bantam rooster to the four-star general, is to strut." But "not for the Negro male. The 'sassy nigger' was lynched."

Moynihan went on, however, to argue that slavery and Jim Crow were not the only sources of contemporary black social ills. The urbanization of the black population, which advanced in the twentieth century, was "immensely disruptive of social patterns." Drawing on Frazier and on his own writing in *Beyond the Melting Pot*, he declared, "It was this abrupt transition that produced the wild Irish slums of the 19th-Century Northeast. Drunkenness, crime, corruption, discrimination, family disorganization, and juvenile delinquency were the routine of that era. In our own time, the same sudden transition has produced the Negro slum—different from, but hardly better than its predecessors, and fundamentally the result of the same process."[4]

After citing Frazier at length, Moynihan featured a bar graph showing that "ONE THIRD OF NONWHITE CHILDREN LIVE IN BROKEN HOMES," compared with only 10 percent of white children. The highest percentages were in urban areas. He then summed up his own view: "In every index of family pathology—divorce, separation, and desertion, female family head, children in broken homes, and illegitimacy—the contrast between the urban and rural environment for Negro families is unmistakable."

The closing pages of "The Roots of the Problem" devoted considerable space to "Unemployment and Poverty." Moynihan focused on the impact of structural forces impeding black Americans. Four large bar graphs illustrated the close causal connection between nonwhite male unemployment rates and illegitimacy and family disruption.

Here, as throughout the report, it was the plight of black *men* rather than that of women that especially disturbed him. Rates of black male joblessness, he showed, had grown since World War II and had normally been two times higher than those among whites. In 1963, a prosperous year, 29.2 percent of all Negro men in the labor force did not have a job at some point during the year. Almost half of these men were unemployed fifteen weeks or more. Using a favorite word, "fundamental," Moynihan deplored a long-standing situation: "The fundamental, overwhelming fact is that *Negro unemployment*, with the exception of a few years during World War II and the Korean War, *has continued at disaster levels for 35 years*."

One of Moynihan's most striking graphs presented the relationship between the nonwhite male unemployment rate in 1960 and the percentage of nonwhite births out of wedlock in 1963 in various census tracts of the District of Columbia. It indicated that the higher the unemployment, the higher the proportions of nonmarital births three years later. These out-of-wedlock birth proportions were 40 percent or more in tracts with nonwhite male unemployment rates of 12 percent or more. Another graph, again concerning Washington census tracts, showed a similarly close relationship between median nonwhite family incomes and percentages of nonmarital nonwhite births. This statistic was around 12 percent in tracts where median family incomes were $8,000 and above, but neared 40 percent in tracts where the median incomes were below $4,000.

"The Tangle of Pathology," Moynihan's next, longest, and, for his critics, most incendiary chapter, opened by reiterating that the Negro community had "paid a fearful price for the incredible mistreatment to which it has been subjected over the past three centuries." This mistreatment had forced many black families into a "matriarchal structure, which, because it is so out of touch with the rest of American society, seriously retards the progress of the group as a whole, and imposes a crushing burden on the Negro male, and in consequence, on a great many Negro women as well." Moynihan elaborated on this point: there is "no special reason why a society in which males are dominant in family relationships is to be preferred to a matriarchal arrangement. However, it is clearly a disadvantage for a minority group to be operating on one principle, while the great majority of the population, and the one with the most advantages to begin with, is operating on another."

A key and controversial passage followed in which Moynihan explained the complexity of these patterns. It began as he tried to clarify that "not every instance of social pathology afflicting the Negro community can be traced to the weakness of family structure." Indeed, a central theme of the report was that the myriad social ills of the ghetto—products of segregation and discrimination—were environmental and interdependent. He reminded his readers that whites largely controlled organized crime in black communities, and that "the hostility and fear many whites exhibit toward Negroes" also afflicted black lives. He continued, "There is no one Negro community. There is no one Negro problem. There is no one solution." He added:

> Nonetheless, at the center of the tangle of pathology is the weakness
> of the family structure. Once or twice removed, it will be found to be

the principal source of most of the aberrant, inadequate, or anti-social behavior that did not establish, but now serves to perpetuate the cycle of poverty and deprivation.

It was by destroying the Negro family under slavery that white America broke the will of the Negro people. Although that will has re-asserted itself in our time, it is a resurgence doomed to frustration unless the viability of the Negro family is restored.

Much of the rest of the chapter offered statistics on the damaging impact of broken homes, matriarchy, and discrimination on black communities. Black youth, he wrote, performed poorly on the mental tests that are a standard means of measuring ability and performance. In accounting for these differences, Moynihan emphasized that "there is absolutely no question of any genetic differential: intelligence potential is distributed among Negro infants in the same proportion and pattern as among Icelanders or Chinese or any other group. American society, however, impairs the Negro potential."

More than in other parts of the report, Moynihan here evinced a fondness for the sociopsychological explanations that had come to pervade U.S. social science during the postwar years. Briefly discussing delinquency and high crime rates among blacks, he blamed both on the "combined impact of poverty, failure, and isolation among Negro youth." He concluded, however, by citing three studies from psychological journals that supported his core belief in the importance of stable families. "One study," he added, "showed that children from fatherless homes seek immediate gratification of their desires far more than children with fathers present." He cinched his case by citing a favorite source, Thomas Pettigrew, a Harvard psychologist who was among the contributors to the *Daedalus* issues on the "Negro American" and whose *A Profile of the Negro American* (1964) had obviously influenced him. "A warm, supportive home," Pettigrew wrote,

can effectively compensate for many of the restrictions the Negro child faces outside of the ghetto; consequently, the type of home life a Negro enjoys as a child may be far more crucial for governing the influence of segregation upon his personality than the form the segregation takes—legal or informal, Southern or Northern.

Near the end of "The Tangle of Pathology," Moynihan reiterated in an obviously heartfelt manner the argument he had made in his *One-Third of a Nation* report in 1964: blacks had a high failure rate of 56 percent—almost four times that of whites—on the armed forces mental test. If more Negro men had been accepted by the services, their unemployment in 1964 would have been 7 percent instead of 9.1 percent. Moreover, service in the military "is the *only* experience open to the Negro American in which he is truly treated as an equal." Above all, the military

> is an utterly masculine world. Given the strains of the disorganized and matrifocal family life in which so many Negro youth come of age, the Armed Forces are a dramatic and desperately needed change: a world away from women, a world run by strong men of unquestioned authority, where discipline, if harsh, is nonetheless orderly and predictable, and where rewards, if limited, are granted on the basis of performance.

Moynihan concluded, "The theme of a current Army recruiting message states it as clearly as can be: 'In the U.S. Army you get to know what it means to feel like a man.'"

Peppering the chapter with additional psychologically based observations, Moynihan moved on to a section titled "Alienation." Here, too, he emphasized the interdependence of problems. It recorded a number of worrisome developments: low and decreasing labor force participation rates among nonwhite men, "almost unbelievable" unemployment rates, and high rates of narcotic addiction. All these indicated that "large numbers of Negro youth appear to be withdrawing from American society."

Racial segregation, he added, also had worsened. Moynihan lamented especially the spread of "vast white, middle- and lower-middle-class suburbs around all of the Nation's cities. Increasingly the inner cities have been left to Negroes—who now share almost no community life with whites." Citing *Beyond the Melting Pot*, he wrote, "The present generation of Negro youth growing up in the urban ghettos has probably less personal contact with the white world than any generation in the history of the Negro American."

Two paragraphs near the end brought religion into the picture. "Observers," Moynihan wrote, "report that the Negro churches have all but lost contact with men in the Northern cities." The sole exception according to him was the rise of the Black Muslims, "the only religious movement that appears to have enlisted a considerable number of lower-class Negro males in northern cities of late." This is a "movement based on total rejection of white society, even though it emulates whites more." A short sentence ended the chapter: "In a word: the tangle of pathology is tightening."

Until this point, Moynihan had said little about specific programs that might unravel this tangle of pathology. He had focused instead on diagnosing and describing the problems so that government officials would take notice and begin seriously collecting the information necessary to fashion remedies. Only in his passages concerning the armed forces had he tipped his hand—black men would profit greatly from joining the services. But as in *One-Third of a Nation*, he did not maintain that the qualifying tests were biased against blacks. On the contrary, his perception was that the cognitive difficulties of blacks, stemming from familial and social problems, were deeply embedded. If there were easy answers, they were as yet undiscovered. Moynihan did not claim to know them.

The closest he came to such answers was in his final chapter, "The Case for National Action." It was only a page and a half—a brief space considering the systemic and pernicious problems he hoped to solve. He began by giving three reasons the report was written to define a situation rather than propose solutions to it. First, "there are many persons, within and without the Government, who do not feel the problem exists, at least in any serious degree." They need to be informed. Second, "the problem is so inter-related, one thing with another, that any list of program proposals would necessarily be incomplete and would distract attention from the main point of inter-relatedness." He also emphasized, "Where we should break into this cycle, and how, are the most difficult domestic questions facing the United States. We must first reach agreement on what the problem is, then we will know what questions must be answered."

The third reason, Moynihan lamented, was that "our study has produced some clear indications that the situation may indeed have begun to feed on itself." To emphasize this point, which a graph had indicated earlier, he described the statistical relationship between welfare and unemployment, later dubbed "Moynihan's scissors," that he and Barton had found so stunning. For most of the postwar period, he wrote, "male Negro unemployment and the

number of new AFDC cases rose and fell together as if connected by a chain."
In 1960, however, and again in 1963 and 1964, "unemployment declined, but
the number of new AFDC cases rose."

It is clear from Moynihan's strategic placement of this relationship—and
his memorable metaphor about the situation perhaps feeding on itself—that
it worried him greatly. He illustrated it in detail in the last of the twenty-two
tables of his appendix. He repeated his concern:

> Three centuries of injustice have brought about deep-seated structural
> dislocations in the life of the Negro American. At this point, the present
> tangle of pathology is capable of perpetuating itself without assistance
> from the white world.

By pointing to structural dislocations, Moynihan was reiterating an argument by Frazier, Myrdal, Clark, Young, and Silberman: racist oppression over
the centuries, along with economic changes following industrialization and
urbanization, had badly damaged black people, especially black men. Indeed,
he emphasized that the plight of many lower-class black *males*, rendering them
unable or unwilling to marry or support families, intensified already problem-
atic gender relationships. By using conditional language—the problem "*may*"
have "begun to feed on itself," "the tangle of pathology" is "*capable of* perpetuating itself"—Moynihan stopped short of a flat declaration that the structural dislocations had shattered black culture. Moreover, he was explicit in
arguing that more study was needed. "The possible implications of these and
other data," he warned, "are serious enough that they, too, should be understood before program proposals are made."

That Moynihan did not try to give precise answers to hard questions was
hardly surprising—for some time thereafter, scholars and activists debated
over why the proportion of black children who were born out of wedlock was
rapidly increasing. Indeed, even as he wrote, this proportion was escalating
more dramatically than he might have imagined. By 1970, it had jumped to
38 percent compared with 6 percent among whites. "I did not know then," he
wrote in 1995; "I do not know now" exactly why the scissors effect developed
when it did. "All I had in 1965 was the scissors. Something was happening."

Still, it was obvious in 1965 that he wanted the federal government to act.
He closed the report by insisting the U.S. government make a "national effort":

The policy of the United States is to bring the Negro American to full
and equal sharing in the responsibilities and rewards of citizenship. To
this end, the programs of the Federal government bearing on this objective shall be designed to have the effect, directly or indirectly, of enhancing the stability and resources of the Negro American family.

After the report became public, a number of social scientists, notably Lee
Rainwater and William Yancey, expressed reservations about some of the
harsh language in it. Moynihan, they recognized, knew that many black activists had become proud and assertive, and should have anticipated that they
would object to his statements, forcefully and clinically stated, about sex and
"illegitimacy." Though Moynihan stayed in touch in late 1964 and early 1965
with some black leaders—for instance, Bayard Rustin and Whitney Young—
and though he cited black academics such as Kenneth Clark, he seems not to
have appreciated how angrily the more militant spokesmen might react to his
language. But Rainwater and Yancey had no serious quarrels with his major
conclusions about lower-class black family life. Scholars, Clark included, had
been saying similar things for some time.

Other readers, moreover, offered a number of additional criticisms. Chief
among these were that Moynihan did not set forth programmatic solutions;
that in holding a patriarchal view of family life he focused much more on the
needs of black men than of black women; that he blamed welfare for abetting
out-of-wedlock births and family breakups; that he largely ignored the resourcefulness with which lower-class black families coped and adapted to their
plight; that he oversimplified the subject and thereby exaggerated the seriousness of the situation; and that he emphasized cultural factors, not structural
ones, as the major source of lower-class black problems. The result, they said,
was an overly chilling portrait of deteriorating lower-class black family life
in the ghettos.

The first objection, that Moynihan did not provide solutions to the problems
he so vividly described, was fair. Moynihan admitted as much in his conclusion
and explained why: he was aiming his report at government officials so that
they would become more aware of the crisis and start thinking seriously about
solutions. Later he explained, "A series of recommendations was at first included, then left out. It would have got in the way of the attention-arousing
argument that a crisis was coming and that family stability was the best measure

of success or failure in dealing with it." Had he included such recommendations, he added, he would have highlighted the need for "guaranteed full employment, birth control, adoption services, etc. *But first of all a family allowance.*"

Critics were also accurate in noting that Moynihan focused more on the problems of men than of women. Having grown up (after the age of ten) in a female-headed family, he had strong feelings about the issues he raised, especially the fate of fatherless children in low-income households. Like the vast majority of men in the United States at that time—black as well as white— he assumed that men were supposed to be the breadwinners and heads of families. Malcolm X and Martin Luther King Jr. shared this view along with most black leaders, who dwelt on the needs of black men, not on the circumstances of lower-class black women or beneficiaries of welfare.

As Moynihan stated clearly in the report, he did not maintain that a patriarchal form of family was inherently better than a matriarchal one. Rather, the difficulty stemmed from the fact that female-headed families were at a "distinct disadvantage" in U.S. society. Moreover, he worried greatly about the economic plight of low-income black young men who grew up in fatherless families in the inner city, and he doubted whether it was good for mothers of preschool children to be working outside their homes. But in observing that many black women landed better jobs than black men, he tended to underemphasize their plight. By highlighting increases in welfare rolls, he left an impression that lower-class black women having babies out of wedlock were irresponsible. As a result, it was hardly surprising that black women who heard of the report—already resenting the widespread stigmatization of lower-class black women as oversexed welfare cheats and malingerers—had little use for it or that many feminists and others later denounced his unflattering descriptions of matriarchy.

The third complaint, which alleged that Moynihan blamed welfare for abetting illegitimacy, seems at first justified. As the report made clear, Moynihan regarded the AFDC program as deeply flawed, largely because it failed to cover a great many female-headed families living in poverty. Like many people, he also wondered about the extent to which AFDC, which mainly aided only single-parent families with children, might be contributing to perverse incentives, notably higher out-of-wedlock childbearing and desertions by fathers.

But Moynihan did not vilify welfare or its recipients. His charts, graphs, and statistics did not stigmatize welfare clients or identify AFDC as a cause of the problems of lower-class blacks. Instead, they focused on the relationship between black male unemployment (still the key cause) and AFDC (an effect). Poverty and unemployment, indeed, were the causal forces identified by his model.

It is easy to see why critics would accuse Moynihan of ignoring the resourcefulness of oppressed black families. A liberal who yearned for change, he did not believe that the desperate coping of low-income, female-headed families had done much to alleviate their plight. Indeed, had he dwelt on their adaptiveness—such as reliance on kin networks—he might have faced complaints that he was a conservative who believed lower-class blacks were coping all right by themselves. Though he twice noted the resilience of black families who rose to middle-class status, he otherwise concentrated on the lower classes, dramatizing the seriousness of their situation in order to make his readers take notice and act.

The criticism that Moynihan oversimplified and overdramatized matters had some validity. Those who voiced it, including a number of civil servants in government bureaucracies concerned with social problems, did not charge that his statistics were inaccurate. In fact, they conceded that they were accurate. Some noted that the report was careful to refer to the advances made by middle-class blacks. But they maintained that Moynihan nonetheless downplayed the diversity of the black community and focused too heavily on family problems. As Patricia Harris, a black leader, observed later, the problem with the report was that family issues "became *the* explanation, rather than an explanation of the problems of Negroes." She added, "The primary Negro problem is white discrimination against them, the white assumption of black inferiority."[5]

Some critics, though agreeing that black families were far more troubled than white families (there was no way around the staggering statistics), argued that Moynihan should have included more comparisons of blacks and whites using educational and economic controls. Comparisons of this sort, they maintained, would have made it more clear that income levels were key forces behind variations in family structure, and that many impoverished white families, too, were threatened. (One later observer wrote that a better title for his report would have been "Low-Income Families in America.")[6]

All these problems with the report, some government officials thought, revealed that Moynihan was oversimplifying to demonstrate that existing federal programs were failing and that the plight of low-income blacks was therefore getting worse. But were the programs so bad? Welfare administrators, though conceding the inadequacies of AFDC, nonetheless maintained that the program was essential. Moreover, welfare policies could be reformed. Was the situation really getting worse? After all, groundbreaking civil rights legislation had just been passed, the economy was booming, and unemployment was down. Blacks were finding work in niches of the labor market closed to them in the past. Southern black migrants to the city, Labor Department researchers believed, were managing reasonably well. Why conclude, as Moynihan had, that the civil rights acts could not be fine-tuned to build on improvements already occurring?

It is clear why the final criticism was aimed at Moynihan: that he saw the collapse of black culture as a key source of the problems of black families. As his citation of Elkins indicated, he did believe that historically powerful racism and economic discrimination had left abiding scars that had ravaged the ambitions and behavior of many black people. Relying on Clark and various psychological studies, he had sketched a portrait of cumulative, long-range damage. Stating that the situation may have begun to feed on itself, he implied that developments had become so harmful that lower-class black people, though restless and angry, were becoming virtually unable to cope.

No word stung black critics more strongly than "pathology," which of course signified disease. In retrospect, he would have done better to describe a tangle of inequality to dramatize his main theme. Still, Moynihan did not go quite as far as Michael Harrington, for instance, who had previously concluded that an intergenerational culture of poverty had afflicted millions of poor people.

Moynihan's historical passages notwithstanding, his central message blamed white racism and structural forces, especially high rates of poverty and unemployment among young black men and the isolation of ever larger numbers of distressed people in highly crowded and segregated inner cities. Indeed, his description of contemporary black family ills and of their structural roots in some ways rendered his speculations about historical causes, notably slavery, superfluous. His conclusion, gloomy though it was, held out a bit of hope: the situation in the ghettos was frightening, but it might not be too late for the nation, led by its government, to take action that would promote equality of economic results.

No writer can foresee everything, and Moynihan was no exception. His report, like all reports, was time-bound. Concentrating on racial matters, it did not anticipate the growth of a strong women's movement or of rising economic inequality in the United States, much of it hastened by rapid increases in the numbers of female-headed families, white as well as black. Nor did he foresee—few people did in early 1965—enormous expansion of the drug trade, mass incarceration of young black men, or dramatic changes in sexual mores and family patterns. Because of these and other developments, the miseries he described in 1965 became considerably more serious—and increasingly multiracial—over time.

Still, the Moynihan Report was a prescient document. Powerfully argued, it drew widespread attention to the dawn of what was later recognized as a much-discussed social trend in the country: the frightening growth of a host of interrelated problems affecting lower-class urban family life in the United States.

Criticisms aside, there was much to recommend the report. Moynihan was correct in insisting that the travails of lower-class black families had a long history, that they were in many ways unique, that they had a deep neighborhood or ecological structure, that they were rooted in white racism and economic inequality, that they were causing "crumbling," that federal officials needed to develop a clearer understanding of the depth and interrelatedness of the situation, and that the crisis had to be met before it was too late. Clark had offered a comparably dismal portrait of the ghettos—and had used the phrase "tangle of pathology"—but he had not focused on family issues, and (perhaps because he was black) he had received no flak. Had Moynihan's report remained an internal document discussed by well-intentioned liberal policymakers, it might well have stimulated useful thinking—and action—to better the quality of lower-class black family life in the United States.

Instead, when it later leaked to the public, it fueled a firestorm of controversy that threw Moynihan and his allies on the defensive, thereby stymieing well-intended efforts to deal with one of the nation's most serious social problems.

CHAPTER 4

"The Moment Lost"

L ittle constructive action concerning black family life occurred either upon the Moynihan Report's release in the summer of 1965 or for many years thereafter. Indeed, the ideas of the report, even though stirringly endorsed by President Johnson at Howard University on June 4, quickly fell victim to a host of events and misunderstandings.

As Moynihan later pointed out in an aptly titled essay, "The President and the Negro: The Moment Lost," the public acrimony that broke out that summer was deeply dispiriting not only for advocates of programs to promote greater social equality for blacks but also for liberalism in general. At this pivotal time, a historic moment for reforms to improve race relations may indeed have been lost.[1]

In the wake of the euphoria that followed Johnson's speech at Howard, this extraordinary turnabout could hardly have been anticipated. Top civil rights leaders had praised the text of his address when speechwriter Richard Goodwin had read it to them in advance of delivery. Writer Ralph Ellison was one of hundreds who wrote enthusiastic letters about the speech to the White House. Martin Luther King Jr. lauded the oration in a public statement. These positive reactions were fully justified, for LBJ's address had indeed laid out a path toward a "new and more profound stage of the battle for civil rights."

The voting rights bill, moreover, was moving toward passage—LBJ would sign the far-reaching measure on August 6, 1965.

Moynihan, having cowritten the speech with Goodwin, did not stay long with the administration thereafter. Instead, anxious to try his hand at elective politics, he resigned his post at the Labor Department in mid-July and campaigned over the next two months for the office of president of the New York City Council. But he, too, had been hopeful for action, helping in early July to arrange a series of meetings between Johnson staffers and social scientists—many of whom were joining him as authors of articles for the forthcoming *Daedalus* articles on "The Negro American." Kenneth Clark and Bayard Rustin were among the invitees. Their goal: to prepare for the fall conference, "To Fulfill These Rights," that Johnson had called for in his speech.[2]

Planning for the conference, however, did not make much progress in July, and as time passed, militant civil rights leaders began to fret. Their expectations, already high, had been further whetted by Johnson's speech, and they became ever more impatient for action. Many, tiring of white leadership, were also eager to wrest control of the movement from Johnson and his fellow politicos in Washington. LBJ, moreover, had other concerns at the time. In late July, he announced plans for a highly costly military escalation in Vietnam. Antiwar protestors, who had already staged demonstrations and teach-ins, now turned sharply against the administration. Given these absorbing developments, it became increasingly difficult for Johnson to concentrate on fulfilling the promises he had made at Howard.

Also in late July, news reporters began speculating about the sources of Johnson's address and about the administration's plans to prepare for a conference. These articles, which clearly relied on leaks, tended to emphasize one of two points: first, the administration was busy following up on the speech at Howard; and second, blacks ought to assume more responsibility for self-improvement. The first was an exaggeration—little was in fact being done—and the second, irritating civil rights leaders, misinterpreted Johnson's (and Moynihan's) argument.

The White House, though aware of these distortions, did not challenge them. Instead, it quietly decided to outflank the leaks by making the Moynihan Report widely available. The Government Printing Office (GPO) would print more copies (no longer marked "For Official Use Only"). These, printed on eight-and-a-half by eleven-inch paper and bound in a black paper cover and back sheet, would be sold upon request at 45¢ apiece when ready in mid-August.

The press beat them to it. Before copies could be printed, *Newsweek* on August 9 published a four-page story that for the first time offered a fairly full summary of the report and that listed Moynihan—identified as a candidate for president of the New York City Council—as an author of it. Titled "The New Crisis: The Negro Family," it stated accurately that the report had been the basis for Johnson's speech at Howard.

Newsweek's story was alarmist to say the least. It featured a photograph of black kids in Harlem tossing bottles, under which a caption read, "A time bomb ticks in the ghetto." It added that a confidential report from the Labor Department "has set off a quiet revolution in the basic White House approach to the continuing American dilemma of race." "Seventy-eight fastidiously documented pages" identify the "social roots: the splintering Negro family." Noting the emphasis on matriarchy in the report, black unemployment ("an appalling 29 percent"), and high rates of violent crime in the inner cities, *Newsweek* warned, "The disintegration of Negro families may have fallen into a self-sustaining vicious cycle."

The story included charts taken from the report, one of which dealt with "the rising rate of non-white illegitimacy." Another plotted the "runaway curve in child welfare cases" against the nonwhite male unemployment rate—that is, what became known as the "scissors effect." Passages in the article quoted directly from the report, including Moynihan's apocalyptic prediction that "there will be no social peace in the United States for generations" if the crisis was not soon addressed.

Who was leaking this information? Journalist Nicholas Lemann, having interviewed many government officials who were parties to discussions about the report in 1965, suggested later that it was Moynihan himself, who hoped to highlight his reputation as a reformer in order to advance his ongoing candidacy in New York City. Others who knew Moynihan—and who perceived him as an able political opportunist—agreed that he might well have been the source.

Moynihan denied such allegations. Though he told Rainwater and Yancey in late 1965 that he had given copies of the report to "one or two persons very privately who had been called to the White House for consultation" (one of whom was Kenneth Clark), he disavowed leaking the report to journalists.

He also claimed that he had not given a copy to *Newsweek* (but he did tell Rainwater and Yancey that he had talked to its reporters off the record). Though he said he did not know who had leaked the report to *Newsweek*, he later stated that the White House did leak it soon afterward, following the outbreak of rioting on August 11 in the predominantly black Watts area of Los Angeles. It did so, he maintained, in order to claim that administration officials had been aware of the discontent seething in the ghettos.[3]

The source or sources for the leaks may never be known. Nor, ultimately, is it vital to know. What really made a difference to the reception of the report at the time was not the early media coverage but rather the rioting in Watts. Following an altercation between police and a black man who resisted arrest for drunken driving, unrest among black residents exploded into a huge and enormously destructive spate of looting, burning, and violent confrontations between black people and law enforcement officials. For the next five days, television stations throughout the country carried live coverage of one horrific scene after another. Before 13,900 National Guard troops finally put an end to most of the disturbances, a total of 34 people had been killed, all but five of them black, and 1,000 had been reported injured. More than 600 buildings, most of them white-owned, had been burned or looted, causing $200 million or more in damage. It was the worst urban violence in U.S. history.

Widespread black grievances rooted in economic distress had helped to fuel the uprising, which enjoyed considerable popular support in the area— it was later estimated that 35,000 adults had taken part in the disturbances. The violent confrontations made it even more glaringly clear than earlier that racial hostilities were by no means confined to the South. Many blacks in Los Angeles insisted that what had happened was not a riot but rather a long-overdue rebellion against police brutality and systemic racism that had deprived black people of decent job opportunities, schools, and housing. Many outraged American whites, however, preferred to downplay or to ignore these sources of black frustrations. California Governor Edmund "Pat" Brown, a Democrat, exclaimed that "hoodlums and juvenile delinquents" had led the outbreak. Oscar Handlin, a Pulitzer Prize–winning Harvard historian (and one of the contributors to the *Daedalus* volumes on the American Negro) agreed, branding the rioters as "disorderly elements taking advantage of an occasion for looting."[4]

However it was explained, the Watts Riot was one of the most shocking events of a historically pivotal summer. As Moynihan wrote in 1967, it was "the real blow. It threw the civil rights movement entirely off balance." This was surely the case, for the riot—followed by nearly two dozen racial disturbances in other U.S. cities that summer—transformed the national conversation concerning civil rights legislation into one that focused on racial confrontations. Watts was in fact a key to the development of what Moynihan identified in 1967 as the "Moment Lost." Masses of black people, feeling proud and entitled, were no longer willing to forgo violence or to trust whites as leaders—or (as in Moynihan's case) as messengers. Freedom was indeed not enough—beyond legal protections, black Americans demanded jobs and social equality.

Mainline civil rights leaders, caught off guard by the uprising, struggled to cope with the new situation. James Farmer, national director of the Congress of Racial Equality (CORE), later conceded, "Civil rights organizations have failed. No one had any roots in the ghetto." Rustin added, "We must hold ourselves responsible for not reaching them. . . . We've done plenty to get votes in the South and seats in the lunchrooms, but we've had no programs for these youngsters." When King flew into Los Angeles to calm the scene, walking the streets and preaching nonviolence, many Watts residents, still irate, ignored him. When he addressed a meeting of local people, one shouted, "We don't need your dreams; we need jobs!" King told Rustin that night, "I worked to get these people the right to eat hamburgers, and now I've got to do something . . . to help them get the money to buy them."[5]

Though Johnson, after the smaller urban disturbances that had occurred in 1964, had initiated intra-administration discussions about dealing with unrest in the cities, he still had not done much to follow up on his speech at Howard, and he, too, was unprepared for the scope of the violence in Watts. At his Texas ranch when Watts exploded, he reacted with anger and self-pity. "How is it possible?" he asked an aide. "After all we've accomplished. How can it be?" Refusing to read cables from Los Angeles that urged him to dispatch National Guard units to the area, he took no action. Joseph Califano, a young aide, lamented later, "He just refused to accept it." It was Califano, risking his job, who facilitated the sending of forces to Watts.

A week later Johnson heeded King's call for government assistance by authorizing $25 million for emergency aid to area residents. He knew, however, as did King, that such a modest sum would do little for blacks in the area. Anticipating passage in September of a bill that would establish a new department, Housing and Urban Development, the president held out some hope for the future. But he remained furious with the rioters, whom he denounced publicly in late August. "A rioter with a Molotov cocktail in his hands," he exclaimed, "is not fighting for civil rights any more than a Klansman with a sheet on his back and a mask on his face. They are both . . . lawbreakers, destroyers of constitutional rights and liberties, and ultimately destroyers of a free America." "Negroes," he complained privately to Califano, "will end up pissing in the aisles of the Senate."[6]

The Watts Riot did more than expose the depth of black anger and the scrambling of civil rights and government leaders. It shocked and terrified white Americans, including a number of white liberals who had enthusiastically and in some cases bravely backed nonviolent, interracial civil rights activities. Henceforth, some of these whites were not so sure about inner-city blacks, whose violence in Watts had cost them the moral high ground they earlier had enjoyed. As Moynihan put it later, long-suffering black people prior to Watts had been widely perceived as "victims." After Watts, "the black urban population became, in effect, an aggressor."

It was in this explosive social context that the White House finally began releasing GPO copies of Moynihan's report on request. It did so only after a fair amount of last-minute debate, for top officials, having by then read the report, had feared that release of it might spark a barrage of attacks from all quarters. John Leslie, head of the Labor Department's Office of Information, Publication, and Reports, worried privately that the report could be "used out of context to prove this or that point depending on the slant of the individual who uses it." A colleague, Leslie added, "thinks that parts of it will be picked up by the segregationists and used against the Negro as a political document." LBJ general counsel Lee White, consulted by Moyers, finally advised that because rumors of the report's existence were already circulating in the press, it should be released so that no one would accuse the administration of hiding it.[7]

At about the same time, journalist Robert Novak got hold of a copy—perhaps from Bill Moyers, perhaps in some other way. When Novak called Moynihan for more information, the two men talked, whereupon Novak rushed his information into print the next day. Thus, on August 18, a story titled "The Moynihan Report" appeared in the widely syndicated column "Inside Report" that Novak wrote with his collaborator, Rowland Evans. "That," Moynihan said later, "is when it became 'The Moynihan Report.'"

Publication of *The Negro Family*—along with the Evans and Novak column— helped unleash what became a virtual avalanche of scholarship as well as a torrent of public acrimony. A careful historian, Steve Estes, later estimated that between 1965 and 1980 "more than fifty books and five hundred journal articles addressed the effects of poverty and discrimination on black families." Few of these rested on fresh field observation. Another historian, Walter Jackson, described a more immediate effect of the column and of release of the report as "one of the most turbulent public controversies ever generated by a social scientist." The result, he added, was a "donnybrook."[8]

Evans and Novak supplied considerable pertinent information about the report, explaining that the "much-suppressed, much-leaked Labor Department document . . . strips away usual equivocations and exposes the ugly truth about the big-city Negro's plight." They also noted correctly that the president had used the report as a source for his speech at Howard, and that Moynihan had wondered "why in a time of decreasing unemployment, the plight of the urban Negro was getting worse—not better." The column was not hostile to Moynihan or to his ideas, and Moynihan did not object to it.

Still, the "Inside Report" column was misleading in some respects. Most important, Evans and Novak asserted that the Moynihan Report, viewed by some administration officials as a "time bomb," brought up "the most taboo subject in civil rights: preferential treatment for the Negroes." Though Moynihan had described the plight of low-income urban blacks as profoundly different from that of other poor people, and though he did in fact favor "preferential treatment" (in the form of social legislation, not of racial quotas), he had not presented specific remedies in the report. Evans and Novak also failed to emphasize Moynihan's basic point that the troubles afflicting low-income Negro families stemmed above all from economic sources. As the report had stated, "The fundamental overwhelming fact is that *Negro unemployment*, except for a few years during World War II and the Korean War, *has continued at disaster levels for 35 years.*"

The Evans and Novak column did not persuade all readers. (Many liberals, indeed, already referred to the reporters as "Errors and No Facts.") But it did make Moynihan something of a household name. Above all, its alarmist tone—reflecting post-Watts fears of racial violence—was echoed in a host of subsequent media accounts. It proved increasingly difficult after Watts for many commentators to discuss Moynihan's ideas—now circulating in an agitated public arena—in the thoughtful and constructive manner he had hoped to generate when he had put together the report earlier in the year.

During the next few weeks, a number of additional news stories about the report appeared in major newspapers, including the *Washington Post* and the *New York Times*. Some of these, too, seemed to rely in part either on leaks or on other news stories. Indeed, the report itself was not actually published within the covers of a book until Rainwater and Yancey's *The Moynihan Report and the Politics of Controversy* appeared in 1967. As Douglas Massey and Robert Sampson, sociologists, pointed out in 2009, "The Moynihan Report is probably the most famous piece of social scientific analysis never published."[9]

Moynihan, meanwhile, was busy campaigning until September 14, primary day in New York City. Having resigned from the Johnson administration, he was in no position to represent it in attempts to respond to stories such as these. Nonetheless, he defended himself by writing a newspaper article in early September about the riots, titled "Jobless Negroes and the Boom." Statistics showing nonwhite economic progress, he agreed, were accurate. But unemployment rates for black men and women remained very high. "Massive general prosperity," he wrote, "can conceal utter calamity in the Negro world." Cities, he warned, "must begin insisting on national programs directed specifically to this issue. I do not believe there is a single serious social problem facing them [the cities] of which unemployment is not one of the root causes."[10]

He also wrote a longer piece, "A Family Policy for the Nation," which appeared on September 18 in *America*, a Jesuit weekly. Using language from his report, he offered as vivid a reminder of the importance of family life to the health of society as any he ever wrote:

> From the wild Irish slums of the 19th-century Eastern seaboard, to the
> riot-torn suburbs of Los Angeles, there is one unmistakable lesson in
> American history: a community that allows a large number of men to
> grow up in broken families, dominated by women, never acquiring any
> stable relationship to male authority, never acquiring any set of rational
> expectations about the future—that community asks for and gets chaos.

Crime, violence, unrest, disorder—most particularly the furious, un-restrained lashing out at the whole social structure—that is not only to be expected; it is very near to inevitable. And it is richly deserved.

In support of this argument, Moynihan again drew on his scholarly under-standing of ethnicity to contrast the familial experiences of various U.S. ethnic groups. Immigrants from Japan and China, he wrote, had been very poor on arrival in the United States but over time had managed to do reasonably well. So had Jews. "And what have all three groups in common? A singularly stable, cohesive, and enlightened family life." The situation among Negroes, how-ever, differed greatly. In particular, they suffered from "savage unemploy-ment." The rate of joblessness for Negro men at that time, at 7.6 percent, was twice that of white men.

A third expression of Moynihan's views at this time appeared in *Daedalus*, which published his previously prepared article, "Employment, Income, and the Ordeal of the Negro Family." It was one of fifteen essays in *Daedalus*'s fall issue, the first of two consecutive *Daedalus* volumes on the subject of "The Negro American." Kenneth Clark was coeditor with Harvard sociologist Tal-cott Parsons of the issues, which also included essays by James Q. Wilson, Thomas Pettigrew, John Hope Franklin, Rainwater, and Clark himself. Pres-ident Johnson contributed a foreword to the fall issue.[11]

Moynihan's article in *Daedalus* was more scholarly in tone than his report. Still, it opened by reiterating his main point: in civil rights matters, the United States must move beyond the provision of liberty toward securing equality of results. Emphasizing the seriousness of family problems among Negroes, he stressed, as in his report, that nearly 24 percent of all nonwhite births in 1963 had been out of wedlock. This was a "disastrous number." His essay repeated other arguments from his report, noting, "It is quite possible the Negro com-munity is moving in two directions, or rather that two Negro communities are moving in opposite ones." Describing the scissors effect, he concluded, "The linkage between problems of employment and the range of social pa-thology that afflicts the Negro is unmistakable."[12]

While Moynihan was trying to cope with criticisms, he lost his race in the New York City primary that took place in mid-September. Though this was a blow, it was not a surprise, and he did not remain at loose ends for long. On the same day as the primary, novelist Paul Horgan, director of the Center for Advanced Studies at Wesleyan University, offered him an academic-year post as a fellow there. With Liz and the children, Moynihan moved to Middletown, Connecticut, for what turned out to be a pleasurable but temporary experience for him and his family. While at Wesleyan he taught a seminar concerning racial issues, traveled to a number of colleges and universities to speak on the subject, and organized a scholarly conference about it. He also began drafting a book, tentatively titled "Toward Equality as a Fact and as a Result: The Dilemma of Negro Family Structure," only to abandon the idea of getting it published because, as he later put it, "all I had achieved was a description of the problem."[13]

While he was at Wesleyan, comments and articles about his report proliferated. By no means were all of these commentaries hostile to it. Indeed, then as later, many writers publicly shared his concerns. In September, the editor of *Commonweal*, a journal of liberal opinion run by lay Catholics, agreed with Moynihan that civil rights had to include measures promoting social equality, but feared that "with an emerging generation of Negroes becoming entangled in the pathological pattern of family life, this may be a dangerous assumption." Michael Harrington as well as Charles Silberman also defended the report. It was not the case, as Moynihan sometimes implied, that virtually the whole world turned against him.[14]

In October 1965 (as well as on other later occasions) Martin Luther King Jr. also seemed to sympathize with Moynihan. In public addresses, he spoke movingly about the "shattering blows," notably slavery, that had made the Negro family "fragile, deprived, and often psychopathic." King stressed also that the causes of the crisis of the Negro family "are culturally and socially induced. What man has torn down, he can rebuild." Without mentioning Moynihan he seconded his diagnosis of the problem as well as his call for reform. "At the root of the difficulty in Negro life," he said, "is pervasive and persistent want. To grow from within the Negro needs only fair opportunity for jobs, education, housing, and access to culture."[15]

Though support such as this was encouraging to Moynihan, unflattering comments about his report continued to mount, and they peaked late in the fall of 1965. These did not come from conservatives, most of whom shared Moynihan's gloomy understanding of life in the ghettos. Rather, they came from liberal whites and from civil rights militants. Although some of these critics offered thoughtful reservations about the report, others were ill informed or unfair. A few were nasty. These hurt. As his biographer, Godfrey Hodgson, noted later, Moynihan then entered a "crisis of depression, a dark night of the soul."

Some of the hurtful criticisms emanated from government officials who worked in welfare and antipoverty bureaucracies such as the Department of Health, Education, and Welfare (HEW) and the Office of Economic Opportunity (OEO). Perhaps jealous of the access that Moynihan had earlier enjoyed to high-level White House aides, they also resented his criticisms of welfare policies. When Moynihan became fully aware of the enmity of these officials, he was enraged, writing his friend (and White House adviser) Harry McPherson to complain of "the savage reaction of the Federal bureaucracy in H.E.W. and Labor, and to some extent O.E.O."[16]

More worrisome were the reactions of top administration officials, most of whom quickly distanced themselves from the report. Fearful of offending angry black leaders, they treated *The Negro Family* as if it were some sort of conversational Gulag. This was most obviously the case with powerful people who had backed the report in May. If Labor Secretary Wirtz or President Johnson had jumped to Moynihan's defense, he might have fared a little better in the escalating controversy. But relations between Wirtz and Moynihan had cooled by June. Wirtz was also upset that the report had been leaked (he believed by Moynihan), thereby ruining any chance that something useful might have come from intra-administration discussions of it.[17]

Johnson, deeply suspicious by nature, could not forget that Moynihan had supported the senatorial campaign of Robert Kennedy, his most bitter enemy, in 1964. The president told McPherson that Moynihan was "an ingrate and a traitor." When Moynihan tendered his resignation in mid-July, Johnson did not thank him for his service or endorse his candidacy in New York. On August 6, acknowledging receipt of the resignation, he scrawled simply, "Accepted, LBJ." During discussions that summer concerning the forthcoming White House conference, Johnson once asked an aide, "what the hell is he getting out of that?" To another aide, he made it unmistakably clear that civil rights leaders wished to exclude Moynihan from the conference. When the aide nonetheless suggested inviting him, LBJ quickly said no. The aide recalled, "If you thought I was trying to invite a polecat, you would have found no greater resistance. Absolutely not. He [Moynihan] was beyond the pale."[18]

The president, moreover, continued to stew over what he considered the perfidy of black people such as those who had rioted in Watts. Increasingly under fire for escalating the war in Vietnam, he also shrank from engaging in controversies that might harm his already wobbling relationship with civil rights leaders or that might cost him wider political support. Indeed, he acted as if he had never heard of the report. As Moyers later put it, LBJ's attitude was "I don't know what was in there, but whatever it was, stay away from it."[19]

Moynihan seconded Moyers's recollections. The Johnson administration, he wrote later, "promptly dissociated itself from the whole issue." A "vacuum" then developed, he said. "No black would go near the subject. And until one did no white man could do so without incurring the wrath of a community grown rather too accustomed to epithet." More colorfully, he told McPherson (who had tried to calm down the president), "If my head were sticking on a pike at the South-West Gate to the White House grounds, the impression would hardly be greater."[20]

Many civil rights leaders, meanwhile, also backed away from Moynihan and the report. Some of their coolness stemmed from feeling neglected by LBJ after he had spoken in June at Howard. More important, most civil rights leaders, by then well aware of the rage that had motivated the residents of Watts, were in no mood to talk about, much less to endorse, the unflattering renderings of black family life central to the report. Nor did they believe that anything substantial could be done in the short term about family problems, which were obviously deeply entrenched. With a few exceptions these leaders had not been consulted during Moynihan's preparation of the report, and they did not know Moynihan well. Many recognized him (if at all) as just another Democratic politician—or worse, as yet another white man pontificating about their "problems" and preaching to them about how they should behave. Their reactions, too, outraged Moynihan, who wrote McPherson to complain of what he called "the even wilder resentment on the part of what might be called the civil rights left."[21]

If a black person had produced such a report, it might well have received— as Clark's *Dark Ghetto* had—a respectful hearing among people who yearned to fight against racism and poverty in the cities. But coming as it did from a writer who was white—and in the racially charged atmosphere following Watts—it met a hostile reception from black leaders. Its language aside, it suffered from three especially large liabilities: the messenger was white, the report focused on sex and family life, and the timing could hardly have been worse.

Civil rights leaders were especially uncomfortable talking in public about the problems in black families. Though recognizing truth in what Moynihan wrote—a number of black leaders had grown up in broken homes—they nursed hopes, however unrealistically, that Johnson and Congress might still support a far-reaching socioeconomic program for blacks, and they regarded an agenda centered on the "pathologies" of black family life—or on the woes of black "welfare mothers"—as guaranteed to alienate potential supporters of such a plan.[22]

The true pathology, these activists retorted, was racism itself, which had subjected black people to the deliberate, unending, and unbearable humiliations of segregation and discrimination. By highlighting nonmarital births and increasing welfare rolls, moreover, the report reminded blacks of what Whitney Young had called "scars" in their culture. The report, they thought, would serve to confirm what many white people already believed: blacks were deviant. Moynihan, some began to imply, was something of a racist himself for having stressed such matters.[23]

Even civil rights leaders who respected Moynihan's intellect and appreciated his desire for reform shrank from endorsing Moynihan's ideas. Rustin insisted, "I don't agree with the criticisms of Moynihan that he is a racist. I think the racist argument is kind of silly." He added that Moynihan's "intentions were excellent." The report, however, was "incomplete," "gave no suggestions for correcting measures," and "accentuated or exaggerated the negative." "Finally," he said, "we must talk about the poor family, and not simply the Negro family." Whitney Young added that his book *To Be Equal* had "identified the same pathologies in the Negro ghetto. And I called for an urban Marshall Plan, just as the Moynihan Report implies." But, he said, "I think that the title *The Negro Family* was tragic in that as a result it has stigmatized an entire group of people when the majority of that group of people do not fall into the category of the Negro family that Moynihan describes." Martin Luther King Jr., too, expressed reservations. There is a danger, he said, in emphasizing negative accounts of Negro family life. It is that "problems will be attributed to innate Negro weaknesses and used to justify, neglect, and rationalize oppression."[24]

Some white social scientists seconded these warnings. Christopher Jencks, a sociologist who wrote a widely noted critique of the report in the *New York Review of Books* in mid-October, opined that some of Moynihan's critics were "somewhat paranoid," but otherwise came close to arguing that Moynihan was blaming the victim. "Moynihan's analysis," he wrote, "is in the conservative tradition that guided the drafting of the poverty program. . . . The guiding assumption is that social pathology is caused less by basic defects in the social system than by defects in particular individuals and groups which prevent their adjusting to the system. The prescription is therefore to change the deviance, not the system."

At the same time, Herbert Gans, another white sociologist, published an article in *Commonweal* that provided a thorough summary of the report. Favoring a range of activist economic programs, notably provision of government jobs, Gans accepted Moynihan's prescriptions. "In the desert of compassion" that characterized white attitudes toward blacks, he wrote, "the Moynihan Report is a tiny oasis of hope, and if properly interpreted and implemented a first guide to the achievement of equality in the years to come." But he was one among many observers who regretted that Moynihan had not offered a guide to reform. "The vacuum that is created when no recommendations are attached to a policy proposal," he wrote, "can easily be filled by undesirable solutions, and the report's conclusions can be conveniently misinterpreted."

Gans also wondered if Moynihan had been correct in assuming that lower-class black families were wallowing in a pathological state. "However much the picture of family life painted in that report may grate on middle-class moral sensibilities," he wrote, "it may be that instability, illegitimacy, and matriarchy are the most positive adaptations possible to the conditions which Negroes must endure." Moreover, "The matriarchal family structure and the absence of a father has not yet been proven pathological, even for the boys who grow up in it." The "extended kinship system of mothers, grandmothers, aunts, and other female relatives," he concluded, can be "surprisingly stable, at least on the female side."

Gans further argued that the report could be co-opted by opponents of reform. "The inherent sensationality of the data," he wrote, would lead people to focus on disabilities instead of causes. Right-wing and racist groups might trot out the report to support already widespread assumptions of Negro inferiority. Others might cite it to place the onus of reform on blacks themselves.

It would be "tragic," Gans wrote, "if the findings . . . were used to justify demands for Negro self-improvement or the development of a middle-class family structure before further programs to bring about real equality are set up."[25]

Attempting to defuse harsh reactions among civil rights activists, Gans sought assurances from Goodwin that the forthcoming White House conference would not dwell on the miseries of black family life. In reply, Goodwin did his best to calm the waters. The conference, he wrote, "will reach far beyond the problem of the Negro family into the entire structure and pathology of the Negro community. And you can be sure that we will not regard the family structure as an isolated deficiency, but as one that must be tackled along with the conditions that give it life."[26]

Other people who were swept up in the turmoil surrounding the report sympathized with what they understood as Moynihan's liberal objectives. But they, too, wished that he had offered specific programs. They also wondered where government reforms might start—with reform of education? of welfare? of segregation? of all at once? Given the already obvious limitations of the War on Poverty, how were policymakers to expand economic opportunity, let alone promote the equality of result Johnson had called for at Howard? Sexual matters posed special difficulties: how were reformers supposed to go about lowering the numbers of nonmarital births? How many decades would it be before even a massive governmental assault on deeply ingrained family problems might make a difference?

Many analysts who worried that government did not have enough information to take action against such complicated problems were soon known as neoconservatives. But it was not only neoconservatives who began to lower their sights in late 1965. It was during these fateful months, as Johnson's responses indicated, that liberals, too, backed ever farther away from pursuing the dreams the president had outlined at Howard. Indeed, controversy over the Moynihan Report—along with Watts and escalation in Vietnam—was an important reason why liberals began to downscale their once-high hopes. By late 1965, they, too, began to wonder if they had oversold their ability to change the world, especially as they watched billions of dollars poured into support of the war in Vietnam. There seemed to be real limits to the capacity of government to engage in social engineering for domestic purposes.

McPherson had also developed serious doubts by late 1965 about the political possibilities of enacting anything that might lead to major improvements

in lower-class black family life. In 1966, he stressed the existence of an especially large obstacle: the nature of mainstream popular opinion concerning the
very meaning of equality. By and large, McPherson wrote, Americans believed
in equality of opportunity, but not—or not so much—in the establishment
of measures aimed at producing the equality of result LBJ had championed.
Most people, he added, had decided that the civil rights laws, having done a
great deal to conquer official discrimination, had gone far enough. "Once that
was done," he emphasized, "the American idea was that every man was on his
own. No one was supposed to get special treatment. The Irish hadn't; the Italians hadn't; the Jews hadn't. What made the Negro special?"

McPherson continued by arguing that Americans will generously help
people who suffer "observable cruelties" at the hands of "villains." They understand the cruelties involved when racists force people to sit in the back of
a bus, refuse them service in a restaurant, or deny them the right to vote. But
"there were no villains—at least none that strangers could identify—in the
broken homes of the Northern cities where men 'chose' to be unemployed,
women chose welfare, and young people chose heroin."[27]

What he was saying was that in the hearts and minds of many Americans,
the achievement of freedom for blacks *was* in fact enough. If black people
hoped to get ahead, these Americans thought, they should start by doing what
other ethnic groups had done: hold their families together.

Two especially sharp denunciations of Moynihan highlighted the furious controversy over the report that escalated in October and November. Although
these were in many ways ill informed, relying primarily on news stories, they
received considerable publicity and backing from civil rights militants and
their supporters.

The first denunciation came from a minister, Dr. Benjamin Payton, a black
sociologist who was director of the Office of Religion and Race of the Protestant Council of the City of New York. On October 14, he mailed out several
hundred copies of a twenty-two-page critique of the report to people, including "persons [he] knew in universities." This critique relied on newspaper accounts, not on the report itself, which apparently he had not read. Payton's
descriptions of ghetto life did not differ from Moynihan's. But he tore into
the report for its "simplistic logic," the "inadequate empirical evidence it uti-
lizes," and the "erroneous premises on which it is based." A major complaint

of Payton's appeared to be that Moynihan overemphasized black pathology. Misrepresenting what Moynihan had written (and, moreover, what Moynihan had reiterated after the Watts Riot), Payton also maintained that the report had paraded optimistic data about black unemployment and income. His uninformed statements enraged many backers of the report. Charles Silberman, defending Moynihan, later blasted Payton's paper as "the most blatant distortion that I can remember seeing in a long time."[28]

Payton closed by calling for a pre–White House conference to be held in New York on November 9. This was duly attended by some 100 people, who endorsed a number of resolutions, the most important of which demanded changes in the agenda for the conference scheduled for a week later in Washington: "*It is our position that the question of 'family stability' be stricken entirely from that agenda and be approached through an economic and urban analysis of needs in the critical area of jobs, housing, and equality integrated education.*"

The second denunciation of Moynihan's report received even greater attention. William Ryan, a white Boston psychologist and civil rights activist who had worked with CORE, originally wrote it in September after he had read the *Newsweek* article of August 9. In early October, his critique went off to several hundred people, including political figures—White House officials, senators and representatives, and leaders of private organizations. Payton, a recipient, relied on it to compose his attack. Immediately following the conference in mid-November, a slightly shorter version of Ryan's argument appeared in the *Nation* under a title that revealed its tone: "Savage Discovery: The Moynihan Report." *Crisis*, the NAACP's journal, also featured it under the heading "The New Genteel Racism." In 1971, Ryan published a book-length version with a title that captured the essence of his argument: *Blaming the Victim.*

Ryan's piece was an unforgiving attack aimed at killing the messenger. He charged that the report "draws dangerously inexact conclusions from weak and insufficient data," "encourages (no doubt unintentionally) a new form of subtle racism," and "seduces the reader into believing it is not racism and discrimination but the weakness and defects of the Negro himself that account for . . . inequality." Thus the report was "irresponsible nonsense," containing "damnably inaccurate simplicity [which is] surely heresy."

More than most critics, Ryan focused on Moynihan's handling of nonmarital birth statistics. These, he pointed out, had emphasized that blacks were far more likely than whites to have children out of wedlock. Among the many important explanations for such differences, Ryan retorted, were the following: whites had much greater access to contraception and abortion; white hospitals underreported white nonmarital births; and shotgun marriages, more common among whites than blacks, reduced the number of white babies that were "illegitimate." (Whitney Young, in his *To Be Equal*, had raised similar points in 1964.) In Ryan's view, white racism, not deviant behavior by blacks, was the key to understanding the issue.

Ryan had a point in mentioning these explanations for high numbers of nonmarital births among blacks as well as in emphasizing (as Moynihan had) the long history of racial oppression, especially slavery, that had affected the sexual behavior and marital histories of many black people. But as Moynihan's accurate data had made abundantly clear, black nonmarital birth ratios were far higher than those of whites (eight times as high in 1963)—an extraordinary multiple that could in no way be explained away in the manner Ryan was suggesting.

Moreover, though Moynihan's treatment of black births out of wedlock was central to the report, it was not moralistic in tone. His charts, instead, suggested that the high proportions of nonmarital births among nonwhites were associated with exceptionally high nonwhite male unemployment rates and with low income. His purpose, moreover, had been to demonstrate the *outcome* of greater out-of-wedlock childbearing among blacks: higher numbers of female-headed households, in which many children suffered from poverty as well as from a host of related behavioral problems that damaged their lives. There was no way that these problems, which were often devastating, could be dismissed as Ryan had done.[29]

Ryan's assault outraged Moynihan's defenders. Harvard psychologist Thomas Pettigrew, whose publications had informed *The Negro Family*, later charged that Ryan's broadside was "trash . . . replete with errors and written by a man with no past experience in race relations. . . . It was, I fear, the opening shot of a wave of McCarthyism in the United States." Roy Wilkins of the NAACP, distressed that *Crisis* had printed Ryan's attack, wrote Moynihan an apology, saying that "it is a silly and sinister distortion to classify as racist this inevitable discussion of a recognized phase of our own so-called race problem." (Still hurting in 1967, Moynihan included both these comments in his article "The Moment Lost.")

Still, Ryan's piece created a considerable stir in October and November 1965. As Rainwater and Yancey pointed out, his assault was "widely regarded among critics as a definitive social science critique of the report." Even more than Payton's effort, it added firepower to the arsenal of weapons that many people, especially black people, had been amassing as they armed themselves for the long-awaited White House conference in mid-November.

By the time some 200 conferees assembled at Washington's Hilton Hotel, the high expectations that had flourished at the time of the Howard address five months earlier had dissipated. Johnson had already downgraded the function of the meeting, describing it as a planning session to prepare for a conference in June 1966. Many who attended in November wondered why any sort of conference had been called before policies had been drafted for discussion. One sardonic observer quipped, "It may be that the Hilton Hotel is not fertile ground for the planning of a revolution."[30]

The conferees also arrived with the knowledge that the sessions—as Payton had demanded—would devote little attention to issues involving the Negro family. The organizers scheduled eight panels, only one of which was to concern such matters. The executive director of the conference, White House aide Berl Bernhard, smiling broadly and hoping to set a light tone, announced at the start, "I want you to know that I have been reliably informed that no such person as Daniel Patrick Moynihan exists."

Moynihan did attend, however, traveling from Wesleyan to sit in on the family panel. This featured a scholarly paper by Hylan Lewis, a black sociologist from Howard University whom Moynihan had earlier consulted about family issues. Lewis reminded his audience that there was great diversity among black families, no single type of which was necessarily better than another, and that poverty accounted for most of the differences between the structures of black and white families. Without confronting Moynihan's report directly, he argued against the view that black families were crumbling or enmeshed in a self-perpetuating tangle of pathology. He noted that the proportion of female-headed black households had risen from 18.8 percent in 1949 to only 23.2 percent in 1962, or by roughly one-third of one percentage point per year. Though Lewis's emphasis on economic causes as well as his approach to remedies (he recommended full employment measures and the establishment of "rational family policy") approximated Moynihan's, the thrust of his presentation was to urge his listeners not to buy into a crisis-oriented view (such as Moynihan's) of trends in black family life.[31]

Moynihan did not speak on the first day. On the second, however, he rose to ask Payton how he could have failed to see that the report in fact emphasized unemployment as the key source of black family problems. (Later, in "The Moment Lost," Moynihan charged that Payton's paper "bordered on the psychopathological.") Payton held his ground, quoting Moynihan's statement in the report that the deterioration of the Negro family is "the fundamental source of weakness of the Negro community at the present time."

Further exchanges ensued, but the confrontation, though dramatic, probably did not change anyone's mind. It did, however, reveal a fact apparent since rumors about *The Negro Family* had begun to appear in July and August: phrases and sentences could be leaked or lifted from the report to frame it in a variety of ways. How people represented or misrepresented it depended in considerable part on where they were coming from and what they hoped to prove.

Other comments at the conference also received coverage in the media, notably those of Mary Keyserling, director of the Department of Labor's Women's Bureau. Keyserling challenged Moynihan's idea that black women were overemployed or that it would help families if black men took the place of black women in certain areas of employment. Especially as agitation for women's rights rose to the fore in U.S. political life within the next few years, criticism of the report as having endorsed patriarchal family life resonated more broadly.

The debates at the meeting as well as corridor conversations revealed that nothing could bridge the gulf that had deepened during the previous few months between angry civil rights leaders and defenders of the report. Four days after the meeting, Ryan's harsh attack, "Savage Discovery," appeared in the *Nation* magazine. A day later, Young, who had earlier endorsed the main ideas of the report, gave a speech in Washington in which he emphasized the role of white racism. The United States, he said, "can no longer discuss the pathology of Negro society without discussing also the pathology of the white society that permits that pathology to develop."

No one hammered Moynihan harder than James Farmer of CORE. In the past, like other black leaders, he had deplored the persistence of black family ills. Less so in December. In two columns that he wrote that month for the *Amsterdam News*, a black paper, he exclaimed that Moynihan had "provided a massive academic cop-out for the white conscience." The report clearly implied, Farmer added, that "Negroes in this nation will never secure a substantial measure of freedom until we learn to behave ourselves and stop buying Cadillacs instead of bread." Farmer said that the report, "when studied carefully, emerges in my mind as the most serious threat to the ultimate freedom of American Negroes to appear in print in recent memory."[32]

Moynihan, having moved to Wesleyan, had been somewhat sheltered from the blasts slamming the report since September. At the conference, he learned firsthand how passionate some of his critics had become. Moreover, it then became even more obvious to him than earlier that leading officials in the Johnson administration, shaken by the militancy of civil rights leaders, desperately yearned for the controversy over the report to go away altogether. As Moynihan noted, Johnson's State of the Union address in January 1966 devoted only a little attention to civil rights and none at all to concerns about the black family. Gone were the dreams of racial equality as so loftily expressed in "To Fulfill These Rights" at Howard. That splendid moment was now lost for certain.

As Moynihan was recovering from the conference, he derived some consolation from letters of support. Theologian Reinhold Niebuhr assured him that his report was a "terrifyingly accurate study of the disintegration of the Negro family."[33] But Moynihan was nonetheless deeply hurt by the abuse he had received. "The whole affair," he explained to Mrs. Niebuhr, "has become a nightmare of misunderstanding, misinterpretation, and misstatement." But he also knew that if he hoped to rise again from the depths—and to make himself heard—he had to try to defend his report.

So he entered the fray. In late November and December, he wrote an article for the *Washington Post* and eagerly accepted interviews for stories in the *New York Times*, *Life*, and *Newsweek*. He sat down for a long interview with Rainwater and Yancey, who were already working on their book about the report and the controversy that followed. He also appeared on television's *Meet the Press*. Having done these things, he explained to friends, "I am going to sulk a little and write out my hostilities [in the book that he was still planning to put together] in the next six months."[34]

The ample and generally favorable coverage these interviewers gave him again made it obvious, as earlier, that mainline media sources shared Moynihan's pessimism about the pathology—a word that they, too, often used—that gripped the ghettos. To rebut the notion that the report sustained racism, *Newsweek* even included a comment from Kenneth Clark deploring the negative reception of Moynihan's report: "It's kind of a wolf pack operating in a very undignified way. If Pat is a racist, I am. He highlights the total pattern of segregation and discrimination. Is a doctor responsible for a disease simply because he diagnoses it?" Thanking Clark for standing by him, Moynihan replied, "In moments of fury I sometimes think we are about to repeat the tragedy of Reconstruction: Liberty Without Equality."[35]

No newspaper at the time gave Moynihan more space than the *New York Times*, which on December 12 devoted six columns (and a photograph of him) to an admiring profile. In the course of it reporter John Herbers noted that Moynihan, thirty-eight years old and "with hair beginning to gray," had three children. Moynihan's "open, friendly face," however, "reddens a bit when he talks about the controversy over family stability." Most of the article then let Moynihan speak for himself. Given the opportunity, he drew attention to Johnson's speech at Howard and to his essay "A Family Policy for the Nation" that he had published in *America* in September. The United States, he repeated, was the "only industrial democracy in the world that does not recognize the welfare and stability of family life as a principal object of social policy."

Moynihan tried especially hard to make sure that readers understood the magnitude of the family issues he had dramatized in his report. The proportion of children born out of wedlock in New York City, he told Herbers, had risen from 3 percent in 1946 to 12 percent in 1964. The rate in Harlem in 1964 was 44 percent.

As if to cinch his case, he defended his personal understanding of family disruption. "I grew up in Hell's Kitchen," he said. "My father was a drunk. I know what this life is like."

CHAPTER 5

Families, Welfare, and Race, 1966–1968

On June 1, 1966—almost a year to the day after Johnson's clarion call at Howard University for racial equality—the White House conference, "To Fulfill These Rights," finally convened at the Sheraton Park Hotel in Washington. Attended by some 2,500 delegates, the size of the conference might have impressed uninformed passersby.

In fact, the conference was a humdrum two-day affair that accomplished nothing of substance. In agreeing at last to set it up, Johnson acted only because he had promised at Howard to do so. His heart was not in it, and his handpicked organizers made sure that moderates dominated the list of invitees and that the Moynihan Report would not be discussed. As Ben Heineman, the business leader LBJ designated chair of the conference, later noted, "Both the blacks and the whites were in agreement that it would not be put on the agenda."

President Johnson gave a speech, as did A. Philip Randolph, Roy Wilkins, and Thurgood Marshall. But members of the Student Nonviolent Coordinating Committee (SNCC) refused to attend. There was no real dialogue about issues. Moynihan, calling upon his knowledge of naval terminology, complained to Rainwater, "There was no plenary session. We were dumped into separate, watertight compartments, in the manner of damage control techniques on a battleship."

Literature about race relations was on display in a room at the meeting. Conspicuously absent from the collection, however, was the Moynihan Report, which Johnson administration officials, like most civil rights leaders, had long since consigned to oblivion. "The family," White House staffer Clifford Alexander explained to Moynihan, "is not an action topic for a can-do conference."[1]

Notwithstanding episodes such as this, some liberals in mid-1966 tried to maintain hopes for the future. After all, many of the landmark programs of the Great Society, notably the Civil Rights and Voting Rights acts, federal aid to public education, Medicare, Medicaid, and immigration reform, survived as important governmental initiatives. The economy continued to boom. Official government measurements of poverty reported dramatic declines, from 22 percent of the population in 1959 to 17 percent in 1965. Blacks, too, benefited from the thriving economy: the percentage of nonwhites officially identified as poor had plunged from 55 percent in 1959 to 40 percent in 1966 (and even to 32 percent by 1969).

But as the inconclusive conference had revealed, liberalism, having crested at high tide in June 1965, now remained in the doldrums in which it had been stranded by early 1966. The seismic events of the previous year—notably the Watts Riot and escalation of the Vietnam War—had shattered the nonviolent, interracial civil rights movement. Militants were embracing Black Power ideas. Controversy over the Moynihan Report had helped bury the hopes LBJ's speech at Howard had aroused. Still bitter, Moynihan wrote a friend in September 1966, "The super liberals chose to start a silly and sterile controversy about the report itself so that the program clearly implied by it has never been enacted, and has not even been formulated."[2]

As if emboldened by the troubles of liberalism, white racists did not hesitate at the time to fire off their grievances to Moynihan. Some of the many people who wrote him following yet another admiring portrait of him in the *New York Times* in July (it reported that he had received three honorary degrees that spring and had been elected to the National Academy of Arts and Letters) told him that he had been foolish to support the aspirations of lower-class blacks. One New Jersey man declared, "There [is] a simple, logical, and accurate explanation for most of the Negroes' troubles, their character, intelligence, and behavior. They are still primitive, even though a few generations removed from the savagery of the African jungle."[3] A month later, a Louisiana woman lit into him, "People like you make me sick. You go to school most of your life and have a lot of book learning, but you know about as much about the negro as I know about Eskimos." She added,

> There has never been a negro family to deteriorate, that is, not a family as white people know a family and I've known negroes all my life and they have never been any different. As they themselves say, they just "take up," and of course they "take up" numbers of times, so a bunch of negro kids may have five or six daddy's in a life time. Mostly their mama's don't know who their real Pa's are.[4]

Moreover, though many black people continued to move upward into the middle classes, large numbers of inner-city blacks remained deeply troubled during the late 1960s. For urban black men aged sixteen to nineteen, the rate of unemployment was estimated in 1967 at around 30 percent—or roughly three times the rate among urban whites of the same age group. Rising rates of violent crime in the ghettos—most of it black on black—especially afflicted working-class African Americans who struggled to protect their families.

The Johnson administration, however, was increasingly absorbed by the Vietnam War, and turned a largely deaf ear to advocates, notably Randolph and Bayard Rustin, who continued to press for massive programs to aid low-income people. It was a sign of the times that Kenneth Clark, who had long championed interracial solutions, seemed to be giving up on whites. The Negro, he wrote in 1966, "must be aware that no fundamental change in his status can come about through deference to or patronage from whites."

Most worrisome of all, an ominous restlessness continued to unsettle black communities in the inner cities. Most of these areas were not as desolate as they were to become during the economic "stagflation" of the 1970s or during the increasingly drug- and crime-ridden 1980s; the worst of the "crumbling" Moynihan had anticipated lay a little bit ahead. But as he had warned in his report, and as the Watts Riot had revealed, the civil rights movement had greatly lifted the expectations of black people. Demanding decent jobs, schools, and housing, they would tolerate rotten conditions no longer.

Many did not: racial disturbances surged. Already rising alarmingly in 1966, these peaked in the summer of 1967, when looting and burning afflicted a number of cities and ravaged Newark and Detroit. Thrown onto the defensive,

Johnson agreed after the troubles in Newark and Detroit to the appointment of a National Advisory Commission on Civil Disorders, which concluded in March 1968 that white racism lay at the root of the nation's racial problems and that the United States was "moving toward two societies, one black, one white—separate and unequal." Citing the Moynihan Report's emphasis on "slavery and . . . long periods of male unemployment afterwards," it concluded that "the Negro family structure had become matriarchal; the man played a secondary and marginal role in his family." In many ways, notably its central point that the United States was becoming divided into two nations—one black, one white—the commission echoed the alarm Johnson had expressed at Howard in June 1965. LBJ, however, insisted that lawless black conspirators had sparked the riots and that the commission was blaming him for the country's racial problems. He refused even to receive its report.[5]

The year 1968 was indeed an especially tumultuous time for Americans. Following the so-called Tet Offensive in January, antiwar demonstrations escalated dramatically. Johnson, tired and depressed, announced in late March that he would not run for president again. On April 4, Martin Luther King Jr. was assassinated, whereupon rioting broke out anew, notably in Washington, D.C. An assassin killed Robert F. Kennedy in June. Democrats met for a chaotic convention in late August and selected Vice President Hubert Humphrey as their presidential nominee. But the party was deeply divided, mainly over the war, and Humphrey lost in November to Richard Nixon.

For Great Society liberals, on the defensive since the "moment" had passed during the summer of 1965, Nixon's election was the last straw. It also appeared to extinguish all chances for easing racial hostilities. Indeed, white backlash against black activists had become powerful. Polls in August 1968 revealed widespread white resentment of blacks: 67 percent said that "Negroes are asking for more than they are ready for," 63 percent that "Negroes have less ambition than whites," and 49 percent that Negroes "want to live off handouts."

The riot commission report also noted the racial issue that had so troubled Moynihan in 1965: deteriorating family life among low-income blacks in the cities. Indeed, statistics concerning black out-of-wedlock childbearing, female-headed families, and increases in welfare rolls during the late 1960s and early 1970s were stunning. These more than confirmed Moynihan's conclusions that black families differed substantially from white families in these respects, and that the dire situation of many lower-class black families had "begun to feed on itself." By the 1970s they presented a portrait that made Moynihan's findings in 1965 appear bland by comparison.

Statistics concerning out-of-wedlock childbirth were especially striking in these years. They indicated that the proportion of white births to unmarried women had risen from 2 percent in 1950 and 1960 to 4 percent in 1965 and to 6 percent in 1970. Because this proportion had been so small in the 1950s, the relative increase—up by 300 percent—was very high. The absolute proportions of black births out of wedlock, however, rose enormously in the same years, from 18 percent in 1950, to 23.6 percent in 1963 (the figure that Moynihan had cited in his report), to 28 percent in 1965, and to 38 percent in 1970. This was a smaller percentage increase than that among whites, but—and this was the trend that frightened Moynihan and others of his persuasion—it showed a strikingly sharp upturn compared with the more gradual increases of the 1940s and 1950s.

Later developments, moreover, made it clear that the increases of the late 1960s were more than a blip. The proportion of births that were out of wedlock in the United States continued to rise rapidly between the mid-1970s and mid-1990s. Though these proportions leveled off from then until 2002 (at which point the overall proportion stood at 34 percent), they then shot upward again. In 2007, 39.7 percent of all births in the United States (including 72 percent of black births) were to unmarried women. This was a total of 1,714,643 out-of-wedlock babies, compared with 89,500 in 1940, 290,000 in 1965, 665,747 in 1980, and 1,365,966 in 2002.[6]

As demographers later concluded—approaching consensus concerning the question of *why* these proportions increased—three main trends spiked them. One development was substantial increases in birthrates among unmarried women of childbearing age (normally defined as fifteen to forty-four). This rate rose from 7 births per 1,000 unmarried women in 1940, to 23.4 births per 1,000 in 1965, to 45.1 births per 1,000 in 1995. This was a doubling of the overall birthrate among unmarried women during these thirty years. The jump was still greater among young unmarried women, leaping among teenagers aged fifteen to nineteen from 16.7 in 1965 to 44.4 in 1995. (Births to unmarried teens accounted for 50 percent of all unmarried births in 1970.) Among unmarried women aged twenty to twenty-four, birthrates rose from 39.6 in 1965 to 70.3 in 1995.

The second powerful trend was a sharp decrease in the proportion of women of childbearing age who were married. Overall, the marriage rate (the number of marriages per year per 1,000 unmarried adult women) dropped by 43 percent between 1960 and 1996. Unsurprisingly, demographers and others often label this dramatic development "The Decline of Marriage." In 1965, nearly two-thirds of all women aged twenty to twenty-four in the United States were married. By 1993, this percentage had plummeted to 34. Similarly, in 1965, almost 90 percent of women aged twenty-five to twenty-nine were married—a percentage that had shrunk by 1993 to 58. Percentages of black women who were married, always smaller than those among whites, dropped to lows throughout the period: by 1993, they had sunk to 19 percent among women twenty to twenty-four and to 43 percent among women twenty-five to twenty-nine.

The third relevant trend was a considerable drop in birthrates among the shrinking pool of married women. This decline, too, was considerable. In 1965, by which time the baby boom had ended, there were 130 births per 1,000 married women in the United States. Over the ensuing ten years, the birthrate among married women fell rapidly, and by 1996, having dropped by a third since 1965, it had settled to a low of 83.9. The number of children born to married couples dropped from 3.47 million in 1965 to 2.65 million in 1995, whereas the number born to unmarried women during these years more than quadrupled, from 290,000 in 1965 to 1.25 million in 1995.[7]

There was little policymakers (or moralists) could do about dynamic demographic trends such as these. After all, it was the baby boom, which began in 1946 and ended in 1964, that accounted for one of these key trends: great increases in the number of women who entered their prime childbearing ages during the years between 1965 and 1985. Largely because steadily higher percentages of these women decided to postpone marriage or to remain single, the proportion of all women who were unmarried rose greatly during that time. A range of developments that continued to be strong after the mid-1960s—notably, significant increases in the percentages of women who finished school, went to college, and entered the workforce—helped prompt these decisions and bolstered this trend. Meanwhile, among married women the spread of effective contraception and an increase in abortions were among the many social and cultural forces that helped reduce the high birthrates that had promoted the baby boom.

The decline of marriage and rise of births out of wedlock stemmed in turn from a number of powerful cultural changes that neither government nor private efforts could overcome. Highly influential was a development beginning to receive serious notice when Moynihan wrote his report: a surge of more casual attitudes, especially among the young, toward sex. Many, it seemed, took literally the Beatles' 1967 song "All You Need Is Love." Young women, some of whom followed a surging women's movement, increasingly believed that they could manage all right alone and that they no longer "had" to get married if they became pregnant. These new mores spread rapidly during the late 1960s—a time when the contagious power of rights-conscious activism interacted with unprecedented prosperity to drive grand popular expectations about life, as well as rebellion against more conservative social norms. Though the economy faltered during the 1970s and at other times thereafter, the new sexual mores—and the grand expectations—continued to flourish: millions of increasingly rights-conscious and individualistic Americans zealously pursued self-discovery, personal happiness, and greater sexual freedom.

Prior to the 1960s, many single women who became pregnant were forced into "shotgun" marriages. As of the 1970s, that was far less likely to happen. To be sure, the age-old stigma of illegitimacy did not disappear, especially among whites. Among blacks, where the stigma had never been as strong as among whites, pregnancy before marriage sometimes continued to be a source of intrafamily embarrassment, at least among grandparents. But by the mid-1970s relatively few young women, white or black, any longer considered it shameful to bear a child out of wedlock. Indeed, the stigma of illegitimacy lost force with astonishing speed, resulting in a rapid decline in forced marriages.[8]

As Moynihan had pointed out in his report, increases in the proportions of nonmarital births were showing up in the early 1960s among low-income black women, especially those in their teens. Within a few years, considerable increases also appeared among older black women and among low-income white women. By 1980, it was becoming clear that young, lower-class black women in the 1960s had formed the leading edge of broad-based, long-term changes in family formation in the United States—the decline of marriage and the concomitant rise of nonmarital fertility. These changes—among the most important demographic developments of the late twentieth century in the United States—also appeared throughout much of the economically developed world.[9]

Matters of social class, which have always affected the way people approach sex and marriage, are also important to an understanding of these developments. Well-educated, middle-class women were, and are, far more likely than less educated, low-income women to follow a prudent "life script"—one that parents and the culture repeatedly impress upon them. This script has always been clear: if you want to have children, wait until you are ready to marry and have the will and the means to raise them. By contrast, low-income women—less likely to have access to reliable contraception—are more likely to experience unintended pregnancy. Imagining bleak futures with the low-income, ill-educated men who impregnate them, they (like the men) are also more likely to shy away from the altar.[10]

Though the relative influence of these varied and interdependent forces—demographic, economic, and cultural—was disputed in the mid-1960s (and later), it was no wonder Moynihan and others worried about the direction of the trends. The consequences are serious. For a variety of reasons, babies delivered by unmarried mothers are at higher risk of having adverse outcomes such as low birth weight (often as a result of prematurity) or death in infancy. As Moynihan had emphasized, babies that survive are also far more likely to grow up in impoverished single-mother households.

Statistics concerning black female-headed families in the late 1960s reflected these prognoses. The proportion of white families headed by women, with no man present, fluctuated a little during the early postwar years, but rose only slightly—from 8.5 percent in 1950, to 8.1 percent in 1960, to 9.0 percent in 1965, and to 9.1 percent by 1970. The proportion of black families headed by women, however, jumped during these years—from 17.6 percent in 1950, to 21.7 percent in 1960, to 24.9 percent in 1965, and to 28.3 percent in 1970. By then, 31 percent of black children (and 9 percent of white children) were living in such families, most of which were poor. These figures did not alarm everyone—after all, two parents (some of them cohabiting) still headed more than two-thirds of all black families in 1970. But the relentlessly upward trend, driven by especially high percentages of children born to single mothers in the black ghettos, was unmistakable.[11]

Discussions in the 1960s and later about the rise in out-of-wedlock births, finally, often left a key question up for debate: why did these proportions become so much higher among blacks in these years than they did among whites? Relevant to an answer is the fact that the very different numbers for blacks and whites were nothing new: from the slavery era onward, marriage rates among black women had always been lower—and birthrates among unmarried black women higher—than they were among white women. Still, the question remained. Because out-of-wedlock childbearing among blacks rose so steeply between the early 1960s and the early 1990s, arguments over this question, as over the Moynihan Report, continued in later years—often sharpened by racist whites who attributed the differences to the amoral and overheated sexuality of black people.

Moynihan, no demographer, admitted in his report that he did not have the answers to such matters, but he clearly believed that the impact of slavery, followed by the long history of white racism in the United States, had become so overwhelming that the "situation" (as he had put it) of inner-city black families was feeding on itself. Many liberals and civil rights leaders, however, continued in the late 1960s and later to reject the notion that long-range historical forces such as slavery—or "black culture"—were the keys to contemporary changes in black family formation. The most powerful sources of increases in nonmarital births among blacks, they insisted, were relatively recent—and largely economic in nature. Post–World War II socioeconomic forces, notably massive south-to-north migrations of unskilled and poorly educated African Americans, had vastly increased the populations of already crowded black ghettos. Secure employment, moreover, often proved elusive. Liberals insisted that well-targeted economic policies attacking black unemployment, along with civil rights policies to crack the isolation caused by racial segregation, were necessary if these trends were to be arrested.

Moynihan, too, recognized that these economic forces had become especially damaging to family solidarity in the ghettos. After all, his report had stated, "*Negro unemployment*, with the exception of a few years during World War II and the Korean War, *has continued at disaster levels for 35 years*." He had also stressed that the people most affected by low education and unemployment were young black *men*. In short, his response to the question of why nonmarital black childbearing was becoming so much greater than that among whites, though highlighting long-range historical forces, was not much different from that of many of his liberal critics: if an unemployed and ill-educated black man impregnates a girlfriend, he is far less likely to commit to marriage than if he has stable, living-wage work. The girl, in turn, thinks twice before marrying such a poor prospect: better to go it alone, relying on welfare, help from kin, and/or low-income work—and cherish the child.

Statistics concerning welfare rolls in these years were equally graphic. The number of Americans receiving assistance from Aid to Families with Dependent Children (AFDC) increased from 3.1 million in 1960, to 4.4 million in 1965, to 6.1 million in 1968—and (following economic decline in the early 1970s) to 10.8 million in 1975. Moreover, the number of black families in the AFDC program began to increase considerably in the mid-1960s. By 1967, 46 percent of the families on AFDC were black, compared with 41 percent in 1961 and 32 percent in 1950. White families on AFDC in 1967 still outnumbered black families. But considering the fact that nearly nine out of ten families were white in those years, it was obvious that blacks were far more likely to end up on welfare than whites.

A number of developments helped to cause these increases in the welfare rolls, among them the considerable increase (thanks to the baby boom) in the number of young women who were reaching childbearing age as of the mid-1960s. A liberalizing of AFDC's eligibility rules championed by reformers in the late 1960s further swelled the rolls. Pressure for more generous welfare also mounted from single mothers; like other Americans, they were becoming considerably more rights-conscious. Unorganized politically and stigmatized by their situations, they had tended in the past to acquiesce in stringent administrative decisions concerning eligibility. Not so as of the late 1960s, by which time they were demanding welfare as a human right.[12]

As a result, the expense of AFDC grew considerably in the late 1960s. Between 1960 and 1970, the total cost of the program (shared by the federal government and the states) rose from $1.06 billion to $4.85 billion. These were far from lavish outlays—by themselves, AFDC benefits did not come close to pulling people out of poverty. But it was becoming increasingly evident that serious family problems in the inner cities, notably the rise of out-of-wedlock childbearing, were driving these well-publicized increases in tax dollars spent on welfare.

Many critics, especially conservatives, continued to complain that AFDC spurred perverse incentives. The availability of aid, they maintained, virtually invited low-income women (few of whom had access to reliable contraception) to have babies. Racists snarled that oversexed black women were ripping off the system. What incentive was there, these critics asked, for such women to stay in school or go to work? Why should welfare mothers receive taxpayer dollars while millions of low-income working people struggled to stay afloat? Worst of all, critics added, AFDC, which in many states denied aid to needy two-parent families in which the father was unable to find work, offered an incentive for the fathers to desert the home so that the mothers of their children might receive benefits. Liberals retorted correctly that this was not a common occurrence. But an incentive existed. An authoritative study later concluded that AFDC remained a program that was "antifamily and antiwork."[13]

So it was that a tangle of hotly contested issues in the mid- and late 1960s concerning black families, especially low-income black families, heated up the already combustible mix of controversies inflaming contentious race relations. Skirmishes over welfare, intensified by lurid exposés of black sexual behavior, constantly agitated the political scene until legislation in 1996 abolished AFDC.[14] The worrisome trends in black family structure that escalated in the late 1960s and thereafter, moreover, made the much-maligned Moynihan Report seem prophetic. Given his continuing concern with such issues, it was inevitable that he would make himself heard during the late 1960s.

In doing so, Moynihan was generally a little more careful from 1966 to 1968 about what he said than he had been in his report of 1965. At that time, as he wrote a scholar in 1967, he had resorted to dramatic language because he "was trying to rouse the administration to a state of crisis." (The riots, he added, indicated that he had been "right in this.") But "the more I learned about the subject, the fewer adjectives [he mentioned 'crumbling' as one] I might have used."[15]

Still, Moynihan was hardly silent in those years, during which he became widely known as head of the Harvard-MIT Joint Center for Urban Studies. In addition, he held a tenured professorship in education and urban politics at Harvard. That he landed such prestigious positions in 1966 was the result in considerable part of his good connections. His friend and outgoing head of the center, James Q. Wilson, was key in marshaling support at Harvard for these appointments.

Delighted, the Moynihans moved to Cambridge in time for Harvard's fall semester of 1966. There they rented a large university-owned house near the campus. Liz later described it as a "huge white elephant"—it had three stories with seven bedrooms on the second floor. Liz had the top floor fixed up as an apartment, in which a series of graduate students lived over the years, rent-free, in return for which they shoveled snow, put out the trash, and if needed watched over the three Moynihan children, Tim, Maura, and John. Until 1977, when Pat entered the U.S. Senate, this (along with his farm in New York State, where during the summers he did much of his writing) was the home base of his family. Though he was away from Cambridge a good deal—on leave from Harvard for five of the years between 1969 and the end of 1976—it was a prestigious base that enabled him to widen his connections with scholars and politicians, and to deepen his friendships with academic colleagues and neighbors such as Nathan Glazer, James Wilson, and their families.[16]

Owing to his continuing notoriety as author of *The Negro Family*, however, Moynihan and his family did not always have an easy time of it in the liberal environs of Cambridge. Liz recalls some nasty episodes. On one occasion, the mother of a playmate of Tim, learning that he was Pat's son, refused to let him enter her house for a play date. Nor did she call Liz to tell her so; Tim had to walk home alone. On another occasion, a schoolmate of Maura whose mother was a black activist showed her a book listing Pat as someone who had to be killed if blacks were to make progress. Later, Liz and some of her friends were at a party where a woman she did not know learned that Pat was her husband. The woman exclaimed, "How awful," and turned away. Appalled, friends told Liz that she would do better to stay at home to avoid rebuffs at social events.

While at Harvard, Moynihan taught a course called "Education and Urban Politics" to undergraduates. Taking advantage of his prestigious post at the center, he also cultivated contacts with journalists, many of whom in those years of urban unrest were eager to interview him. In July 1967, at the time of the rioting in Newark and Detroit, the *New York Times* ran an especially flattering story about his expertise concerning urban and racial matters. *Time*, seeking his wisdom at the same time, published a cover story on him titled "URBANOLOGIST PAT MOYNIHAN," in the course of which the magazine reminded readers that his report in 1965 had been "sensational" but also that criticism of it was unfounded. Devoting considerable space to his ideas, it highlighted his belief that blacks needed jobs and that black boys had to have more contact with authoritative male role models. "When these Negro GIs come back from Viet Nam," Moynihan said, "I would meet them with a real estate agent, a girl who looks like Diahann Carroll, and a list of jobs. I'd try to get half of them into grade schools, teaching kids who've never had anyone but women telling them what to do." *Time* concluded, "Few have articulated the urban crisis so well, and few have put forth so many thoughtful, or at least ingenious remedies."[17]

Not to be outdone, *Life* ran a six-page feature story about Moynihan in November 1967. Titled "Idea Broker in the Race Crisis," it included a full-page photograph of him under which a caption read, "A Troubled Nation Turns to Pat Moynihan." Three additional photos of him followed. Like many other mainline media profiles that appeared in later years—profiles that highlighted his "Celtic wit" and "Irish charm"—*Life*'s admiring article praised his personal qualities, describing him as a "huge, 6-foot-5 Irishman with a wide-open, red-cheeked face and eyes that are soft and full of humor, but that nonetheless burn into you." Reflecting the angst many Americans felt in the aftermath of urban rioting, *Life* wrote, "His sort of forward thinking may be the best hope—perhaps even the only hope—for any sort of long-term solution short of out-and-out civil war."

Aside from puffery of this sort, *Life*'s article set aside considerable space for Moynihan to advance his ideas. He began by refuting the proposition that race problems in the United States could be blamed (as the Commission on Civil Disorders later did) on "evil racists" or on the "power structure." On the contrary, Moynihan argued, the woes of blacks in the city were "systemic." Noting that many blacks in their senior year of high school in New York City were performing at the sixth-grade level, he exclaimed, "The outcomes are not willed. It's happening, and there's no point in looking around and trying to find the son of a bitch behind it all."

He also reiterated his long-standing advocacy of a generous, bureaucratically simple system of family allowances, without means testing, for all families with children aged seventeen or under. That would mean, he conceded, that nonpoor families, regardless of race, would also receive aid. Such a program would be costly and politically vulnerable. But, he argued, many recipients would be members of the working classes, which by and large had been left out of what he later called the "recent spate of government programs."

Above all, Moynihan insisted, family allowances would help needy children—this was as ever at the heart of his approach to social welfare. The allowances, he estimated, might cost approximately $9 billion per year, minus sums of money that would otherwise have been spent on welfare. In fact, such a sum, divided among the millions of families with children under seventeen, would have done little to help the poor. Given that federal spending (much of it for the war in Vietnam) had mushroomed—from $118 billion in fiscal 1965 to $158 billion in 1967—his proposals had no chance whatever of being accepted by the administration. Still, in *Life*'s profile, as in others, he had done his best to make his ideas known.

Moynihan understandably welcomed the positive exposure that these articles (as well as TV appearances) gave him while he was teaching at Harvard and running the urban center. But during these years he also spent much of his time writing essays aimed at scholars, opinionmakers, and political leaders concerned with race relations and social policies. These did not represent original scholarship, and they did not appear in refereed journals. But his essays appeared in a wide range of publications—*Atlantic Monthly*, *The American Scholar*, *Saturday Evening Post*, *Commonweal*, *Commentary*, *Architectural Forum*, *Catholic Home*, *The Public Interest*, *New Leader*—and widened his already considerable visibility as a commentator about some of the most controversial issues of the time.[18]

Not all of the attention was flattering. Many liberals, including some who could not forgive him for his report in 1965, refused to show him the respect he received from publications such as the *New York Times*, *Time*, and *Life*. Some continued to typecast him as an evil genius or as either a blatant or subtle racist. Garry Wills, who later described him as a "combination of Oxford don and Colonel Blimp," complained that he wrote a "clumsy prose that almost begs to be understood." Other readers could scarcely endure what one saw as his proclivity for "large and confident assertions combined with soft qualifications to account for the complexity of the facts."

Peter Steinfels, who later wrote a discerning study of neoconservatives, was a little kinder, agreeing that Moynihan was a quick study, skilled at absorbing "'facts' that he needs from all kinds of sources" in order to craft an argument, and that he displayed "extraordinary intelligence and experience—and a gift for language." But, Steinfels continued, Moynihan also had a habit of referring grandly to "firsts," "defining qualities," "new classes," "clashes of opposing ideals and theories," and "announcing new eras or the passing of old ones." Moynihan was "a man who tosses off general formulations as a comedian does one-liners, who gravitates to the battleground of ideas as naturally as a Dubliner to a pub, who cannot resist the intricate or oblique example, the startling or even inflammatory phrase."

Steinfels, like some others, also found Moynihan's writing uneven—at best, "genuinely witty and eloquent," at worst, "pretentious patter." He had a point about the pretentiousness, for Moynihan could not resist parading his wide-ranging reading of famous authors: historians Richard Hofstadter and Eugene Genovese, poets Archibald MacLeish, T. S. Eliot, and William Butler Yeats, sociologists (and friends) Nathan Glazer and James Q. Wilson, as well as Alexis de Tocqueville, George Orwell, Jean-Jacques Rousseau, Benjamin Disraeli, James Joyce, Herbert Marcuse, Reinhold Niebuhr, William Buckley, and many, many others. As Steinfels put it, Moynihan was sometimes a writer who "flaunted the professorial" and who could be guilty of producing a "masterpiece of manner over matter."

These criticisms aside, there was no denying that Moynihan's facts were generally accurate and relevant, and that many editors were happy to publish his efforts. Later, after Moynihan had become a widely known senator, Michael Barone, coauthor of the *Almanac of American Politics*, described him as "the nation's best thinker among politicians since Lincoln, and its best politician among thinkers since Jefferson."

This description is debatable, to say the least. It would be more accurate to conclude that Moynihan offered smoothly written and strongly argued observations about a considerable range of urgent social issues. On matters concerning race relations, social welfare, and the role of social science in policymaking, he was indeed an idea broker, mixing his own strong opinions with the theories of others (generally those who agreed with him) to track contemporary social and political trends and to ask probing questions about the possibilities of public policy. It was no wonder his opinions attracted a great deal of interest or that by 1969 some contemporaries were rating him as the country's most prominent public intellectual.

The simplest and in general most accurate label for Moynihan's ideas during these years following the release of his report on black family life is that they had become moderately neoconservative. Hence Moynihan's appeal to readers of journals such as *Commentary* and *The Public Interest* (which he had helped to found and on which he served as a member of the Publication Committee).[19] Hence, too, his close association with leading neoconservatives such as Glazer, Wilson, and Irving Kristol.

Moynihan's new associations did not mean that he recanted his support of liberal initiatives: as in his recommendations in *Life*, he wrote often of the need for a "system of income equalization" that would include full employment policies and family allowances. Unlike most neoconservatives, he continued to identify himself as a Democrat, backing Robert F. Kennedy for president after Johnson pulled out of the race in March 1968.

But Moynihan still seethed with resentment at the critics who had condemned his report in 1965. Militant advocates of Black Power especially enraged him, causing him to accuse them in early 1967 of being "caught up in a frenzy of arrogance and nihilism." "The great, guilty, hateful secret," he countered, "is that Negroes are not swingers. They are Southern Protestants. They like jobs in the civil service. They support the war in Vietnam, approve the draft, [and] support the President."

Liberal activists also infuriated him. After the spate of rioting in the summer of 1967, which stoked his fears and hardened his resentments, Moynihan wrote, "Liberals must somehow overcome the curious condescension that takes the form of defending or explaining away anything, however outrageous, which Negroes, individually and collectively, might do." As in his article about the moment lost, he complained that many liberals were "preoccupied with white racism" and wallowing in "white guilt." Other liberals, he complained, blamed the "system"—a way of thinking, he retorted tartly, that was "not an act of analysis; it is too often the opposite." "With all its virtues as a secular conscience," he concluded, the "liberal left can be as rigid and destructive as any force in American life."

In rejecting the views of liberals such as these, Moynihan called in late 1967 for a "politics of stability." This would require liberals to ally with conservatives to keep the nation from veering off on a radical course. It was a shame, he wrote, that "in America we don't have a conservative class. . . . This is not healthy." Liberals should "divest themselves of the notion that the nation—and especially the cities of the nation—can be run from agencies in Washington."[20]

A few common themes united many of his potshots at government policy-makers in these years. One was central to the message of neoconservatism, which by 1969 was seriously challenging LBJ-style big-government liberalism. This was that mediating institutions—families, churches, local civil organizations—were vitally important in protecting and enhancing social stability and that federal government policymakers, who were "good at collecting revenues but rather bad at disbursing services," did not know enough to accomplish some of the grandiose projects they were undertaking. Policymakers must act cautiously lest they run afoul of the bane of large-scale governmental social programs: the unforeseen and unintended consequences of public action. As Moynihan phrased it later, echoing the views of other neocons, "the role of social science lies not in the formulation of social policy but in the measurement of results."[21]

Moynihan was especially forceful in making such statements after he had digested in early 1967 a landmark study of American schooling, *Equality of Educational Opportunity*. Overseen by Johns Hopkins University sociologist James Coleman, a friend whom he greatly admired, and published in mid-1966, it was the focus of an eagerly attended, nationally discussed faculty seminar on education and related matters that Moynihan organized and codirected at Harvard in 1966 and 1967.[22] Perhaps no work of U.S. social science published during Moynihan's lifetime did more to bolster his already strongly held view that the quality of family life was the key to good society.

Coleman agreed that the "social environment of the schools—the educational backgrounds of other students and teachers"—was important in advancing educational achievement. Clearly, he emphasized, low-income and minority children deserved better schooling. But, he insisted, the cognitive development of children did not depend alone on what happened in the schools. He wrote, "*The sources of inequality in educational opportunity appear to lie first in the home itself, then they lie in the school's ineffectiveness to free achievement from the impact of the home, and in the school's homogeneity, which perpetuates the social influences of the home and its environs.*"[23] Given the power of home and neighborhood forces, Coleman concluded, increases in per-student spending for school facilities would not necessarily make a large difference in student achievement. A committed advocate of civil rights and of racial desegregation of schools (he had been arrested during protests in Baltimore), he was shaken by what he found. In early 1967, he scrawled an anguished letter to Moynihan that expressed his alarm.

> I think now is the time for designing some really radical alternatives to the present system of education—alternatives that, in one way or another, release Negro children from the environment in which the accident of birth has located them—meaning not only introduction of whites into that environment, but also replacing that environment (including the home and neighborhood) to a very large extent with different ones—e.g., things like daytime group homes, with plenty of middle-class white mothers around, for very young children.[24]

As this letter indicated, Coleman was deeply pessimistic about the life chances of lower-class urban black children. The impact of deeply entrenched socioeconomic disabilities that plagued them could not be disentangled from the ill effects of inadequate schools—both should be considered when evaluating variations in achievement test scores and in charting reform—but problems of home and neighborhood obviously mattered enormously.

Moynihan agreed wholeheartedly and enthusiastically with Coleman's conclusions, which added considerable scholarly heft to his insistence that children in lower-class black families suffered from enormous cognitive disadvantages even before they entered school. (A story has it that a friend confided to him when Coleman was compiling the data, "Have you heard what Coleman is finding? It's all family.")[25] Moreover, the report was the sort of social science Moynihan most admired: an evaluation of existing governmental efforts. It encouraged him to become even more outspoken in emphasizing the seriousness of lower-class family ills and in expressing reservations about overly zealous liberal policymaking. "Our existing social science," he maintained, "cannot explain what is going on." Policymakers, therefore, must understand "how difficult it is to change things and to change people." "The great failing of this time," he wrote in 1968, "is constantly to over-promise and to overstate, and thereby constantly to appear to under-perform."

Above all, Moynihan argued, policymakers must be clear about the meaning of their proposals. Lack of clarity was his major complaint about community action programs, which he continued to blame for having excited unrealistic expectations.[26] There remained a need, he wrote, "for sustained, longitudinal studies of the poverty population to try to determine which factors lead into welfare dependency, and which lead out." Instead, he maintained, antipoverty warriors had tossed off high-flying claims about the virtues of community action. These "raised the level of perceived and validated discontent among poor persons, without improving the conditions of life of the poor in anything like a comparable degree." In a characteristically elliptical and provocative way, he asked, "Can it be that this process has not somehow contributed to and validated the onset of urban violence?"

Another main theme Moynihan emphasized in these especially prolific years of writing concerned the "crises in welfare" arising from the "AFDC explosion." Rebutting conservatives, he argued that women did not get pregnant because they expected to live on welfare: impoverished female-headed families, trapped in bleak environments, would have to receive help from government. But, he argued, welfare professionals were covering up the explosion in payments "to protect the good name of their clients." Minority group leaders were making matters worse, in effect saying, "'Let's not do anything about it.'" Overall, he wrote, there was a "near-obsessive concern to locate the 'blame' for poverty, especially Negro poverty, on forces and institutions beyond the community concerned." The result was what Moynihan called "the great silence" concerning the vicissitudes of low-income family life in the United States.[27]

Silence about what he termed the "recognizable problem of black lower-class behavior" greatly frustrated him. Returning to a main theme of his report of 1965, he declared, "The heart of the [welfare] problem is dependent children from broken families." Thus a "vast Negro underclass" has grown up in northern cities—"a disorganized, hurt group of persons easily given to self-destructive violence." Partly to blame for this doleful trend, he said, were liberal Protestants "who speak with scorn of 'Victorian' notions about broken homes." As a result, he sniped, "somehow or other, the idea that sexual repression is bad has gotten mixed up with the idea that illegitimacy, or whatever, is good."

As earlier, Moynihan did not go so far as to argue that lower-class black people were living in an intergenerational, unbreakable culture of poverty. Poverty, he insisted, was "not a trait but a condition." Thus, though the sons of the ghetto might end up acting like their fathers, poverty and behavioral excesses were not indelibly heritable: "Each succeeding generation can re-create the patterns of the previous one without there being any specifically intergenerational transition in the process." He also believed there was a common value system for all Americans that rich and poor alike understood and hoped to live by. But, he emphasized, "conforming to norms requires certain kinds of social and logistic[al] support." Because many blacks, Mexican Americans, and Puerto Ricans were "poor in ways that other groups were not," enormous governmental resources had to be mobilized on their behalf.

Again and again, therefore, he argued that while the United States must try to advance equality of results, as LBJ had advocated at Howard, it must also find ways to curb the spread of dysfunctional behaviors. Concerning the issue of nonmarital childbearing, he concluded that there had to be "sharp curtailment of the freedom now enjoyed by low-income groups to produce children they cannot support." The nation, he said, should support a "massive dissemination of birth control knowledge and practice among low-income groups."[28]

Moynihan's arguments about the limitations of contemporary social science and about the perils of overeager liberal policymaking were well taken. His understanding of poverty was nuanced, reflecting the sophisticated ideas of sociologists such as his friend Lee Rainwater. Furthermore, some of his complaints about the cravenness of white liberals and the posturing of black militants were justified. Above all, he was correct in deploring the silence that Americans—notably liberals, black and white—had helped impose on informed discussion of lower-class black family problems. In charging that these liberals were dealing in denial, he was delivering inconvenient but necessary truths.

Given Moynihan's insistence that social scientists and policymakers needed to know more about poverty, however, it was evident he was on shaky ground in advancing his own policy recommendations. Indeed, it was obvious that formidable problems of politics and of implementation continued to stand in the way of significant job creation and family allowance programs. Then as earlier, many conservatives, stereotyping black "welfare mothers" in highly unflattering terms, strongly opposed large-scale government programs on their behalf. As Rainwater warned Moynihan, moreover, the funding he sought for his family allowance proposals would have fallen far short of what would be necessary to make much difference in people's lives. Other friends reminded him that there was no way the government, engaged in enormously expensive efforts to win in Vietnam, could or would find the money to fund public jobs for the millions of troubled Americans who needed living-wage work. In short, the hurdles facing large-scale socioeconomic programs to aid lower-class black people continued to be immense.

Many liberals, moreover, continued to pay Moynihan no heed. From 1966 to 1968, as in 1965, some deemed him the infamous author of *The Negro Family*. Black leaders continued to resent his frank depiction of lower-class black family life. Still others, noting his reservations about strong affirmative action programs concerning universities (Jews, he pointed out, had suffered in the past from quotas), distrusted him. Many critics simply brushed him off as a neoconservative windbag who liked to hear himself talk.

For all these reasons, Moynihan knew all too well by late 1968 that his recommendations for policies to aid inner-city black families stood no chance of passage. When Nixon won the election of 1968, it seemed even more unlikely than in the past that political leaders would listen to him.

CHAPTER 6

Moynihan, Nixon, and the Family Assistance Plan

D aniel Patrick Moynihan liked to tell friends that he was "baptized a Catholic and born a Democrat." Richard Nixon, however, was a Protestant and about as partisan a Republican as one could be. Many Democrats, perceiving him as a vindictive and deeply suspicious man—and recalling his support of Senator Joseph McCarthy in the 1950s—detested him.

Black civil rights leaders, too, expected the worst when Nixon took office in January 1969. Though he professed to be an advocate of civil rights, he joined many other Republicans who employed code language as part of a "Southern strategy" aimed at winning over white voters who resented Black Power rhetoric and deplored urban rioting. Many Republicans (like many blue-collar Democrats) spoke angrily and often about crime in the streets, mothers on welfare, and the need for law and order. The Southern strategy, refined by Republican leaders in the years to come, ultimately moved the GOP well to the right, intensified political partisanship, and transformed the geography of U.S. politics.

Given these circumstances, it would have seemed bizarre in late 1968 to imagine that Nixon would ask Moynihan to join his administration or that Moynihan would accept. Indeed, Nixon often raged against intellectuals. "Professors," he later lectured Henry Kissinger (who had been one), "are the enemy. Write that on a blackboard 100 times and never forget it." But ask

Nixon did, and Moynihan said yes. From January 1969, when Nixon took office, through December 1970, Moynihan not only served as a loyal trooper in Nixon's camp but also occupied an office in the west basement of the White House, at first as executive secretary of a newly created Urban Affairs Council. When Nixon set up the council, he had in mind that it would become for many domestic matters the equivalent of the National Security Council, which had been established in 1947 to advise the president concerning issues of international import. Nixon himself was chair of the new council, and all cabinet members except the secretaries of state, defense, and treasury were members.

Still, the question lingers: why did Nixon choose Moynihan, a Democrat, and why did Moynihan accept? The first question is relatively easy to answer. Though Nixon had often stormed about eastern, urban "elitists" such as scholars at ultraliberal Harvard, he wished to have it known that prominent intellectuals like Moynihan (and Kissinger) would be willing to sign on with him. It was also obvious to Nixon that his administration would have to deal with racial antagonisms that threatened to pull the country apart. And on many domestic issues, about which he cared little, he was open to a number of liberal ideas, including environmental reforms and proposals to establish a national health insurance plan. More than a year before the election of 1968, some of his advisers had brought Moynihan's speeches and articles about welfare and race relations to his attention. Much of what Moynihan was saying, notably his arguments for development of a more bipartisan politics of stability and against the "adversary culture" of the Left, intrigued and impressed him. Appointing Moynihan, a Democrat widely hailed as the nation's preeminent expert on urban matters, seemed to make good political sense.[1]

When rumors started circulating in late September 1968 that Moynihan might sign on with Nixon, friends wrote him in dismay. One was Harry McPherson, who asked him, "Do you know Nixon? Do you know who will run the government for him? I fear for liberal intellectuals who think they may regain a voice in policy-making in the Nixon era. There is simply no engine there—not the slightest throb of interest in a country that ought to be." Moynihan reassured him, pointing out that he had "publicly and explicitly" come out for Hubert Humphrey during the presidential campaign. He added, "Have no fear that I will accept the job. I have life tenure at Harvard University and make twice as much money as a cabinet officer with no particular effort, and have four-month vacations besides!"[2]

In fact, however, Moynihan was eager to serve. Having moved in neoconservative circles during the previous two years, he had burned bridges with many people on the left. He remained disgruntled about the way that they had treated him and his report in 1965. He had also lost hope that Democrats, who by 1968 were widely blamed for "Johnson's War" in Vietnam, were in a position to move the nation ahead.

Equally important, Moynihan had Potomac fever. Having lived away from Washington since the summer of 1965, he was anxious to have a hand in devising public policies concerning families, poverty, and welfare. So he took steps to ingratiate himself. In October, he wrote Nixon, "I was greatly impressed by your radio address on the subject of employment." Having flattered him, he offered to send him material on the issue that would clarify the "relations between unemployment and various forms of social pathology." When Nixon's offer came, he was quick to accept, even though Liz, a lifelong Democrat, decided not to take the children out of their schools and move from Cambridge to Washington. Wasting no time, he found an apartment, got in touch with former associates—notably Paul Barton, who prepared for him a detailed summary of information concerning family life and welfare—and set to work.[3]

Even more than other presidential administrations in modern U.S. history, Nixon's suffered from ideological infighting and bureaucratic intrigue. Moynihan, quickly assembling a team of mostly young and relatively liberal staffers, soon found himself in combat with a more conservative group of presidential advisers surrounding Arthur Burns, an economist and professor whom Nixon had named as his counselor. A fiscal conservative, Burns was also a tenacious defender of his turf. Until late 1969, when he left to become chair of the Federal Reserve, Burns battled Moynihan for access to Nixon's ear. John Ehrlichman, the president's top adviser concerning domestic matters, often had to intercede. Thereafter, replacing Burns as counselor until returning to Harvard in January 1971, Moynihan continued to advise Nixon, but without the executive responsibility he had as head of the staff of the Urban Affairs Council.

Confident of his ability to influence the president, Moynihan thrived in Washington. As early as January 3, when he wrote Nixon a memo advising, "Your task . . . is clear: to restore the authority of American institutions," it was plain he would do more than merely coordinate the actions of the Urban Affairs Council. He operated (in the view of one later scholar) as Nixon's "iconoclast in residence," whipping off lengthy memoranda concerning a host of issues: Washington's public architecture, population control, nominees for Presidential Medals of Freedom, and establishment of a department of higher education and research. At Nixon's request, he gave him a list of ten books to peruse, notably a biography of Benjamin Disraeli, the nineteenth-century English Conservative leader who won historical renown by supporting reforms. Nixon read it. Playing to Nixon's ego, Moynihan may have hoped to entice him into becoming a modern-day Disraeli.[4]

Moynihan also urged the president to "avoid at whatever immediate cost" an "enormous controversy" that would develop if he decided to abolish Johnson's War on Poverty. Though Nixon had no use for the Office of Economic Opportunity (OEO), which was in charge of the initiative, the agency had the support of many liberals. Concluding that doing away with it would hurt him politically, he took Moynihan's advice. The OEO limped along until 1974, when President Gerald Ford transferred its functions to a new agency, the Community Services Administration (CSA).[5]

Though Moynihan made it clear to Nixon that he remained a Democrat and that he opposed the war in Vietnam, the president continued to welcome his iconoclastic prodding. The professor, Nixon thought, was skilled at anchoring ideas about public policies in broad historical and international contexts. He also liked reading Moynihan's memos and talking to him about the issues. In June 1969, he scribbled on one of Moynihan's memoranda, "It's reassuring to have a true intellectual in residence!" As Stephen Ambrose, a biographer of Nixon, later put it, the president was attracted by Moynihan's "gift for gab, by the brilliance of his mind, by his uncompromising honesty, by his pixie qualities, and by the originality of his thought." Also, Ambrose wrote, Moynihan was good at "flattery that was unusual for a Harvard professor and quite welcome to Nixon."[6]

Moynihan, who continued to stay abreast of scholarship and developments concerning black family life, concentrated his efforts in early 1969 on securing one cherished goal: welfare reform. Indeed, while at Harvard he had taken time to serve on a poverty task force for Mayor John Lindsay of New York City and to act as a consultant concerning welfare issues to Governor Nelson Rockefeller of New York. As earlier, he favored creation of a comprehensive but easily administered system of family allowances—these, assisting all families with children, whether rich or poor, would not diminish the incentives of recipients to seek employment. But he knew that any such plan would face heavy opposition, mainly from conservatives who would rail at the cost—and who would maintain, as they had in the past, that it would lead to higher birthrates among the poor.[7]

But since the early 1960s, Moynihan had continued to argue that some sort of fundamental reform of what he called the "welfare mess" in the United States must be undertaken. This meant overhaul of Aid to Families with Dependent Children (AFDC), which was continuing to grow rapidly. As earlier, the size of AFDC benefits varied enormously, with recipients in poorer states, especially in the South, receiving far smaller welfare payments than those in wealthier (and more liberal) urban states of the North.[8] Even more loudly than earlier, city leaders were complaining that hordes of poor people (many of them black) were abandoning the South to take advantage of higher benefits in the North. These migrations, the critics added, were greatly expanding the rolls and the costs to taxpayers.

Conservatives, including many white working-class Americans, also continued to charge that AFDC offered perverse incentives, "coddling welfare mothers" who thereby refused to look for work and who bore one illegitimate child after another. Experts, then as earlier, retorted accurately that AFDC probably had only a small impact on the rise of nonmarital childbearing. Still, the critics intensified their assaults, many of which fanned an often nasty backlash against the behavior of lower-class black men and women.[9]

Many liberals, too, were demanding an overhaul of AFDC by 1969. They complained not only about the state-by-state variations in aid but also, as they had in the past, about benefits that fell far short of meeting the needs of families who received them. This was true not only in the South but also in the higher-benefit states of the North, where the costs of living were much greater. Liberals also bemoaned the fact that many states denied aid to needy families with two unemployed parents, thereby creating the incentive for fathers to desert the home so that mothers and children might become eligible for assistance. Reform of the system, liberals insisted, must at least provide better and more uniform benefits and cover two-parent as well as one-parent families in need.

As these varied criticisms indicated, welfare had come under widespread attack by the time Nixon took office. Many who were demanding changes in the system, including not only liberals but also conservative economist Milton Friedman and a number of business leaders, had begun by that time to support various "negative income tax" or "guaranteed income" proposals. Though these differed, they were alike in seeking establishment of government entitlements that would guarantee families (or at least families with children at home) a minimum annual income. Moynihan did not at first call for such a guarantee, which until April 1969 he thought the administration would not support, but he did urge Nixon to back wholesale reform. The system, he wrote the president in January, "destroys those who receive it, and corrupts those who dispense it." The United States, he said, should move "away from a *services strategy* dealing with the problems of social inequality, toward an *incomes strategy.*" A services strategy, he added, was one "feeding the sparrows by feeding the horses. *An incomes strategy* is something quite different. It begins with the assumption that what the poor and near poor lack most is money."[10]

The key to enacting any kind of major reform of welfare, of course, would be winning the president's support—a goal Moynihan tirelessly pursued. Recognizing that Nixon was angry about reports of corruption in the existing system, he also reminded him that an incomes plan would greatly appeal to northern governors who were struggling under the burden of contributing state funds to AFDC. Moynihan also told the president that some sort of guaranteed income plan that could be relatively easily administrated would enable him to eliminate "tens of thousands of social workers from the government payroll," whereupon, a White House staffer recalled, "Nixon's eyes lit up."[11]

In his appeals to Nixon, Moynihan often highlighted the role of racial concerns. One of the reasons many white Americans might support overturning the existing welfare system, he explained, was that they believed AFDC mainly benefited blacks. But it was also clear that Moynihan hoped to accomplish what his report in 1965 had failed to inspire: bettering the conditions of poor black families. Welfare reform, he explained to Nixon, would assist the "whole effort the nation is making to respond to the needs of the black urban lower class."[12]

The struggle to develop a comprehensive plan, to override objections from Burns and other conservatives, and finally to get the president to support a specific proposal took the better part of six months. But it succeeded. Nixon, alarmed by the rising costs of AFDC, was persuaded above all that the incentives of the existing welfare system perversely penalized work effort. By supporting a plan that would both abolish AFDC and offer working-class people help, he thought, he could win over white working-class voters to the Republican Party. As Moynihan had recognized, Nixon also yearned to take aim at the liberal social workers and government bureaucrats that administered AFDC: the new program, the plan anticipated, would be run by a small team of experts in the Social Security Administration. Political motives aside, the president strongly supported scrapping AFDC. "This whole thing [welfare] smells to high heaven and we should get charging on it immediately," he had expostulated in January.

Convinced of the political possibilities for change, Nixon went ahead in Auguest 1969 to announce that he backed a major new program named the Family Assistance Plan (FAP). "My God!" Moynihan later exclaimed. "I didn't think any Republican administration would go for any more than that!"[13]

Moynihan's exclamation was understandable, for FAP promised to be the boldest effort ever undertaken in the United States toward establishing widespread cash entitlements for low-income people. Estimated to cost $5 billion when set into operation for the 1971 fiscal year, it offered guaranteed annual incomes not only to the AFDC population but also to millions of people in low-income working families. A two-parent family of four, for example, would receive basic FAP payments—the floor—of $500 per parent per year, and children $300 each, for a total of $1,600. Poor families of that size with earned income would be entitled to retain earnings of up to $60 per month ($720 per year) without losing such payments (the so-called income disregard). A four-person family with annual earnings of $720, therefore, would have a guaranteed total income for the year of $2,320—the $720 in disregarded earnings plus the $1,600 from FAP.

To sustain work incentives for parents of families with earnings above the income disregards, the planners had to struggle to find a formula. What they were devising, after all, was a shot in the dark that would rest on assumptions about how people would react to cash incentives. In retrospect, it is evident that a large-scale experiment in social planning such as FAP would have benefited from what might have been learned from the results of a considerable number of smaller-scale trials.

Presidents, however, are attracted to fashioning bold and headline-grabbing initiatives. Nixon was no exception once he had been convinced that revision of the welfare system would help him politically. With his support, FAP featured a formula the planners hoped would sustain work incentives for families that earned more than the income disregards. For every dollar a family of four earned between $720 and $3,920 (a cutoff point slightly above a poverty line for such families at which FAP payments would cease), its basic entitlement of $1,600 would be cut by 50 cents. The formula was aimed at ensuring two goals. The first was that the continuation of FAP payments to low-income working families (those earning up to the cutoff point) would preserve work incentives. The second was that by cropping the payments as incomes rose and stopping them when a family earned a better-than-poverty-level amount, FAP would mainly assist the most needy—and in the process, control costs.

As Moynihan and others conceded, FAP would not affect everyone—only low-income families with children. Very few of the elderly, who were 20 percent of the poverty population, would benefit from it. Nor would the plan help single people or families—no matter their incomes—without children eighteen or under. Moreover, as Nixon himself emphasized to appeal to working-class people, relatively little of the money to be allotted would go to the poor on welfare. Indeed, the proposed income guarantees were hardly generous: as Moynihan ruefully admitted, the floor of $1,600 for an eligible family of four was in most areas less than half the poverty line for such families, and (in all but six southern states) a lower amount than four-person AFDC families had been getting. Liberals also complained that the plan would require employable heads of recipient families (those not elderly, disabled, or caring for preschool children) to register for training or job placement. (For these people, the plan did not in fact guarantee an annual income without strings.)

Supporters of Nixon's plan, however, pointed out that it required states (aided by federal fiscal relief) to pay supplemental benefits equal at least to the difference between the proposed minimum standards under FAP and the states' present levels of welfare support. Eligible families, therefore, would be at least as well-off as they had been under the federal-state AFDC system. Defending the plan, Moynihan argued that it would reach some 20 million people per year—roughly twice the number then on AFDC—and that it would be a godsend to the South, the nation's poorest region. The program promised to triple the number of southerners who received governmental assistance, of whom 40 percent would be black.[14]

For good reason, Moynihan later maintained that FAP was "the most startling proposal to help poor persons ever made by a modern democratic government." Other experts agreed, noting that the guarantees represented a dramatic new entitlement that advanced income supports to a higher ground. FAP, unlike AFDC, also proposed to guarantee benefits to all eligible two-parent as well as one-parent families. Many years later, in 2008, a leading student of social policy, Gary Burtless, described FAP as "revolutionary"—a "high water mark for support of European-style social welfare in the United States."[15]

Burtless, echoing many other analysts of FAP, was correct. By including welfare families—historically the "undeserving" poor—in a larger program that also benefited the more "deserving" working poor, backers of FAP hoped to lessen the stigma borne by the "undeserving" and to better the circumstances of many low-income people, especially in the South. Above all, it broke ground by guaranteeing income levels for millions of Americans. In so doing, it promised to broaden the meaning of liberalism, which in the area of social welfare policy had relied in the past primarily on the provision of rehabilitative services to individuals in order to widen the doors to opportunity. FAP, by contrast, sought to build floors under the incomes of large groups of people, thereby moving toward the goal Johnson (coached by Moynihan) had outlined at Howard in 1965: *greater equality of result.*[16]

For a time, it appeared FAP might receive congressional approval. Administration officials, including Donald Rumsfeld, Nixon's director of OEO, gave it vigorous support. In April 1970, the House of Representatives passed it by a vote of 243 to 155. George H. W. Bush, a Republican representative from Texas, was one of many Republicans who voted for it. Over the summer, however, it became apparent that FAP faced serious opposition both from the Right and from the Left. The U.S. Chamber of Commerce, helping to lead a conservative onslaught, argued that government wage supports would make workers dependent. It took out full-page newspaper ads that proclaimed, "FAP would triple our welfare rolls. Double our welfare costs." Russell Long of Louisiana, chair of the Senate Finance Committee (which was in charge of evaluating the measure), was one of many southern conservatives who worried that the program would exert upward pressure on wage rates, which were low in the region. Expressing a widely held stereotype of AFDC recipients, he referred to mothers on welfare as "brood mares." Asserting that poor people were already relying on welfare instead of working, he added, "I can't get anybody to iron my shirts."[17]

Still other obstacles slowed the bill's journey in the Senate. John Williams of Delaware, a staunch fiscal conservative—also a member of the finance committee—came up with figures indicating that other federal programs would complicate the issue of work incentives. Rising numbers of poor families were by then benefiting from noncash (in-kind), means-tested programs such as Medicaid, Food Stamps, and public housing. If working heads of families received cash payments from FAP, Williams demonstrated, their incomes would increase, potentially endangering their eligibility for the in-kind benefits. FAP beneficiaries, he exclaimed, would be "better off just to spit in the boss's face to guard against a pay raise."[18]

Though supporters of FAP managed to fine-tune the plan, thereby minimizing the glitches, Williams's intervention showed that technical and bureaucratic issues might complicate any far-reaching initiative to reform welfare. This was so, for as subsequent efforts (notably during the Carter years) revealed, the labyrinthine interconnections of varied U.S. social programs—and the lobbies with turf to defend—greatly hindered the struggles of social reformers. Joseph Califano, who led Carter's efforts as secretary of Health, Education, and Welfare (HEW), famously lamented that welfare reform was the "Middle East of domestic politics."

FAP, moreover, unsettled some liberals, including those in organized interest groups. Labor union leaders did not oppose the plan, but they worried that it might jeopardize their hard-won standing as protectors, via collective bargaining, of workers' rights and benefits. In 1970, they offered little more than faint praise for the proposal. Many social workers, confronted with a plan that seemed to threaten their jobs, were lukewarm. They declared that their expertise provided a more individualized kind of aid than cold cash. Poor people, they pointed out, have varying needs and problems and need personalized attention.

Many liberals worried especially that provisions in the legislation calling upon able-bodied adult recipients to register for training or placement might be rigorously enforced, thus turning FAP into a punitive "workfare" program. U.S. Representative Shirley Chisholm of New York, who had been the only black representative to vote against the plan in April, exclaimed that the "compulsory work qualifications" bordered on "involuntary servitude." In truth, most recipients—including, of course, all children—would have been exempted from such provisions. And it was widely believed, especially by conservatives, that the training and job placement provisions would be virtually unenforceable.

But the fears of liberals persisted. Many, moreover, demanded funding in the legislation to create public-sector jobs—so that recipients who received training might subsequently find employment. (The administration, refusing to make government the employer of last resort, would not go that far.) Other liberals, loathing Nixon, rejected any reform for which he might claim credit. Still others asserted that the basic entitlements were much too low to sustain a decent standard of living for the majority of needy families with children, notably those headed by large numbers of single mothers in the inner cities of the North, where the costs of living far exceeded those in the South.

With the program bogged down in the Senate, militants from the National Welfare Rights Organization (NWRO), a recently established pressure group mainly representing black welfare mothers from the North, mounted fierce opposition to it. The NWRO was hardly a large lobby, and at first it received little support from civil rights leaders, most of whom (like Moynihan in 1965) continued to focus on the problems of black men. Indeed, many of these leaders, defensive in the face of negative stereotypes of mothers on welfare, at first shied away from the NWRO. But black women activists deeply resented descriptions of welfare recipients as lazy, incompetent, and oversexed. Some had responded bitterly to Moynihan's report in 1965, viewing as slurs his comments about matriarchy. Others, including many who later rallied to the NWRO, had railed at the report because it had argued that black women, faring better than black men, did not need as much help. Michele Wallace, a young black feminist who conceded that Moynihan had been correct about the special problems of black men, nonetheless observed later, "Everybody wanted to cut Daniel Moynihan's heart out and feed it to the dogs."[19]

The NWRO activists, demanding their rights as citizens, were feisty. Most of the funding from FAP, they charged angrily, would go to white workers, not to black welfare recipients. Their fury rising over the course of the Senate debates, they hiked their demands for a guaranteed adequate income to a high (as of 1971) of $6,500 (plus increases to keep pace with inflation) for an eligible family of four. Branding FAP a "Family Annihilation Plan," they exclaimed,

"ZAP FAP." NWRO's magazine, the *Welfare Fighter*, ran a cartoon that featured two tattered charwomen. One asked, "What's that FAP mean?" Her coworker replied, "Fuck America's Poor."[20]

In seeking to secure their far more costly demands, these militants were politically unrealistic. Still, the basic case of the NWRO—that proposed FAP payments to welfare mothers were modest—was hard for many liberals to ignore, among them Senators George McGovern of South Dakota and Eugene McCarthy of Minnesota. The Urban League, which was hardly a radical organization, and which, courted by Moynihan, had signaled interest in the plan in 1969, felt obliged in 1970 to testify on behalf of the NWRO's position, whereupon Nixon raged privately at its director, Whitney Young. "He is hopelessly partisan," he scrawled on a memo that Moynihan had sent him. "Can't some of our people who help finance the Urban League hit him? See if we can't get someone on this."[21] When the Senate Finance Committee finally voted on the plan in November 1970, it turned it down by a vote of ten to six. Three of the ten opponents on the committee (joining seven Republicans) were Democratic liberals—a fact Moynihan never forgot.

Yet the Senate liberals were obviously not the only ones to blame for what killed FAP. Well before this vote, the president had ceased to press for action. Absorbed by foreign policy matters (especially Vietnam), he seemed to lose interest altogether in the fight, which had wearied him after the plan began to suffer attacks. Though he reintroduced FAP in 1971, his clearly lukewarm stance helped destroy whatever slim chances there might have been at that time for passage. Whipsawed by conservatives as well as liberals, the proposal failed again in the Senate Finance Committee in late 1972, never reaching the Senate floor. Another "moment" for reform to help the poor had been lost.

The defeat of FAP did not mean that social welfare policies languished during the Nixon years, during which time liberal Democrats controlled Congress. Major programs such as Medicare, Medicaid, and Food Stamps grew during these and later years, affecting ever more people. Shortly before the election of 1972, moreover, Congress passed legislation indexing Social Security benefits for inflation. This was an important change. Congress also approved a major new initiative, Supplementary Security Income (SSI), which replaced existing federal-state programs aiding low-income elderly, blind, and disabled people with a wholly federal—and therefore uniform—system of benefits.

These benefits, too, were increased and indexed for inflation. Nixon, courting the senior vote, signed SSI into law, establishing what amounted to a guaranteed annual income for millions of low-income Americans.

Later, in 1975, Congress also established an Earned Income Tax Credit (EITC) program, which offered tax credits to the working poor, thereby supplementing their incomes. Resembling Nixon's proposals under FAP for the working poor, it passed Congress with comfortable bipartisan majorities. And it expanded greatly over the years. Thanks in part to programs such as SSI and EITC, the percentage of people in poverty, which hit an all-time modern low of 11 percent in 1973, continued thereafter to remain well below the proportion (around 20 percent) that had existed in the early 1960s.

Still, having zapped FAP, the fact remained that Congress did not enact a national program to guarantee aid for low-income families with dependent children. These Americans, unlike the seniors and people with disabilities who were henceforth covered by SSI, or the low-income working families who later benefited from EITC, were—as ever—the "undeserving" poor. As earlier, they remained isolated as a category of people who would have to depend on welfare—that is, on the unreformed and inadequate policies of AFDC.

Nixon, moreover, proceeded to abort subsequent efforts on behalf of needy children. In December 1971, he infuriated liberals by vetoing a Democratic bill that promised to establish a comprehensive system of federally supported day-care centers. Explaining his veto, which rested upon the traditional belief that parents should take full responsibility for their children, the president exclaimed that the bill "would commit the vast moral authority of the National Government to the side of communal approaches to child care over against the family-centered approach."

The fate of FAP offered instructive lessons about policymaking for poor families without working parents. It indicated how hard it was—and might continue to be—to fashion a congressional coalition that would be able to pass anything like a guaranteed income program for such families. A major obstacle to such enactment arose from differing regional responses, which had helped to sink FAP. Another obstacle stemmed from the fact that FAP was presented as a single, comprehensive piece of legislation that aimed to help low-income working people as well as welfare families. Inclusion of welfare recipients in the plan, though laudable in intent, enabled conservative opponents to tar the entire proposal and to deliver votes that helped to defeat it.

These political considerations reflected larger ideological matters regarding the role in the United States of government and the meaning of equality. At least since the enactment of FDR's New Deal in the 1930s, most Americans had come to believe—at least rhetorically—that government should advance greater equality of opportunity. They had backed modest federal funding for rehabilitative programs—service initiatives ranging from casework to job training to Head Start. Thanks to the power of the civil rights movement, Americans subsequently came to embrace the idea that the government should guarantee people freedom from discrimination. But freedom, many Americans continued to believe, was enough! As the fate of FAP revealed, Congress was leery of guaranteeing tax-supported floors under incomes, especially for mothers on welfare, or of approving plans that might significantly redistribute income or wealth. The message Moynihan had scripted and LBJ had delivered at Howard University—that government should act to provide poor people with equality of result—was one that Congress was not ready to endorse.

Moreover, low-income families have always had minimal political influence. Women on welfare, especially black women, have always been stigmatized. So it was that Senator Long and others, unafraid of political reprisals, were able to disparage welfare recipients as malingerers, bums, and brood mares. Liberal advocates of welfare reform have often lamented that programs targeted to assist poor people alone are likely to end up as poor programs. This is because negative stereotypes of people living on welfare, especially black people, are so strong that opponents of high levels of welfare support will succeed in cutting aid to the needy. These laments are well taken: when a major welfare bill finally passed in 1996, eliminating AFDC in the process, many liberals were appalled.[22]

In retrospect, one may also wonder about the larger assumptions that proponents of the guaranteed income idea held in 1969 and 1970. Because FAP represented a sharp departure from existing programs dealing with welfare and poverty, it was hard at the time for policymakers to know in what ways a guaranteed receipt of cash might affect the personal behavior or work effort of recipients. Would FAP, if implemented, have resulted in higher numbers of out-of-wedlock births and family breakups? Would income guarantees have weakened work incentives and led to more people living off the "narcotic"— as FDR had called it—of the dole?

Hoping to answer these questions, federally financed local experiments involving guaranteed income plans—notably in Seattle, Denver, and New Jersey—were instituted in the late 1960s and early 1970s. Preliminary results of these pathbreaking, randomized experiments seemed to indicate that income guarantees moderately reduced work effort among recipients, especially among working wives. Though these findings unsettled some analysts, others thought that this might be a good thing—the mothers, after all, would have more time at home with their families. Initial reviews of findings, however, also suggested that a guarantee of income led to higher rates among black families of marital breakup and divorce. Then and later, a number of scholars retorted that negative conclusions such as these were premature. The impact of guaranteed income plans on work effort or family life, they insisted, would depend upon a number of factors, notably the level of support offered by any given program. Politicians with their own conservative agendas, some scholars charged, tweaked the data to sully the whole idea of guaranteed income policies.[23]

Moynihan, studying these results, was nonetheless among the many observers who later became troubled by evidence concerning family dissolution. When the Carter administration supported an ambitious guaranteed income program, Moynihan as a U.S. senator convened hearings to examine the outcomes of the experiments. Some of the findings indicated that rates of marital breakup among recipients of income guarantees were considerably higher than the rates among control groups. What did this mean? Again, answers to this question differed. A number of analysts thought that income guarantees had enabled some participants, especially women, to become more independent and to leave unsatisfactory relationships. Others, however, were alarmed. Moynihan agreed with them. "We were wrong about guaranteed income!" he exclaimed. "Seemingly it is calamitous. It increases family dissolution by 70 per cent, decreases work, etc." Putting on his scholarly hat, he added, "Such is now the state of science, and it seems to me we are honor-bound to abide by it at this moment."[24] Moynihan's reaction, which many others shared, dealt a final blow to the possibility—already minimal—that Congress might give serious consideration at that time to such an initiative. Carter's plan never reached the floor of either chamber. Though liberals continued thereafter to support a range of federal policies to improve social services—and to better

low-income family life—their sights were narrowed, and the trails they followed were bumpy.

During his support of FAP, Moynihan suffered painfully from a leak that, like
the release of his report in 1965, tarnished his image—already dim—among
black civil rights leaders and white liberals.

The leak was of a thoughtful nine-page memo—one of many he prepared
for Nixon concerning racial questions—dated January 16, 1970. It repeated
an encouraging point he had made in 1965 and in several earlier memos to
Nixon: increasing percentages of U.S. blacks were moving into the middle
classes. The incomes of young, two-parent black families in the North were
achieving parity with those of young two-parent white families. "There is a
silent black majority," he added, "as well as a white one."

But, the memo continued, proportions of births that were out of wedlock,
especially among blacks, were rapidly rising, and an increasing percentage of
female-headed black families lived in poverty. There was a great deal of "social pathology" and "virulent . . . anti-white feeling" among the black lower
classes. Militant groups such as the Black Panthers were exhibiting "social
alienation." Moynihan added, "It would be difficult to over-estimate the degree to which young, well-educated blacks detest white America."

Having sketched a predominantly gloomy racial scene that in many ways
resembled his report of 1965, Moynihan advised Nixon what his response
should be. Deploring the excesses of black militants and the political stupidity
of conservative Republicans (he probably had Vice President Spiro Agnew
in mind) who were angrily denouncing them, he recommended that top administration officials talk quietly among themselves about racial issues and
conduct more research on crime. He also concluded, most problematically for
his future reputation, "The time may have come when the issue of race could
benefit from a period of 'benign neglect.' The subject has been too much
talked about. The forum has been too much taken over to hysterics, paranoids,
and boodlers on all sides. We may need a period in which Negro progress
continues and racial rhetoric fades."[25]

Nixon loved the memo, underlining his copy and scribbling "I agree" over
the words "benign neglect." At the bottom, he scrawled, "K note?!" presumably to have the memo shown to Kissinger. Moynihan probably anticipated
Nixon's favorable reaction. Moreover, his political advice was sound: as he

wrote, reliance by Republicans on overheated "racial rhetoric" would make matters worse for the administration. As Moynihan had written in his very first memo to the president on January 3, 1969, Nixon would do better to focus on other issues in the hope that racial tensions might soften in time.

But Moynihan soon learned that Nixon planned to circulate the memo, with his annotations on it, to the cabinet. Fearing a leak, he called presidential aide H. R. Haldeman and pleaded, "Get those annotated copies back." Haldeman did so, and distributed clean copies of it instead. One of these, however, was nevertheless leaked and appeared in newspapers, including a complete version of it on March 1, 1970 (with photo of Moynihan) in the *New York Times*. Neither then nor afterward did Moynihan discover who did the leaking. (Later, he simply snorted, "Washington.") But it did not matter, for the damage was done.

Many black civil rights leaders and liberals leapt on the phrase "benign neglect" and accused him of advocating the abandonment of efforts to promote racial justice. Kenneth Clark, who had stood by Moynihan in 1965, was now among his critics. The *New York Times* called Moynihan a "political pixie" and added, "This rumpled refugee from academia has always doted on clothing his thoughts in such elegance and extravagance of expression that the thoughts often get lost in a phraseological fog." The "benign neglect" memo, it editorialized, supplied a "sophisticated rationale for racial retrogression, a high polish for the cruder arguments put forward by open practitioners of the Administration's 'Southern Strategy.'"[26]

Blindsided, Moynihan stewed over the beating he was receiving. "It won't ever go away, will it?" he mourned to a *Newsweek* writer at the time. Eighteen months later, he vented his continuing bitterness in an article for the *New York Times Magazine*. It exactly reflected Nixon's own rage at elitists and liberal intellectuals. Complaining of the "disproportionate amount of political influence exercised by an elitist minority in this country," Moynihan wrote, "Its definition of politics is so colored, so affected by a near loathing for the country itself that nothing very healthy comes out of it." As he had done in his "benign neglect" memo, he urged that the nation "calm down a little bit."[27]

In retrospect, the controversy over Moynihan's "benign neglect" memo was unimportant. It did not affect policy. Nor did it prevent admiring news reporters from writing flattering things about him. David Broder of the *Washington Post* wrote in July 1970, "Moynihan's rich Celtic prose stands out like an exotic bloom in the lunar landscape of shapeless, gray language that is employed by almost everyone else in the Nixon Administration except Spiro Agnew." Nonetheless, the fracas indicated Moynihan's unfortunate habit of phrasing things in ways that could be misconstrued. The leak further alienated him from the very groups he had hoped to help.[28]

The memo was correct, however, in lamenting that a politics of polarization was taking hold during the Nixon years. Fights over school desegregation were intensifying, the killing in Vietnam wore on, and antiwar protests multiplied. In May 1970, after four students had been killed at Kent State University, Moynihan heard that the Students for a Democratic Society (SDS) were planning to burn down his house in Cambridge. As his family, urged by the university, evacuated their home, he sent a memo marked "CONFIDENTIAL" to Nixon that assured the president he would remain in Washington. "I'm sticking here," he said. "I am choosing the interests of the administration over the interests of my children." But Moynihan added, "This would be the act of a fool if I did not feel free to tell you exactly what I think, and to feel that you were at least hearing me out." He urged the president to "call a halt to the vulgar partisanship . . . and hysterical demagoguery (e.g., Agnew) of people theoretically on your team. . . . At the very least, you need to call off attacks on groups whose support, or at least acquiescence, you need."[29]

As it happened, no one attacked the Moynihans' house. Nor did his anguished, even critical memo of May 1970 damage his standing with Nixon, who had dispatched Secret Service agents to Cambridge to protect Moynihan's family. Indeed, their relations continued to be solid. When Moynihan resigned in December 1970—to protect his tenure at Harvard—he accepted a continuing role as consultant to the president. At a widely noted farewell ceremony in the East Room of the White House, he gave a speech praising Nixon for having "moved swiftly to endorse the profoundly important, but fundamentally unfulfilled, commitments, especially to the poor and the oppressed, which the nation had made in the 1960s." Referring to Nixon and his top aides, he added, "This has been a company of honorable and able men, led by a President of singular courage and compassion."[30]

This was flattery to be sure, but Moynihan proudly released it to the newspapers, some of which labeled his speech as "Dr. Moynihan's Farewell Address" and printed selections from his remarks. And he continued thereafter to state his high opinion of Nixon. Six months later, interviewed in the *New*

York Times, he conceded that the war in Vietnam had been a "disaster," but that it was too early to tell whether the administration's policy of slow deescalation had been a mistake. Praising the president, he called him a "civil man with a sustained capacity to understand that not everybody agrees with him." As he was to do in his book on the subject published in 1973, Moynihan also lauded the president for supporting FAP.[31] There, as earlier, he mainly blamed liberals for defeat of the plan, glossing more quietly over the fact that Nixon had lost interest in the struggle by 1970.

Back at Harvard, now as a professor of government, Moynihan continued to ensure that the president was aware of his good feelings. In March 1971, he wrote Nixon to say, "Really dreadful things occurred when my party [the Democratic Party] was in power," but that these errors had been corrected during "your brilliant first year in office." In an interview in *Life* in September 1972, he all but endorsed Nixon for reelection by hailing him as "a man of peace successfully building a new world order" and a person "in his own way, as much an intellectual as any President in modern times."[32]

Whether flattery of this sort greatly affected Nixon, a gruff and self-contained man, is hard to say. But it surely did not hurt Moynihan's standing with him. Indeed, Nixon began to rely on him concerning foreign policy matters. As early as summer 1970, he had asked him to serve as U.S. ambassador to the United Nations—an offer Moynihan, anxious to retain his tenure at Harvard, had declined. In 1972, the president tapped him to become U.S. ambassador to India. This time, Moynihan, having protected his tenure, accepted. Taking another leave from Harvard, he went to India in 1973 and stayed there for two years.

While teaching again at Harvard in early 1975, Moynihan was chosen by President Gerald Ford via the recommendation of Secretary of State Kissinger to serve as U.S. ambassador to the United Nations. There, he made headlines as an ardent foe of dictatorship and as a hard-liner critical of Kissinger's policy of "détente" with the Soviet Union. He received wonderfully good press in New York by denouncing a UN resolution that equated Zionism with "racism and discrimination." The resolution, he proclaimed, was an "obscene criticism" that put the United Nations at the point of "officially endorsing anti-Semitism." *Time*, heralding the ambassador's toughness, placed him on its cover in January 1976, with the caption "GIVING THEM HELL AT THE U.N."

Having run afoul of Kissinger, Moynihan left his UN post and returned again to Harvard in early 1976. As he well knew, however, his widely hailed rhetoric as ambassador to the United Nations had greatly advanced his political standing in New York. Though he had never been elected to public office, he had lived in New York City as a child and in Albany and Syracuse as a young man. He still owned the farm in upstate New York. He had also been careful to nurture good relations with political leaders throughout the state. Thus he made a decision in early 1976 that was to alter the course of his life: to run for a seat in the Senate as a Democrat from New York. At the age of forty-nine in March, his seven-year flirtation with the Republican Party had come to an end. Winning in November, he moved to Washington, where in January 1977 his twenty-four-year career as U.S. senator from New York began.[33]

CHAPTER 7

Unproductive Dialogue, 1971–1983

In the aftermath of the Family Assistance Plan's demise, Moynihan continued to ruminate over his ill-fated report on black family life. He made this especially clear in 1972, when he published an essay on the subject. Titled "The Schism in Black America," it cited W. E. B. Du Bois and others to demonstrate the long history of scholarship that had supported his understanding of the issues. A schism, he argued, was still widening between young, two-parent black families in the North, most of which were flourishing, and those in the lower classes, increasing percentages of which were female headed and poverty-stricken. Kenneth Clark, he wrote, had been correct to speak of a "tangle of pathology" in the ghettos. Resorting to italics, Moynihan emphasized, *"poverty is now inextricably associated with family structure."*[1]

Still hoping to promote public dialogue on his signature issue, Moynihan then reflected directly on *The Negro Family*. He wrote,

> It is now almost a decade since my policy paper and its analysis. As forecasting goes, it would seem to have held up. . . . This has been accompanied by a psychological reaction which I did not foresee, and for which I may in part be to blame. . . . I did not know I would prove to be so correct. Had I known, I might have said nothing, realizing that the subject would become unbearable, and rational discussion close to

impossible. I accept that in the social sciences some things are better
left unsaid.

During the next ten to twelve years, Moynihan continued to reflect sadly—
and correctly—about the poor quality of public discussion concerning developments in lower-class black family life. Indeed, a convergence of historical,
sociological, and activist thought in these years stymied productive public dialogue about the complex sources of such troubles in the United States. Two
lines of thinking were especially powerful—one forged by liberals, the other
by conservatives.

Liberal critics of Moynihan's ideas, bolstered by new scholarship, for the
most part reiterated the already widespread criticisms black activists and others had leveled at him in 1965: that white racism caused black family troubles
and that he had blamed the victim. To be sure, some scholars dissented from
these assaults: Orlando Patterson, a Jamaican-born sociologist, forcefully denounced the "ethnic chauvinism" of Moynihan's detractors and highlighted
the point that Du Bois, E. Franklin Frazier, and others had made concerning
the "catastrophic" impact of slavery on black family life.[2] A few other scholars, moreover, published impressive ethnographic accounts of lower-class
black life in the cities that tended to reinforce Moynihan's gloomy conclusions.[3] But by the late 1970s, widespread rejection by liberal scholars of *The
Negro Family* had not only perpetuated the great silence Moynihan had
lamented in the late 1960s, it had also hardened into an orthodoxy that virtually
excused lower-class black people from much if any responsibility for their
own difficulties and that discouraged white scholars, fearing to be pilloried as
racists, from raising the subject of black family problems.

The second obstacle to meaningful dialogue arose in the 1970s and early
1980s from the efforts of ever more outspoken "family values" spokespeople
on the political right, most of whom demanded that black people take action
to help themselves. Their largely negative depictions of black lower-class behavior further stymied the efforts of Moynihan and others who clung to the
belief that well-crafted governmental programs might help the black poor.

Many of the liberals who looked at black family issues in these years stressed
an earlier complaint: that Moynihan, in parading the pathologies of the black
lower classes, had slighted the power of institutional forces—both economic

and racist—that had held black people down. A related liberal argument, however, also gained force amidst the cultural and intellectual turbulence of the late 1960s and 1970s. Rooted in the explosion of racial and ethnic pride that accompanied Black Power thinking, it held that African Americans, no matter how oppressed, were not psychologically damaged. On the contrary, advocates of this point of view proclaimed, black Americans had always shown admirable creativity and courage in resisting their white oppressors.

This argument for the fortitude of poor black Americans relied in considerable part on the work of scholars, many of whom were sociologists. An early thrust came in 1968 from Andrew Billingsley, a black scholar who took deliberate aim at the Moynihan Report. The black family in the United States, Billingsley insisted, far from having been shattered by slavery and other developments, had always been a "strong and resilient institution." Robert Staples, another black sociologist, echoed this argument when he charged in 1971 that Moynihan had "made a generalized indictment of all Black families." In so doing Moynihan had "shifted the burden of Black deprivation onto the Black family rather than [onto] the social structure of the United States."[4]

Strong words, yet hardly unusual at the time. Joyce Ladner, a young black sociologist who had participated in civil rights activity in Mississippi during the mid-1960s, joined the fray in 1971 with *Tomorrow's Tomorrow: The Black Woman*. Confessing that she could not be objective, Ladner made it clear that she had little faith in white perspectives concerning black family life. Black scholars, she said, must "develop a total intellectual offensive against the false universality of white concepts whether they are expressed by William Styron or Daniel P. Moynihan."[5] She added, using Billingsley as a source, "My primary concern here is with depicting the strengths of the Black family and Black girls within the family structure." These strengths, she stressed, were powerful and enduring: even after slavery, many African survivals were evident, notably in the form of spirituals and of jazz. These enabled blacks to establish a "distinct and viable set of cultural mechanisms because discrimination acted as an agent to perpetuate instead of to destroy the culture."[6]

Carol Stack, a white anthropologist, pursued a similar line of thought in an ethnological study, *All Our Kin*, of an unidentified black community in the Midwest. Identifying Moynihan and E. Franklin Frazier as writers who had "overlooked the interdependence and cooperation of kinsmen in black communities," she wrote that many black families "maintain a steady state of three generations of kin," with grandparents playing especially valuable roles in holding families together. So fortified, the "black urban family, embedded in cooperative domestic exchange, proves to be an organized tenacious, active, lifelong network."[7]

Historians, too, became active in exploring black family issues during these years. Some of their most enduring work carefully studied the evolution of black inner-city life. In 1966, Gilbert Osofsky traced the rise of the black ghetto in Harlem between 1890 and 1930, and other books dealing with the evolution of ghettos in Chicago, Cleveland, and Milwaukee appeared between 1967 and the mid-1980s. All these historical studies, highlighting the power of white racism, offered grim pictures of black communities. Like the studies of Billingsley, Stack, and others, however, they were at variance with Moynihan's emphasis on black pathology. Though black people suffered grievously from racial discrimination and economic hardship, they were nonetheless resourceful as well as determined in establishing and nurturing their own institutions.[8]

New histories of slavery were especially important in bolstering the view among scholars that blacks in the United States, far from having been psychologically damaged, had always been resilient. Many of these histories took particularly sharp issue with the horrific portrait of black family life Frazier had painted in 1939, Elkins had darkened in 1959, and black leaders as different as Malcolm X and James Baldwin had embraced in the early 1960s. Some of these, of course, were portraits upon which Moynihan had relied in his report. Instead, the new histories offered a "survivalist" approach. Slave communities, they said, had retained some of their African traditions (notably the important role of extended kin relationships). Resisting white domination (usually nonviolently), slaves had not internalized white values, and they had cherished their family ties.

John Blassingame, a black historian at Yale, was among the first of these practitioners. Relying on retrospective slave narratives, he argued in 1972 that black families had been functioning institutions. "The Southern plantation," he said, "was unique in the New World because it permitted the development of a more monogamous slave family." Two years later, Eugene Genovese, whose antiwar politics had already made him a highly controversial historian, published a prize-winning study of U.S. slavery, *Roll Jordan Roll: The World the Slaves Made*, which concluded that many slave-owners had been paternalistic. As the subtitle indicated, it emphasized also that slaves were able to carve out substantial social space for themselves. Genovese, after noting the "terrible toll of slavery," spoke of the "impressive norms of [slave] family life, including as much of a nuclear family as conditions permitted."

Toward the end of his book, Genovese referred directly to the controversy over the Moynihan Report and warned, "Historians and sociologists, black and white . . . have been led astray in two ways. First, they have read the story of the twentieth-century black ghettos backward in time and have assumed a historical continuity with slavery days. Second, they have looked too closely at slave law and at the externals of family life and not closely enough at the actual temper of the quarters."

Other historical studies, too, dissented from the near-apocalyptic interpretations of slavery upon which Moynihan had depended. In 1974, Robert Fogel and Stanley Engerman employed sophisticated quantitative methods to argue that slavery in the United States had often been profitable. Many plantation owners, eager to protect their valuable investments in slaves, had tried to treat their slaves decently. Fogel and Engerman estimated that some two-thirds of slave unions on large southeastern plantations during the last decades of slavery had included a father, a mother, and children. Rejecting the notion that slave families tended to be matriarchal, Fogel and Engerman discovered what they called a "healthy sexual equality" between slave men and women.[9]

Though some historians sharply criticized Fogel and Engerman's book— among other things, the notion that slavery was profitable for plantation owners did not sit well—it rested on an array of economic data hard to refute. (In 1993, Fogel won a Nobel Prize in economics.) Robert Staples, citing that book and others (including Genovese's), announced in 1974 that the authors had "demonstrated that the Black family was a stable institution during slavery and in the immediate post-slavery years." Out-of-wedlock and female-headed families among blacks rose sharply only later, as "concomitants of twentieth-century ghettos."

No one did more to shape this approach to the understanding of slave family life than Herbert Gutman, a social historian who had published a short book that challenged Fogel and Engerman's assertions about the profitability of slavery. Moynihan's unflattering depiction of black family life, however, deeply offended him, and he plunged into historical records to explore its accuracy. After examining census data, diaries, and other primary sources, he completed his labors in 1976. The result was a long and impressively footnoted book, *The Black Family in Slavery and Freedom, 1750–1925*.

Like others who championed the genre of social history in the 1960s and later, Gutman did not chronicle the activities of elites. In his opinion, the story of the past must also be told from the bottom up—that is, from the perspective of ordinary folk. Sympathetic with the poor and oppressed, Gutman admired the courage and creativity of black people. Despite subjugation, he insisted, slaves had preserved many of their own institutions and ways of life. In support of this position, he quoted Ralph Ellison, the author of *Invisible Man*, who had later asked (in 1964), "Can a people . . . live and develop over 300 years by simply reacting? . . . Are American Negroes simply the creation of white men, or have they at least helped create themselves out of what they found around them? Men have made a way of life in caves and upon cliffs, why cannot Negroes have made a life upon the horn of the white man's dilemma?"

Zeroing in on the Moynihan Report, Gutman stressed that neither slavery nor Jim Crow had savaged black families. On the contrary, he wrote, blacks had always cherished their blood relations and had regularly named their children after kin. After emancipation, they had trudged long distances to locate and reunite with their spouses and children. Using manuscript census data, he asserted that husbands and wives, or fathers alone, headed at least 70 percent of black households between 1855 and 1880. Other census data indicated that similar percentages still existed in Buffalo in 1905 and 1925. Summarizing, Gutman wrote, "In the 50 years following emancipation, most African-American families were headed by a husband and wife, most eventually married, and most children lived with both parents." Evidence such as this clearly revealed "the adaptive capacities of the slaves and their immediate descendants."

Turning to the recent past, Gutman agreed that statistics concerning black out-of-wedlock births and family breakup—including those used by Moynihan—showed that black families as of the 1960s had been more likely than earlier to break up. Why, he asked? His reply was that increases in nonmarital births and family disunion among blacks had been of relatively recent origin—the result of highly disruptive twentieth-century black migrations to cities and the decline of living-wage jobs thereafter. Moynihan had "confused the problems of poor blacks in the second half of the twentieth century with those of their great-grandparents in the first half of the nineteenth century."

Gutman charged also that the Moynihan Report, in focusing on race, had paid too little attention to matters of class. Whereas his own statistics (like those of Du Bois, Frazier, and other scholars) indicated that the proportions of postemancipation black female-headed families had always been considerably higher than those of white families, he argued that these differences diminished greatly when controlled by income. Though slavery had indeed been harsh, he asserted that the difficulties of blacks in the 1960s were not, as Moynihan had claimed, rooted in a three-century "cycle of self-perpetuating pathology."

Some of Gutman's conclusions may have been misleading. His own findings, for instance, made it clear that black families in the United States between 1860 and 1880 were three times more likely than white families to be single-parented. Far from slighting twentieth-century developments, moreover, Moynihan was among the many scholars (notably Frazier) who had written about the shocks of urbanization and industrialization.

Still, the work of Gutman and others who studied black history, like that of sociologists arriving at similar conclusions about the present, was useful in reminding readers that black people in the United States had always been important actors in their own right. They had surely not become infantilized. In so doing the new scholarship provided a sizable body of scholarly evidence— or so it seemed to many admirers at the time—to the effect that Moynihan had exaggerated the destructiveness of slavery on black culture.[10] Black scholars in particular hailed Gutman's effort, which supported their own proud assertions about the adaptive capacities of black people.

Most important, the new black history of Gutman and other scholars reinforced the already widely held insistence by black activists that institutionalized racism and economic change in the twentieth century, not long-range historical forces, had driven blacks down. It followed, at least to some, that low-income black people bore relatively little responsibility for the spread within their communities of behavioral manifestations of trouble such as dropping out of school, crime, drug abuse, and nonmarital pregnancy.

Most white liberals endorsed these arguments or, fearful of being identified as racists (as Moynihan had been), they spoke no evil. Indeed, although Moynihan continued to keep informed of developments in scholarship, he recognized the temper of the times, and he prudently made no serious effort in these years to refute the sociologists and historians who criticized him. As the sociologists Douglas Massey and Robert Sampson later observed in revisiting the Moynihan Report, criticisms of the report had a "chilling effect on social science over the next two decades. Sociologists avoided studying controversial issues related to race, culture, and intelligence."[11] It was hardly surprising that Moynihan, having to deal with such a strong and sometimes chauvinistic climate of opinion, believed in the 1970s that rational debate about developments in lower-class black family life was impossible.

Moynihan was correct to worry about the quality of dialogue for another reason: statistics concerning black families in the 1970s and early 1980s revealed trends that were even more alarming than before. Disgusted and outraged by such trends, many conservatives adopted a stance poles apart from that of scholars on the left such as Gutman. Far from highlighting the resilience of black culture, they tended to blame blacks themselves for their problems. Moynihan, who tried to steer a middle course that recognized the power of institutionalized racism as well as self-defeating behavioral developments within the ghettos, was caught in the middle.

The statistics concerning grim developments within black communities in these years were indeed striking. Figures showing nonmarital birth ratios became especially stunning. When Moynihan produced his report in 1965, he had shown that 4 percent of white births and 23.6 percent of black births had been out of wedlock in 1963. By 1970 these numbers had risen to 6 percent and 38 percent, respectively. By 1984, they had jumped to 13 percent and 60 percent. Between 1980 and 1990, the proportion of all births out of wedlock increased in the United States from 18.4 percent to 28 percent. A total of 665,747 U.S. births were to unmarried women in 1980—a number that nearly doubled (to 1,165,384) in 1990.

As in the 1960s, when these increases began to accelerate, they were closely linked to poverty and income levels. As Moynihan pointed out in 1972, there was indeed a great schism dividing poor from middle-class black people. Though the percentage of people in poverty overall leveled off between the mid-1970s and late 1980s—fluctuating with the ups and downs of the economy, it hovered between 13 and 15 percent of the population—this leveling was mainly because of the decline in poverty among the elderly, who benefited from the indexing of SSI and Social Security approved in 1972. Thanks in large part to the spread of female-headed families, however, the poverty rate among children increased considerably during these years—from 15 percent in the early 1970s to 22 percent by the end of the 1980s—or by nearly 50 percent. This was then the highest rate in the industrialized world. As in earlier years, poverty among blacks was especially high in the inner cities, and it remained roughly three times as high (at around 31 percent in the late 1980s) as it was among whites. More than 8.9 million black people lived below the official poverty line in 1985.

The rise in the proportions of births outside of marriage, as earlier, reflected abiding economic, demographic, and cultural forces: lower percentages of women of childbearing age (especially black women) were choosing to marry, birthrates among unmarried women were rising, and birthrates among married women, having fallen sharply between 1965 and 1975, remained low. Divorce rates, skyrocketing during the 1970s, further increased the number of children who were brought up in single-parent (usually female-headed) families. In 1971, 31 percent of black children were growing up in such families—a figure that leapt to 54 percent by 1984.[12]

Why were smaller percentages of women (especially black women) getting married in the 1970s and 1980s? It was clear, as earlier, that economic forces continued to have a considerable effect on the decisions of people about marriage. Employment among black women, who continued to do better than black men in school, increased. But as the U.S. manufacturing sector faltered in the economically troubled 1970s, living-wage blue-collar jobs once available for less educated, low-skilled men became harder to get in some of the cities. The drug trade, which had been relatively modest in the ghettos of the 1960s, had also grown rapidly since then, rendering many young black men unfit for employment.

Driven in part by developments such as these, the unemployment rate among eighteen- to nineteen-year-old black males, which had been 19 percent in 1969, skyrocketed to 35 percent in 1977. This was more than twice as high as it was among white males of the same age. Among black men aged twenty through twenty-four, the rates were lower (around 23 percent between 1977 and 1981) but also more than twice as high as they were among white men of the same age. Young men such as these were hardly ready for marriage, nor were black women eager to marry them. As earlier, many women who became pregnant concluded they were better off raising their babies themselves.

By the 1980s, it had also become obvious that the decline of marriage, having swelled since the mid-1960s, was deeply cultural in nature. Attitudes about sex and marriage were continuing to liberalize. Though Americans told pollsters they opposed cohabitation or out-of-wedlock pregnancy when it involved their own daughters, they proved increasingly tolerant about the trend in the society at large. One-third of people in 1974 said that it was okay for women to have children out of marriage; one-half approved ten years later. It was later estimated that the number of cohabiting couples—some 440,000 in 1960—had become ten times as high—4.2 million—by 1998. These trends reflected forces that from the 1960s onward had a huge impact on the values and behavior of people—especially young people—throughout much of the industrially developed world. Rising expectations from life, bolstered by rights consciousness, continued to drive people to assert their individuality and their freedom from moral standards and conventions that had constrained their behaviors in the past.

Though it was clear in the late 1970s and early 1980s that these economic and cultural forces were affecting whites as well as blacks, a great many media accounts—often citing nonmarital birth statistics—were homing in on the widening disorder affecting families in the ghettos. Many of these accounts offered vivid descriptions of "social deviancy" among blacks: of young people sleeping around; teenaged girls who deliberately got pregnant because they wanted babies; black students who maintained that it was "white" to do well in school; "lazy" black men who refused to work; and gang members, drug addicts, and antisocial young men who were feeding an epidemic of violent crime—much of it black on black. Other stories, extolling the virtues of hardworking immigrants making a success of their lives, demanded to know why blacks were not trying to do the same.

A number of conservative writers, convinced that blacks had only themselves to blame, made no effort to hide their disgust about the way lower-class blacks in the inner cities were behaving. George Gilder, author of *Sexual Suicide* (1981), pointed the finger not at joblessness but at "unsocialized black males" who refused to shoulder their responsibilities. In so doing, Gilder was one of a number of writers on the right who cited Moynihan's observations about matriarchy. Black men, Gilder added, had all too often grown up in fatherless families. Lacking positive male role models, they were "less able to defer gratification, less interested in achievement, more prone to crime, and, even, as other studies have shown, lower in IQ." They were also likely to "exert their masculinity through group violence and through male patterns of sexual activity." The "worst parts of the ghetto," Gilder argued, "present a rather typical pattern of female domination," with "women in charge of the family, and male gangs away on the hunt."

Other conservatives who lamented developments such as these helped lead a surge for organized political action. In 1979, Beverly LaHaye, a San Diego housewife and best-selling author, formed Concerned Women for America (CWA), which waged a crusade against abortion, the Equal Rights Amendment, and no-fault divorce laws. CWA activists emphasized that they were "profamily," by which they meant they sought to return to the patriarchal family of the past. Women who left home to work, they said, upset domestic harmony and prevented men from finding employment. CWA struck a chord with a great many American women at the time. By the mid-1980s, it had a membership estimated at 500,000—far larger than the much more liberal National Organization for Women (NOW).

Distressing developments in family life also sparked the interest of an ascendant Religious Right. James Dobson, a devoutly evangelical child psychologist who had a doctorate in child development, started his long and influential career as a conservative organizer in 1977 when he founded Focus on the Family. Each gender, he maintained, has a biologically mandated role. Women with children under the age of eighteen, he insisted, ought to stay home and assume their role of mothering. In 1981, Dobson established the Family Research Council as a political arm to spearhead a fight for the restoration of traditional "family values" in the United States. "Culture wars" in the 1980s and thereafter, many of them waged by organizers active in the Religious Right, centered on family issues such as divorce, abortion, and out-of-wedlock childbearing, and helped reshape the politics of the nation.

Though Moynihan, still liberal in his politics, strongly disagreed with conservative activists such as Gilder, LaHaye, and Dobson, he did not imagine he could do much to undermine their popularity with people on the right. Like most experts, he realized the trends that were breaking up families stemmed both from economic forces and from cultural developments that were transforming other industrialized nations as well as the United States. He was correct: millions of families—white as well as black, rich as well as poor, in western Europe as well as in the United States—were confronting a wide and bewildering array of obstacles to stability. As Christopher Jencks, a well-regarded social scientist, later commented, these trends could be observed in Beverly Hills as well as in Watts.

Debates over family life in the 1970s and 1980s inevitably sharpened long-standing controversies over the role of AFDC. Most advocates for the poor continued to insist that the program—along with other means-tested benefits such as Medicaid and Food Stamps—remained vital to single mothers and their children, which is why Moynihan regularly denounced efforts to cut back the welfare state in these years. Liberals, Moynihan included, also pushed for expansion of the Earned Income Tax Credit (EITC) program, which in subsequent years offered steadily larger tax credits to low-income working families with children. Growing considerably (especially in the 1990s), EITCs ultimately filled part of the gap in social support that the Family Assistance Program had been intended to provide for the working poor.

Complaints about mothers on welfare nonetheless became especially heated during the politically conservative 1980s. None attracted more attention than those of Charles Murray, whose book, *Losing Ground: American Social Policy, 1950–1980*, set off widespread debate when published in 1984. Earlier (in 1968), Murray had called Moynihan "one of the most perceptive social scientists in the country." By 1984, however, Murray had become known as a contentious critic of virtually all government social programs. Moreover, by then he had more ammunition to fire because more than a decade had passed since the welfare explosion of the late 1960s and early 1970s. Newspaper and magazine articles had thus been able to trace the fates of the children who had grown up in poverty-stricken AFDC families. As these articles showed, considerable numbers of these children, deprived of cognitive enrichment, had struggled in school and had dropped out. Increasing numbers of the boys were landing in jail or prison. Many girls, as if emulating their mothers, had become pregnant and landed on the dole. Life on welfare, it seemed, was producing dismal intergenerational consequences.

Murray was unromantic about the natural instincts of people—most human beings, he maintained, were neither moral nor hardworking. Instead, they were shrewd and rational calculators of their own self-interests. Social welfare programs, he argued, perversely encouraged the most opportunistic of these calculators. Without welfare, Food Stamps, and Medicaid, he asserted, women would be far less likely to have babies out of wedlock. Provoking outraged responses from the Left, Murray set forth cost-benefit analyses to call for the abolition of all three programs.

Advocates of more generous social welfare policies fought back. The U.S. social safety net, they complained, continued to be far less reliable than those in most western European nations. Full of holes people in poverty tumbled through, it hardly promoted widespread idleness or long-term reliance on the dole. Because the real value of AFDC benefits was declining during the highly inflationary years of the late 1970s and early 1980s, the program could hardly be the reason larger percentages of babies were being born out of wedlock. Increases in nonmarital childbearing among the poor, liberals said, stemmed not from the lure of welfare but primarily from poverty, poor education, and (among blacks) the miseries of inner-city existence. The majority of impoverished single mothers who turned to welfare for help, they emphasized, did so because their social and economic circumstances had left them little choice.

Formidable barriers, however, continued to block liberal reformers in the 1970s and early 1980s. One that Moynihan's neoconservative reflections had earlier revealed was the sense among many people, especially conservatives, that many of Lyndon Johnson's Great Society programs had failed to deliver on their promises. As a broad generalization, this perception was flawed—the boldest initiatives, notably in civil rights and health care, had survived and improved the quality of life for millions of people. Still, some policies—notably the War on Poverty—had been oversold. Liberals, falling onto the defensive in the 1970s and 1980s, remained an inviting target for critics on the right.

Another obstacle to reform in these years was the economy, which began to falter badly in the early 1970s. By the close of the decade, double-digit unemployment along with inflation—"stagflation"—mystified economists and came close to crippling the economy. The slump persisted in the recessionary early 1980s—unemployment peaked in 1982 at 10.8 percent. Government revenues dropped amidst the economic doldrums and failed to keep pace with spending. Large public deficits mounted at the federal and state levels.

President Gerald Ford, a fiscal conservative, turned a generally blind eye during his brief tenure on proposals to increase federal spending for social programs. President Jimmy Carter was similarly a fiscal conservative. Outraging many liberals, he publicly doubted the capacity of the federal government to devise effective social policies. "Government," he stated in his second State of the Union address, "cannot solve our problems. . . . It cannot eliminate poverty, or provide a bountiful economy, or reduce inflation, or cure illiteracy, or provide energy." Though he briefly encouraged proponents of a new guaranteed income plan—one that would also provide government jobs—his proposal was poorly prepared, and he backed off after confronted with staunch conservative opposition and with estimates of high budgetary costs.

When Ronald Reagan entered the White House in 1981, there was no doubt where he stood about AFDC. Highly critical of federal public assistance programs, he denounced "welfare queens" who manipulated them. "We fought a war against poverty," he liked to declare, "and poverty won." Government, he added, "is like a baby, an alimentary canal with a big appetite at one end and no sense of responsibility at the other." He quipped, "The nine most terrifying words in the English language are, 'I'm from the government, and I'm here to help.'"

Reagan's bark was a little worse than his bite. Though he managed to secure reductions in aid to the poor, he was unable to arrest the growth of the nation's largest social entitlements, Social Security and Medicare. These were insurance programs (not means-tested) that benefited millions of middle-class people as well as the poor. Highly prized by the elderly, these remained what many observers called the "third rail of American politics." Dare to touch them, Reagan well knew, and you were toast as an officeholder.

Still, Reagan's politically strong presence seriously stymied liberals. Greatly increasing the defense budget, he also cut taxes, thereby running up large deficits that he tried to curb mainly by trimming social programs. Many state legislatures, bowing to well-organized conservative lobbies, began cutting their funding of cash welfare and imposing work or job training requirements on applicants. Though articles about the miseries of the black underclasses started to proliferate, no significant measures to ameliorate their problems came close to reaching the statute books.

From January 1977 on, Moynihan was a U.S. senator. Vividly remembering how the Senate Finance Committee—a power base on Capitol Hill—had played a major role in defeating FAP in 1970, he asked for and received a place on it. Soon, he headed a subcommittee concerned with public assistance. The finance committee, then and later, was where he focused many of his efforts, and where he formed a number of his closest personal relationships in the Senate. Some of these colleagues—Robert Packwood of Oregon and John Chafee of Rhode Island—were Republicans.

Moynihan also attracted a bright corps of aides. Several became well-known: Tim Russert, who acted as his chief of staff and later rose in the television world to chair NBC's *Meet the Press*; Elliott Abrams, who later served in high-ranking posts concerned with foreign relations in the administrations of Ronald Reagan and George W. Bush; and Chester Finn, who had been a graduate student under Moynihan in the Harvard School of Education, and who in the late 1980s played an important role in Reagan's Education Department.

During his early years on Capitol Hill, however, Moynihan was a junior member of the chamber. Like many Democrats, he had little rapport with President Carter, who had a gift for alienating people in Congress. (Later, Moynihan wrote with characteristic acerbity of the "general haplessness of the Carter administration." Carter, he added, was a "decent Southern evangelical politician [who] filled his administration with people not just incapable of political thought, but often as not contemptuous of what was politic."[13]) Carter also angered him by opposing a bill he and Packwood were pushing to give tax credits to parents who sent their children to private (including parochial) schools. Moynihan's support of the bill, which did not pass, revealed his belief that students ought to have viable alternatives to failing public schools. Disenchanted with the president, Moynihan waited until August 1980 before endorsing his run for reelection.

When Reagan took over in 1981, Republicans also won control of the Senate, for the first time since 1955. They held that majority until after the election of 1986. During these years, with conservative Republicans trying to cut social programs, Moynihan grew increasingly frustrated. Indeed, he moved to the left politically—so much so that he gradually alienated many of his neoconservative friends. In 1983, he laid into Reagan in print with a widely heralded article, "Reagan's Revenge," in the *New Republic*. It charged that the president had deliberately run up budget deficits in order to starve the welfare state.

Whatever satisfaction Moynihan might have derived from hammering the president, however, was small, for the needs and problems of lower-class black families continued to distress him. As earlier, he was certain he had been correct when he wrote in 1965 that the sad situation of lower-class black families may have "begun to feed on itself." He also continued to bemoan the fact that black civil rights leaders and white liberals remained reluctant to talk frankly about the need for black parents and community leaders to speak out about the self-inflicted evils that were a part of the problem. Instead, they almost ritualistically continued to blame institutionalized white racism. He also lamented the fact that conservatives, though often citing his report as prophetic, deliberately ignored its subtitle: *The Case for National Action*. Like Reagan, they seemed interested above all in cutting social programs and in pressing poor people to behave better. As of 1984, productive dialogue about lower-class black family life, having been stifled for many years, still struggled to be heard.

CHAPTER 8

Combating the Silence, 1984–1994

E ven as conservatives were amassing political power in the mid-1980s, a number of activists, rallying to Moynihan's cause, began at last to weaken the hold that had strangled productive public dialogue about the ills of lower-class black family life. In these same years, liberal social scientists, benefiting from deeper research into the problems of the underclasses, further advanced knowledge about the social, economic, and cultural forces damaging the lives of people in the ghettos. These were heartening developments.

Still, serious black family problems persisted in the late 1980s and early 1990s. Poverty rates continued to be high—and measurements of cognitive skills low—among black children. Black school dropout rates remained appalling. Unemployment, which increased during a recession in the early 1990s, continued to be far higher among black men than among white men. Rates of violent crime and of incarceration (mostly for drug offenses) among black men had become alarmingly common. Race relations, especially after the outbreak of racial rioting in Los Angeles in 1992, seemed frightful.

The statistics concerning black family life, confirming many of Moynihan's predictions, were eye-opening when compared with those of previous decades. The proportion of black children born out of wedlock, 56 percent in 1980, rose to 67 percent in 1990 and to a record high of 70 percent by 1995. These proportions were also rising rapidly among non-Hispanic whites (and as before at a faster rate than those among blacks), from 11 percent in 1980 to 20 percent in 1990 and to 25 percent in 1995. The overall proportion of nonmarital births in the United States, driven as earlier by economic, demographic, and cultural forces, reached a record high of 32.4 percent in 1996.

It is not difficult to explain why activists in these years managed at last to broaden the conversation about lower-class black family life: as these statistics made glaringly clear, social and behavioral ills in many low-income black neighborhoods had by then become so serious that a growing number of black as well as white leaders finally concluded they must work together and draw greater public attention to workable reforms. A widely noted book by journalist Ken Auletta, *The Underclass* (1982), helped propel them toward a new dialogue.

Auletta deplored the widespread vilification of Moynihan, calling him "prescient." He defined as underclass people who suffered from one or more socioeconomic ills such as long-term poverty, unemployment, welfare dependency, criminal records, drug addiction, and dropping out of school. Reflecting this broad definition, his estimate of the numbers of underclass people in 1980 was high—9 million, 70 percent of whom were nonwhite. (Because the black population in 1980 was 26.5 million, 11.7 percent of the total population, his estimate placed roughly one-quarter of black Americans in the underclass.) Like Moynihan, Auletta focused on economic sources of their difficulties, especially the growth over time of black male unemployment. He also reported that about half of the people in the underclass lived in female-headed households, and that about 70 percent were children under eighteen. "One cannot talk about poverty in America," he wrote, "or about the underclass, without talking about the weakening family structure of the poor."[1]

A few black community leaders, meanwhile, also began to urge blacks to tackle their family problems. The National Urban League started to use the term "underclass." Benjamin Hooks, executive director of the National Association for the Advancement of Colored People (NAACP), placed what he called the "precipitous slide of the black family" at the top of his organization's agenda. The Rev. Jesse Jackson, who made a run for the presidency in 1984, occasionally chimed in to agree.

Starting in 1984, Bill Cosby greatly furthered this effort in an indirect but highly visible way by starring in a hugely popular television sit-com, *The Cosby Show*. Its episodes challenged the notion that virtually all black families were trapped in a tangle of pathology. Cosby, playing an obstetrician, exuded warmth and loving support as the father of five well-behaved, college-bound children. His character's wife (played by Phylicia Rashad) was a successful lawyer. Attracting some 63 million viewers a week, most of whom were white, *The Cosby Show* was the top-rated program for most of the late 1980s. Years later, many people credited the show, which lasted until 1992, with advancing interracial understanding in the United States.

Glenn Loury, a self-styled conservative who had become the first black economist to earn tenure at Harvard, also entered debates over black family life in 1984 by publishing an article, "A New American Dilemma," in the *New Republic*. Citing statistics about low-income black families (79.9 percent of all births in Harlem at the time, he wrote, were out of wedlock), Loury exposed perspectives that few black leaders had been willing to discuss in public, and that some leaders, having been shown a draft of the article, urged him not to publish. "The bottom stratum of the black community," Loury wrote, "has compelling problems which can no longer be blamed solely on white racism, and which force us to confront fundamental failures in black society." He added, "The societal disorganization among poor blacks, the lagging academic performance of black students, the disturbingly high rate of black-on-black crime, and the alarming increase in early unwed pregnancies among blacks now loom as the primary obstacles to black progress."[2]

This was tough language most white liberals did not dare use. A few months later, Loury returned to this theme, again challenging black community leaders to admit that white racism was by no means the only source of inner-city disorders. In an article titled "The Moral Quandary of the Black Community" published in *The Public Interest*, he declared that "too much of the political energy, talent, and imagination abounding in the emergent middle class is being channeled into a struggle against an enemy without, while the enemy within ['family instability and crime'] goes relatively unchecked." There was, he added, "a profound need for moral leadership among blacks."[3]

With the long-moribund debate finally taking on a new life, Samuel Preston, a white demographer, fired yet another salvo in 1984 aimed at scholars and others who had slighted the importance of family issues. In his presidential address to the Population Association of America, he contrasted recent trends in the welfare of seniors with those affecting children. Poverty among the elderly, who enjoyed political clout, had declined considerably since the 1960s,

whereas that among children—who could not vote—had become catastrophic. Children in female-headed families, he wrote, suffered most of all:
62 percent of such children in 1982 lived in poverty as opposed to 13 percent
of children in families with two parents.

Preston found plenty of blame to spread around. AFDC, he wrote, virtually encouraged fathers to leave their families so that the mothers might qualify for aid. Public expenditures for social programs benefiting poor children
had been declining in real dollars since the 1970s. The basic source of child
poverty, he emphasized, was the increase in the number of fatherless families.
Indeed, the United States faced a "disappearing act among fathers." In 1982,
one-half of absent fathers had failed to make child-support payments.

Broad cultural forces, Preston emphasized, had helped accelerate such
trends. At the root of family instability, he argued, was the "increased prevalence of a worldview that legitimizes calculations based on individual self-
interest." Lamenting the increase in divorce rates, he blamed parents for "our
tendency to count only our own interests and not those of children." He predicted that these distressing trends would continue. Two-thirds of U.S. children born in 1980, he said, would experience disruption of their parents'
marriage by the age of seventeen.[4]

Preston's scholarly address, later published in the journal *Demography*, did
not receive as much public attention at the time as Loury's articles, but it influenced scholars entering the debates. No one was more impressed by Preston's scholarship than Moynihan, who cited his research again and again over
the years to make his case that policymakers—whatever else they did—had
to craft better public programs to help fatherless children.

As the debate over black family life was beginning to widen, Moynihan
made himself heard on a larger stage than before. Accepting an invitation to
give a prestigious series of three lectures at the John F. Kennedy School of
Government at Harvard, he used the occasion in April 1985—a month later
than the twentieth anniversary of his report—to focus once again on family
problems (this time, white as well as black). A reporter for *Newsweek* who
attended his opening lecture wrote that he had attracted an overflow crowd
of 500. An accompanying color photo featured him, pink-faced, looking be-
nignly over the top of his glasses at his audience. (Many reporters routinely
likened him to a leprechaun.) His slightly shaggy hair, which had turned
white in the 1970s, flopped across the center of his brow. *Newsweek*'s headline

made it clear where the senator-professor was coming from: "Moynihan: 'I Told You So.'"

In 1986, these lectures were fashioned into a book, *Family and Nation*, that expounded Moynihan's opinions concerning black family life. It cited Loury and Preston regarding the circumstances that were harming children. In Preston's memorable words, Moynihan wrote, these amounted to an "earthquake that [had] shuddered through the American family over the past twenty years." Again following Preston, Moynihan added, "The United States in the 1980s may be the first society in history in which the children are distinctly worse off than the adults."[5]

Though Moynihan approvingly cited Kenneth Clark's use of the term "pathology," he had learned from his battering in 1965 to steer a little more clear of potentially inflammatory language. Indeed, people already familiar with his ideas heard little new material. The title of his first lecture, "The Moment Lost," was the same as the subtitle of the essay he had written for *Commentary* in 1967. It recounted the sad series of events that helped kill the promise of LBJ's soaring address at Howard, "To Fulfill These Rights," and the hammering by angry blacks and liberals of his report. Though he claimed, as he did during his entire career, that social scientists still "do not know many answers," he nonetheless offered a few policy suggestions of his own, which he said reflected the "shared values" of Americans. In so doing, he moved a little beyond his report of 1965, which had stopped short of setting out solutions.

Moynihan's suggestions, reflecting his awareness of the political power of well-funded conservative lobbies at the time, were fairly modest in scope. After all, as a member of the minority party in the Senate, he still hoped to fashion legislation that would pass muster with the Reagan administration. This meant backing social programs that would assist white as well as black families and that would not arouse the hackles of the Right. To that end he called for expansion of relatively noncontroversial public policies such as job training and education initiatives that would help single mothers escape welfare. Delinquent fathers, he added, should be more vigorously chased down and forced to pay child support. Government should fund programs to help unemployed men find work. Income tax exemptions for dependents should be increased. Welfare payments should be indexed for inflation.

Moynihan's lectures received widespread and mostly respectful attention in the media as well as standing ovations from his listeners. It was not so clear, however, that his ideas sparked new thinking about family issues. *Newsweek* reported that Daniel Bell, an acclaimed Harvard sociologist and friend of Moynihan's who attended the lectures, was disappointed to hear him say experts still did not know how to deal with many family ills. "He has to do more than just point to the problem," Bell observed. A *New York Times* reviewer of *Family and Nation* wrote that it did not offer a "careful, well-plotted analytic argument" and that his organization was "anecdotal, discursive, and wandering." Loury, who attended the lectures, reviewed the book for *Commentary*, choosing the occasion to contrast Moynihan's strongly stated opinions in 1965 that had emphasized the serious disadvantages of growing up in a female-headed family with his comments twenty years later. These, Loury wrote, were considerably more circumspect.[6]

Still, a number of well-known advocates—among them, black women—soon began to speak out forthrightly about these issues. One was Eleanor Holmes Norton, a civil rights activist and graduate of Yale Law School whom President Carter had appointed to chair the Equal Employment Opportunity Commission (EEOC). Norton had since then become a law professor at Georgetown University. As far back as the early 1970s she had tried unsuccessfully to get civil rights leaders—most of them men—to pay more attention to the needs of black families. Discouraged by the response, she had defended the Moynihan Report to Auletta, observing sadly, "that it had to come from a white person tells you about the failure of black leadership."

Two months after Moynihan's opening lecture at Harvard, in June 1985, Norton expressed her concerns in an essay published in the *New York Times Magazine*. Her aptly titled article "Restoring the Traditional Black Family" featured statistics on long-term black male joblessness, nonmarital childbearing, and family breakup. The consequence of such developments, she argued, was a "complicated, predatory ghetto subculture."[7] Martin Luther King Jr., she reminded readers, had warned of such developments in 1965, when he had said black families were becoming "fragile, deprived, and often psychopathic." Moynihan, she continued, had then produced a report in which he had used controversial terms, notably "tangle of pathology," in describing lower-class black family life. Stunned, people had ignored Moynihan's concern with remedies, which were "eclipsed." Since that time, "fear of generating a new racism has foreclosed whatever opportunity there may have been to search for relief."

Like Loury, Norton lamented the timidity of black community leaders. She called out scholars who had shown an "almost visceral reaction to mention of black family problems" or who had described such problems as solely the result of white racism. "Talk [by advocates such as Moynihan] of black family weaknesses" had become "tantamount to insult and smear." Unless blacks spoke out, she said, the United States would have a "*lumpenproletariat* (the so-called underclass) without work and without hope." Such a situation could "bring down the great cities" and "sap resources and strength from the entire society." Because Norton (unlike Loury) was well-known as a civil rights activist and as a liberal, black leaders could not easily ignore her admonitions.

Two mass media features in 1986 echoed Norton's warnings. The first was a CBS TV documentary in January that graphically exposed the turbulence of inner-city black life in Newark, New Jersey. Produced by Bill Moyers, who had been Johnson's top aide at the time of the Moynihan Report in 1965, it carried the dramatic title *The Vanishing Family—Crisis in Black America*. A panel discussion on black family issues followed, featuring Loury, Norton, and the Rev. Jesse Jackson as commentators.

The documentary, which included frank interviews with young black people, dwelt on "Timothy," an unmarried black man who had fathered six children with four different women, and on the staggeringly high incidence of nonmarital births and increase of welfare rolls in inner-city black communities. The availability of welfare, one of the women explained, was one of the reasons she went ahead and had children. "Black teenagers," the documentary emphasized, "have the highest pregnancy rate in the industrial world, and in the inner city, practically no teenage mother gets married."

That Moyers, a strong liberal, would film such an exposé of family fragility in black communities spoke volumes about the greater readiness of Americans by then—no matter their political persuasion—to speak frankly about dysfunctions that blacks were partly responsible for bringing on themselves. Reviewers, especially conservatives, hailed the production. Michael Novak, writing for the *National Review*, called it "one of the bravest TV documentaries ever made." Conservative columnist George Will wrote that Timothy was a "paradigm of guiltless sexual irresponsibility." "The 'Timothys,'" he added, "are more of a menace to black progress than the Bull Connors were."

The second mass media account appeared in *Time* on December 1. It was headlined "Today's Native Son," which drew upon the title of Richard

Wright's famous novel *Native Son* (1940). This was a terrifying tale of the ordeal of Bigger Thomas, a teenage black man driven by his environment to the murder of a white girl in Chicago. *Time* quoted Moynihan, who took the opportunity to damn Reagan administration policies. But its story concentrated on terrible conditions in the ghettos. All too many black boys, *Time* reported, were joining gangs, thereby becoming part of the black community's "lost generation." "For many of these youths, fathering children out of wedlock and committing crimes are rites of passage. . . . There are thousands of Native Sons who can be seen hanging out on street corners, talking tough, listening to music boxes, dealing drugs, slipping into lives of crime."

Time, praising the approach of Loury and of other black activists who had begun to speak out, endorsed the efforts in the inner city of local chapters of organizations such as the NAACP and the Urban League. As if confirming that the tide was turning insofar as public conversation about black family life was concerned, *Time* cited approvingly a statement by Mary Frances Berry, a militant black activist, who declared, "We have to get these young males to understand the responsibilities that go along with fathering a child."

No effort in the late 1980s to stimulate serious discussion of ghetto problems, however, made a greater impression than a book by William Julius Wilson, a black sociologist. Already well-known for controversial publications about race relations—Moynihan had cited him in *Family and Nation*—Wilson published *The Truly Disadvantaged: The Inner City, the Underclass, and Public Policy* in 1987. The culmination of substantial on-site research into inner-city life, it documented in considerable detail the rise of a "sizable and growing black underclass" in U.S. cities. His explanations for this development sparked years of reflection and discussion.[8]

Moynihan, Wilson emphasized, had been "prophetic" in 1965. Attacks from his critics, furthermore, had been "vitriolic." These assaults had focused on his "unflattering depiction of the black family in the urban ghetto rather than on the proposed remedies or his historical analysis of the black family's social plight." That Wilson went out of his way to praise Moynihan's interpretation attested to his belief that many black leaders as well as many whites on the left had been guilty of posturing when they condemned Moynihan for blaming the victim. No black scholar of the stature of Wilson had previously dared to say so many positive things about the much-maligned white messenger who had written *The Negro Family*.

Wilson went on to criticize writers and activists who had "failed to address straightforwardly the rise of *social pathologies* in the ghetto" and who had thereby avoided use of the word "underclass."[9] Too many people, he argued, had been silent, afraid to talk about the ever more serious tangle of pathology in the inner city. He documented the worsening situation in detail: the alarming rise in crime, family dissolution, long-term poverty, and welfare dependency. These had roots, he maintained, in "historical discrimination," and therefore could not be blamed entirely on racism in the 1980s. Contemporary racism, Wilson believed, had become less pronounced. The underlying causes of worsening black urban troubles, he reiterated, were macroeconomic forces that in recent years had deepened poverty and had thereby exacerbated behavioral excesses.

Liberals as well as some writers further to the left responded enthusiastically to Wilson's analysis. Michael Harrington wrote that *The Truly Disadvantaged* was a "pathbreaking book, critically important to our current public and political debate as well as to social theory." Moynihan, too, joined the chorus of admirers. His blurb on the book jacket called Wilson's contribution "magisterial. . . . Whilst there are scholars possessed of such extraordinary analytic power there is hope for the rest of us."

The Truly Disadvantaged was indeed important, for unlike a great deal of partisan writing about the subject, this substantial work of scholarship offered impressively documented information rooted in ground-level observation. It emphasized that the failure of liberal scholars and black activists to speak out about the behavioral problems of many lower-class black people had dampened serious research into inner-city concerns. Insisting he was offering a liberal view, Wilson also criticized conservatives who argued that blacks were caught in a culture of poverty. He took special aim at writers such as Charles Murray who were blaming welfare for the breakup of black families.

Wilson endorsed the conclusions of Herbert Gutman and others who had emphasized the role of late twentieth-century economic developments, notably deindustrialization, as key causes of present-day social disorders in the inner city. But he was unromantic about what Carol Stack and other ethnologists in the 1970s had seen as the contributions to family stability of kin networks in the ghettos. Yes, he agreed, these networks represented creative and resource-ful adaptations to poverty, and they had helped to sustain some female-headed families. But they had not appreciably lessened the devastating impact of eco-nomic forces in recent years. Much more help was needed.

Wilson's analysis did not deny the importance of cultural-historical matters such as the long-range impact of slavery. Indeed, he argued (unlike Gutman) that slavery, followed by decades of discrimination, had helped devastate the aspirations of many black men in the past as well as in the present. "Negative attitudes [of black men] toward menial work," he wrote, "cannot be totally dismissed as a contributing factor" to their failure to find or to keep jobs.

But Wilson did not highlight the power of cultural forces. Black people, he recognized, reacted to life in the inner city as individuals. Depending on their backgrounds, circumstances, and skills, they made choices. Moreover, economic pressures, though not all-determining, were the key. Deindustri-alization, he argued, along with the movement of business and industry out of the inner cities since World War II, had heightened a "spatial mismatch" between ghetto-area residence and job opportunities. The rise of high-tech jobs, which excluded poorly educated job seekers, created an "educational mismatch."

Middle-class and "stable working-class" blacks, Wilson added, had for some time been abandoning the ghettos and settling in the suburbs. Young black men who stayed in the inner cities, lacking job opportunities and mid-dle-class role models, suffered from especially high unemployment as well as from "social isolation" in their highly segregated neighborhoods. Thus de-prived, many of these young men despaired of looking for work and left the labor market altogether (and therefore were not included in unemployment statistics). All too many young black men drifted into a street culture of hus-tling, crime, or drug abuse.

Enter, at this point, Wilson's explanation—widely cited though, in time, debated—for the decline of marriage and the rise of fatherless families among blacks in the inner cities. As Moynihan had written in 1965, Wilson pointed out that black women were more likely than black men to finish high school and to find living-wage employment. But, Wilson added, black women who managed to move ahead in life confronted a world that featured a "tragic de-cline in the black male marriageable pool." If a woman became pregnant, she was likely to fall back on AFDC, part-time work, and the assistance of kin rather than marry the unemployed or irresponsible (unmarriageable) man who had fathered her child.

Wilson also offered liberal advice, most of it similar to Moynihan's, to policymakers. Government, he recommended, should devise "short-term targeted programs for the disadvantaged." These could include manpower training, education, and apprenticeships to enhance skills. But the focus of policy should be on long-term programs to attack large structural weaknesses in the economy. These programs should be "universal"—that is, broad enough in reach to cover all categories of people needing economic assistance (not just the black poor). In so arguing, he echoed the belief of many liberal activists that a program for poor people alone was politically a poor program, one that would be stigmatized and underfunded. Reformers must devise "macroeconomic policies designed to promote both economic growth and a tight labor market."

Other useful programs, Wilson added, might include family allowances and more money for child care. Taking aim at the vulnerable welfare system, Wilson backed a number of reforms liberals had been recommending for years: making AFDC a uniform national program instead of one in which benefits differed across the states and providing aid to all needy families with children, not just to those (as was still the case in many states) that had only one parent in the home.

Though Wilson's work influenced liberal scholars, it did not settle debates over the sources of black family problems. Among the many activists, scholars, and policymakers who scrutinized his much-discussed findings within the next few years, some complained he had paid too much attention to economic forces—to jobs and social class—and not enough to racism. One such critic was the Rev. Jeremiah Wright of Trinity United Church of Christ in Chicago, who later lamented Wilson had become one of many "miseducated black brothers." Blaming white people who detested "ghetto culture," critics of this persuasion insisted, as they had earlier, that racial discrimination remained overwhelming.

Some social scientists who questioned Wilson's largely economic interpretation thought he placed too little emphasis on cultural damage that had badly weakened black aspirations. The task of traveling from the inner city to find work in the suburbs, they pointed out, was neither as time-consuming nor as expensive for black men as he made out. Moreover, they said, blacks residing in areas where blue-collar jobs did exist also had high rates of joblessness. The refusal of many young black men to take low-wage jobs, it was suggested, might be at least as important as "spatial mismatch" in explaining why large numbers of black men were not working. As sociologist Orlando Patterson later put the matter, "Work . . . has not disappeared. Rather, what has vanished— from a small, but significant and increasingly troublesome minority of younger, urban Afro-Americans—is the willingness to accept the labor-intensive, 'lousy' jobs available to the poorly educated, and the unwillingness of employers, including Afro-American entrepreneurs, to hire underqualified persons further burdened with soft skills."[10]

Other analysts, though agreeing that many black women rejected such men as unmarriageable, nonetheless argued that the decline in marriage among blacks in inner cities was far greater than the decline in the availability of jobs, and that marriage had fallen almost as much among well-educated black men as among those who were poorly educated. They concluded that something other than economic forces was behind the substantial declines in marriage. Christopher Jencks commented laconically, "marriage must . . . have been losing its charms for non-economic reasons."

Debates also broke out over definitions of "underclass." Some writers, defining it to include not only blacks who were poor but also those who suffered from a wide range of serious behavioral problems, came up with large totals. (Auletta's estimate, for instance, had been 9 million, most of whom were black.) Others, focusing like Wilson on structural-economic forces such as deindustrialization and social isolation in ever more concentrated inner-city neighborhoods, tended instead to define underclass people as those who were poor and living in high-poverty neighborhoods (places where 40 percent or more of the residents were poor). It became clear the term "underclass" was imprecise.

Patterson again offered a helpful view of the subject. All poor people, he wrote, should not be included as members of the underclass. Rather, one should focus on a "small hard core of dangerous people with multiple social problems." Citing Du Bois's study *The Philadelphia Negro* (1899), he reminded his readers that a minority of black men, frozen out of the industrial workforce, had even then turned to crime; since that time, black men acting like that had always been around. The percentage of such men within the black population, Patterson continued, had probably not increased much if at all in recent decades—his estimate in 1997 was around 900,000, at most 10 percent of the African American poor. Still, he noted, the underclass, though smaller than many writers thought, had "certainly become more deadly, taking its toll on the more vulnerable inner-city Afro-American communities."

These debates aside, few informed scholars denied that concentrated poverty and unemployment were ravaging many ghettos, or that behavioral signs of trouble, such as crime and nonmarital pregnancy, having intensified since the 1960s, were far more alarming than they had been even when Kenneth Clark had described them as pathological in *Dark Ghetto* (1964). The issue had become more urgent than ever. The debates, moreover, spilled over into newspaper and magazine stories, some of which, slighting Wilson's emphasis on macroeconomic causes of the troubles, continued to single out welfare policies as especially wasteful and counterproductive. Many stories also emphasized, sometimes sensationally, that teenage women were acting as their mothers had: bearing large numbers of children while unmarried, descending into long-range poverty, and landing on the tax-supported welfare rolls themselves.

What, then, could be done about the black underclasses? Jencks, like other knowledgeable observers, warned in 1991 that it was difficult to be precise in describing them. He noted that there were many underclasses: the impoverished underclass, the educational underclass, the violent (or criminal) underclass, and the reproductive underclass. People should not overgeneralize when talking about class, he maintained. Many individuals or families "are middle class in some respects, working class in others, and underclass in still others." He added, "Everyone who stops to think recognizes that the world is untidy in this sense. We use class labels precisely because we want to make the world seem tidier than it is."[11]

Like Jencks, however, most social scientists, whether liberal or conservative, also tended to agree by the early 1990s that contemporary economic forces, although major causes of poverty and unemployment, were not the only sources of the serious behavioral problems affecting many low-income blacks or residents of ghettos. Other powerful forces also seemed to be at work. As Moynihan had contended in 1965, these included the long and deeply damaging history of racial discrimination, including slavery, that over the years had helped to sabotage black aspirations. More recent consequences of these forces had exacerbated the seriousness of these historically rooted, culturally enduring encumbrances.

Key among these consequences, as Patterson argued, was the one Moynihan had long highlighted: the ascent of out-of-wedlock parenting and therefore of female-headed families and long-term poverty that devastated the life chances of children. Writing in the prosperous year 1997, Patterson observed that the black unemployment rate, having fallen since its high during the early 1990s, was about the same as it had been in 1970. The proportion of female-headed black families, however, had escalated during that time from under 30 percent to over 46 percent. Most of these single mothers had low educational attainment, poor work skills, and little income. Forced to cope with a "misogynistic, 'cool-pose' street culture in which a large majority of sexual predators identify manhood with impregnation and irresponsible fathering," they made a "devastating choice" when they became single parents. Their children suffered badly: Patterson concluded that nearly 60 percent of African American children under the age of eighteen were living in single-parent families and that 45 percent of these households were poor.

When Moynihan had given his lectures on family life in 1985, he had little reason to expect that the Senate, dominated by Republicans, would consider liberal reforms of social policy. In the congressional elections of 1986, however, Democrats (who had enjoyed a majority in the House since 1955) recaptured control of the Senate. In 1987, Moynihan thereupon became chair of a Senate subcommittee on Social Security and family policy. Though Reagan still held the presidency, the arrival of a Democratic majority in the Senate led liberal activists to hope that some expansion of the social welfare system might be in the cards.

In assuming the lead as the architect of such an overhaul in 1987 and 1988, Moynihan surprised Capitol Hill watchers, a number of whom had come to believe that he was more of an intellectual gadfly than a team player. Although many observers admired his ability to highlight important issues, others questioned his capacity for concentrating on one thing at a time, and they doubted that he could bring colleagues in the Senate together. Some senators, indeed, had come to regard him as a pedant—a wordy professorial type with a penchant for larding his orations with academic allusions and offering elegant and often amusing disquisitions on subjects of high purpose. Speaking in what his friend James Q. Wilson called a "clipped, almost stuttering style that must have baffled many of his Senate colleagues," he often paused for effect, sometimes between syllables of impressively lengthy words. (One Moynihan watcher, Elise Shaughnessy, later wrote in *Vanity Fair* that his gestures and speech patterns might lead listeners to believe that he suffered from "intellectual Tourette's syndrome.") Some senators also considered him a diffident and largely ineffectual legislator (except for his politically rewarding efforts—carefully overseen by Liz, his wife—on behalf of the interests of the people of New York).

Other Moynihan watchers—there were many, for as always he attracted the attention of journalists—worried about his tendency to drink too much. In an otherwise friendly feature on him in the *New York Times Magazine* in 1994, a reporter observed that Washington insiders "collect Moynihan drinking stories like baseball cards."[12] Some of Moynihan's staff, moreover, found him a loyal but nevertheless hard-driving and mercurial boss. Then as well as later, his reputation on Capitol Hill, which was mixed, contrasted with the high standing he had among many intellectually engaged citizens. These issue-oriented Americans thanked their stars that there was at least one learned, articulate, and deep-thinking member of the Senate.

Chester Finn, a former Senate aide, later wrote intelligently about this complex mix of reactions. Finn admitted that Moynihan "could be vain and thin-skinned, yes, not to mention quixotic and occasionally impish." But Finn remained an admirer, noting approvingly George Will's comment that Moynihan had written more books than some of his colleagues had read. (Will, a close friend of Moynihan, also declared that his "was the most penetrating intellect to come from New York since Alexander Hamilton.") Finn added, "In the grip of a strong conviction or powerful idea . . . [Moynihan] was resourceful, eloquent, and tenacious." He concluded, "I suspect that his Senate colleagues didn't always enjoy his lectures, but he persisted, coming up with data, examples, quotes, bits of history, more data, and prescient forecasts the like of which few of them encountered anywhere else."[13]

Congressional tussling over reform of welfare in 1987 and 1988 was prolonged, lasting until passage of a law in October 1988. Moynihan, confounding critics who had doubted his willingness to work hard for legislation, walked the halls of Senate office buildings to garner support for the law. The vote on the final bill, which was overwhelming and bipartisan—96 to 1 in the Senate and 347 to 53 in the House—seemed to attest to his success in bringing people together. When Reagan signed it on the eve of the 1988 elections, he proclaimed that the Family Support Act (FSA) was a "reform that will lead to lasting emancipation from welfare dependency." Moynihan exclaimed that it would "bring a generation of women back into the mainstream."

There was reason, or so it seemed at the time, for moderately hopeful prognoses. Though FSA was a far less ambitious effort than Nixon's Family Assistance Program had been, it mandated at last a goal liberals had been seeking for many years: provision by all states of federally subsidized AFDC benefits to needy two-parent families with children in which the father is involuntarily unemployed. FSA also called for stricter enforcement of child-support payments, and it ordered states to set up "welfare-to-work" job training and educational programs for able-bodied adult recipients (those without children under the age of three). These efforts reflected a belief among policymakers—Moynihan included—that recently implemented state-level experiments of that sort had been promising. Advocates hoped that the training programs would wean women from dependency on welfare and endow them with feelings of dignity and self-worth.

It soon became clear, however, that FSA—a compromise measure to please Reagan—was not much of a reform. As before, AFDC remained a federal-state program, thereby continuing to dispense benefits that differed in size across the states. State officials encountered difficulties in establishing effective job programs, which tended to be expensive. Few women in the programs found living-wage work. Many states were slow to appropriate matching money. The federal government kicked in less than states had anticipated.

Conditions for the reform soon worsened. When a recession battered the economy in 1990 and 1991, the AFDC rolls increased (from 10.7 million in 1988 to 14 million in 1993) even as real AFDC funding per recipient continued to slip. In 1991, the average monthly AFDC payment per family was $388, or $4,656 per year—a little less in real dollars than it had been in 1988. At that time the government's official poverty line was $10,873 for a family of three and $13,942 for a family of four.[14]

Even at the time of FSA's passage in 1988, moreover, many liberals doubted it would accomplish a great deal. The act, they said, did not address the roots of the economic problems that afflicted poor families—notably the shortage of living-wage work for men, especially black men. Instead of trying to attack large-scale structural causes of poverty, they added, FSA tinkered with AFDC in the forlorn hope that training programs would manage to get women off of welfare—or at least shorten the long spells of people on it who were absorbing taxpayer dollars. FSA, some critics added, was little more than the latest effort by conservatives to force poverty-stricken mothers to work outside of the home. Far from enhancing the dignity of recipients, they said, it was a punitive experiment in workfare.

Conservative skeptics posed different questions—most of them familiar from debates over FAP and subsequent congressional stabs at reform. (Because Congress continued to slight funding for evaluation of social policies, these questions continued to be difficult to answer.) What evidence existed, critics asked, to indicate that job training programs would develop a strong work ethic among people who participated in them? Or that the programs would manage to train low-income women, most of whom were ill educated, for living-wage jobs? Why should taxpayers contribute to the training and education of welfare recipients when many low-income working people, themselves looking for better-paid jobs, were struggling?

Those who aimed their complaints at Moynihan personally were unfair. A man whose concern for the welfare of families, including black families, was long-standing, he knew that the challenges facing low-income and fatherless families were complicated and profound. He had done what he could to get a law passed that Reagan would sign. But critics were on target in concluding that FSA made little difference in the lives of the welfare poor. What happened on Capitol Hill in 1988 attested to the ongoing strength of a range of political and ideological obstacles, among them budgetary constraints and antiwelfare lobbies. These blocked and would continue to block large-scale programs aimed at promoting what LBJ in 1965 had called "equality as a fact and as a result" in the United States.

Moynihan, like other liberals, was disheartened by new political developments during the next few years. In the election of 1988, George H. W. Bush defeated Democratic candidate Michael Dukakis for the presidency. Bush, who had relatively little interest in social welfare policy, was hamstrung by the recession that arrived in 1990, which magnified already enormous federal deficits and led to urgent and partially successful calls for budgetary restraint. As during the Carter years, a gloomy economic situation worked against passage of costly socioeconomic reforms.

Bush, moreover, found occasions to add his voice to those of conservatives who had been denouncing welfare and lamenting the decline of the traditional family. In his State of the Union address in 1992 he cited FDR's concern that welfare was a "narcotic" and a "subtle destroyer of the spirit." Bush added, "Welfare was never meant to be a lifestyle; it was never meant to be a habit; it was never meant to be passed from generation to generation, like a legacy." Four months later at Notre Dame, he proclaimed, "At the heart of the problems facing our country stands an institution under siege. That institution is the American family. Whatever form our pressing problems may take, ultimately all are related to the disintegration of the American family."

Social conservatives, meanwhile, were becoming even more outspoken over family issues than they had been earlier. Deploring the extent of divorce and out-of-wedlock childbearing, they redoubled their crusades to restore "family values," by which they meant those supposedly dominant in the 1950s. Bush's vice president, Dan Quayle, eagerly embraced this crusade. During the presidential campaign of 1992, he touched off a controversy when he denounced the television character Murphy Brown (played by Candice Bergen in a popular sit-com of that name) for having a baby without getting married and for indicating calmly that the father's identity did not matter. Murphy Brown's behavior, Quayle charged, could not be defended as "just another lifestyle choice."

Critics of Quayle shot back by ridiculing him as a prig and denouncing him as a foe of free expression. Writers for the show responded cheekily by inserting Quayle's criticisms into later episodes, whereupon ratings for the show improved. Still, Quayle and his allies persevered. Indeed, a network of "profamily" organizations became stronger in these years. One was the Institute for American Values, which had been founded in 1987 by a Harvard graduate, David Blankenhorn. One of his many books, published in 1990, left no doubts concerning his message: *Rebuilding the Nest: A New Commitment to the American Family*. Commenting later on the central Democratic campaign slogan in 1992, "It's the Economy, Stupid," Blankenhorn shot back, "It's not 'the economy, stupid.' It's the culture."

Yet another source of activism on behalf of family values in these years was the National Marriage Project housed at Rutgers University. Its codirectors were David Popenoe, a sociology professor and dean at the university, and Barbara Dafoe Whitehead. Popenoe wrote a number of books, including *Disturbing the Nest: Family Change and Decline in Modern Societies* in 1988. As Preston had done in 1984, Popenoe emphasized that parents, no longer heading "child-centered marriages," had increasingly come to place their own desires and needs ahead of those of their offspring. His findings were said to have encouraged Quayle's outburst in 1992. Whitehead, also a prolific writer, published an article, "Dan Quayle Was Right," in *Atlantic Monthly* magazine. Offering an array of statistics concerning family dysfunctions, her article sparked nationwide debate and discussion. Even more than in the 1980s, the culture wars raged in the early 1990s.

Many liberals in these years, though contesting the views of conservatives such as these, continued to agree (as Moyers had demonstrated in 1986) that the increasingly grim realities of lower-class black family life could no longer be ignored. Indeed, some liberals, too, painted gloomy portraits of ghetto conditions in the early 1990s. In 1991, journalist Nicholas Lemann published *The Promised Land*, a widely hailed book that chronicled the generally confused and unsuccessful efforts of Washington warriors against poverty over the years. (Moynihan, portrayed as self-aggrandizing, came out badly in the book.) Lemann focused especially on the experiences of impoverished southern black people who had migrated to Chicago in search of a better life. The Windy City, however, was decidedly not a "promised land." As portrayed by Lemann, black families packed into high-rise projects were plagued not only by rotten housing, poverty, and discrimination but also by aimlessness, infidelity, and crime. Though Lemann was a liberal, his book drew a picture that may have confirmed the worst stereotypes that many conservatives and others held of the inner-city black poor.

Race relations in general were especially tense at that time. In April 1992, an all-white jury acquitted three white Los Angeles police officers who had been accused of beating Rodney King, an African American, during his arrest a year earlier on charges of speeding. Incensed by the verdict, Los Angeles blacks erupted in four days of looting, rioting, burning, and violence. Serious racial disturbances also broke out in Atlanta, Birmingham, Chicago, and Seattle. Andrew Hacker, a white writer, concluded later that year (in the revealingly titled book *Two Nations: Black and White, Separate, Hostile, Unequal*), that "a huge racial chasm remains, and that there are few signs that the coming century will see it closed."[15]

No one expressed greater sadness in these years about race relations than Moynihan's erstwhile guide and friend, Kenneth Clark. In 1993, Clark wrote an extraordinarily bleak summation of his career of battling for civil rights: "I am forced to face the likely possibility that the United States will never rid itself of racism and reach true integration." He added, "I look back and I shudder at how naive we all were in our belief in the steady progress racial minorities would make through programs of litigation and education. While I very much hope for the emergence of a revived civil rights movement with innovative programs and dedicated leaders, I am forced to recognize that my life has, in fact, been a series of glorious defeats."[16]

Black liberals such as Clark, moreover, were not alone in writing pessimistically about race relations and family problems during the early 1990s. Black conservatives, too, began to be heard—predictably with a different message. The most prominent was Shelby Steele, a professor of English literature at San Jose State University. In 1990 he wrote a book that despaired of what he regarded as black posturing. Titled *The Content of Our Character: A New Vision of Race in America*, it blasted black leaders who blamed the difficulties of blacks on white people. Black activists, in turn, assailed him as a turncoat. Still, the book won a National Book Critics Circle award for general nonfiction and established Steele as a leading conservative voice on matters of race.[17]

Like most Americans, Steele professed his pleasure at watching *The Cosby Show*, which presented an upbeat "blackface version of the American dream." Alas, he continued, far too few prominent black Americans acted like the characters Cosby and his television wife played on the screen. Instead, he said, black American leaders too often played the role of "race-holder," one who "whines, or complains indiscriminately, not because he seeks redress but because he seeks the status of a victim, a status that excuses him from what he fears." This stance of victimization not only kept African Americans from realizing their full potential, according to Steele, it also caused them to "neglect the individual initiative that would deliver them from poverty."

Moynihan, too, joined pessimists who bewailed the sorry state of U.S. culture. Unlike Steele, he did not target black community leaders for criticism. (As earlier, this remained a foolhardy thing for whites to do.) Like the pessimists, however, he deplored what he considered the degradation of social standards. In a widely noted essay, "Defining Deviancy Down," he observed in 1993 that deviant behaviors in the United States had so greatly increased in recent years that the American people, unable to deal with the deviance, were no longer willing to recognize it as such. Instead, they defined it down, as more or less normal, thereby seeming to accept all manner of dysfunctional and once-stigmatized activities.[18]

To support his case, Moynihan used the spread of casual attitudes toward rising crime and nonmarital birth, with Preston as a major source of data. People who in effect ignored the disastrous social consequences of such attitudes, he maintained, were defining down the seriousness of dysfunctional behaviors—to the extent that criminals, for instance, were no longer regarded as parasitic or crime as evil. It followed that far too many Americans were accepting deviant behavior. The fetching alliteration of Moynihan's title proved attractive to many commentators in 1993, perhaps because he was an eminently quotable U.S. senator, perhaps because (characteristically) he illustrated his argument by citing eminent sociological theorists (notably Émile Durkheim), and perhaps because his lament seemed to capture the pessimistic mood of the times. The phrase "defining deviancy down," given wide and generally favorable exposure at the time by conservatives and others, entered the American lexicon, where it has retained a fairly prominent place.

It was at this juncture, during the hottest times of the already overheated U.S. culture wars, that extraordinarily fierce political wrangling over welfare reform further polarized the nation's politics. These struggles forced Moynihan to wage the last major political battle of his career on behalf of lower-class black families in the United States and culminated in President Bill Clinton signing a historic welfare law in 1996.

CHAPTER 9

Welfare Reform, Slavery, and Jeremiads

"Everyone hated welfare."

So reflected David Ellwood in 2007, long after he had served as one of President Bill Clinton's top domestic advisers on the subject. Though Ellwood added that the people who "hated it worst" were those struggling to live on it, he knew very well that conservative foes of the existing system, after assailing it for decades, had driven hard to do away with it.

Kill it they finally did. In summer 1996, Congress passed welfare "reform," revealingly titled the Personal Responsibility and Work Opportunity Reconciliation Act (PRWORA). When Clinton signed it into law, angering many liberals, Moynihan blasted the measure as the "most brutal act of social policy since Reconstruction."

In crafting this landmark piece of legislation, which abolished AFDC and established a lifetime limit of five years on receiving public assistance benefits, many members of Congress relied on politically effective challenges to liberal ideas about the black poor. One of these challenges employed long-standing arguments that had identified deep-seated cultural inheritances, notably from slavery, as key sources of the multiple dysfunctions of lower-class black families. Another challenge stemmed from a crescendo of jeremiads, mostly from conservatives, about contemporary cultural trends then afflicting U.S. families, white as well as black. By the early 2000s, when Republicans held all the reins of power in Washington, conservative ideas about the decline of family life were even more powerful politically than they had been in earlier years.

President Clinton might have been expected to be a reliable ally of Moynihan and other Democratic liberals. As governor of Arkansas, he had endorsed Moynihan's efforts to pass the Family Support Act of 1988. As president he enjoyed Democratic majorities in both houses of Congress in 1993 and 1994. But he inherited huge budget deficits that forced him to cut spending and raise taxes in 1993. Recognizing that welfare issues continued to be highly polarizing—Carter, he knew, had failed to resolve them—he also believed Congress would not approve anything like the Family Assistance Plan (FAP) of the Nixon era or appropriate substantial sums for public work.

But Clinton did hope to change AFDC. If elected president, he had declared in 1992, he would "put an end to welfare as we know it." In saying this and in repeating it on later occasions, Clinton was responding in part to long-familiar complaints that the program, by supporting rising numbers of single mothers, had encouraged nonmarital childbearing. In 1991, 1.2 million babies had been born out of wedlock in the United States. More generally, the president was reacting to agitation over welfare costs that had mounted during the recession years of 1990 and 1991. The cost of AFDC benefits had risen—from $18.5 million in 1990 to $22.4 million in 1993. During 1993 alone, 14 million people (9 million of them children) were on welfare at one time or another. In cities with large black populations (Detroit and Philadelphia, for instance), two-thirds of the African American children were then on the rolls. Some 30 percent of new families on AFDC were staying on the dole for five years or more. The welfare situation, critics proclaimed, had gotten out of hand.

Always a cagey politician, Clinton did not specify what he had in mind. But it was fairly clear that he did not intend to go so far as to abolish welfare altogether. Nevertheless, he did aim to shorten to two years the spells of able-bodied people on the rolls and therefore to strike a blow at long-term dependency, a major evil as he saw it. He said, "We'll give them all the help they need for up to two years. But after that, if they're able to work, they'll have to take a job in the private sector or start earning their way through community service."

Aside from limiting dependency, Clinton favored reform that would largely build on the FSA. He hoped to expand job training and education programs for able-bodied women who had been on the dole as well as provide increased funding for Head Start and child care. He was also prepared to go a little beyond that—to support government-subsidized jobs in the private sector or public jobs in community service for many adults who had been on AFDC for two years but who still could not find work.

Most liberals, however, had grander goals. Emphasizing the need for more generous welfare spending, they noted that poverty, hitting a peak of 36.9 million people in 1992 (the highest number since 1962), still afflicted 36.4 million Americans, including 29.3 percent of blacks (9.9 million people), in 1995. Child poverty, at 20.2 percent overall for children under the age of eighteen, continued to be the highest in the Western world, and poverty among black children (41.5 percent) was catastrophic. The United States, the richest nation in the world, could surely afford to do more for its citizens in need.

A number of scholars joined this clamor for better benefits. William Julius Wilson, who wrote the revealingly titled book *When Work Disappears* in 1996, weighed in again about the need to help black people find living-wage employment. Christopher Jencks continued to endorse a variety of programs to target different groups: public jobs for many of the unemployed, a higher minimum wage, expanded funding for the earned income tax credit (EITC) benefiting low-wage working families with children, and more federal money for Food Stamps and child care.

Had Clinton made welfare reform his top priority in 1993, he might have had a chance to reduce long-term welfare dependency while also securing some of these liberal goals. Moynihan, as chair of the Senate Finance Committee, was eager to consider changes, including some that would build on the provisions of the FSA. But Clinton, overly sure of his own political skills, did not defer to him. A Clinton staffer, reflecting the president's cavalier attitude, was quoted in *Time* as saying, "He [Moynihan] can't control Finance. . . . He's cantankerous, but . . . we'll roll right over him if we have to." Moreover, Clinton made the fateful decision to concentrate from 1993 to 1994 on large-scale reform of health care provision. Revision of welfare, he declared, would have to wait. His choice angered Moynihan, who retorted that there was no health care crisis.

In early 1994, Moynihan further irritated the president by criticizing an administration program, Goals 2000, which enumerated grandiose goals for educational progress in the United States. Supporters of the goals, which focused on proposals to raise academic standards, predicted the initiative had the potential to lift the high school graduation rate by the year 2000 to at least 90 percent, and that U.S. students would then be first in the world in mathematics and science achievement. Moynihan, however, continued to be guided by the findings of the Coleman Report of 1966, which had emphasized that low educational achievement stemmed in considerable part from deep-set problems in family and community life.[1] The optimistic predictions of Goals 2000, Moynihan snorted, were utopian—about as credible as Soviet grain production quotas: "avowed but non-constraining." High test scores and graduation rates, he added, correlated well not with high per-pupil expenditures for public education but with high proportions of two-parent families. Noting that these proportions were highest in states closest to Canada, he suggested puckishly that states wishing·to improve schools might try moving toward the border. "This would be difficult, but so would it be to change the parent-pupil ratio."

As wisecracks such as this made clear, Moynihan believed President Clinton was generally inept at legislative leadership. That was indeed the case on occasion—the president's clumsy handling of the health care issue from 1993 to 1994 helped conservatives defeat his plan. Republicans then staged a historic comeback in the 1994 elections. In 1995, as Clinton began at last to give serious thought to tackling welfare issues, the GOP controlled both houses of Congress for the first time since 1954. Save for a one-and-a-half-year interlude in 2001 and 2002, they were to maintain their majorities until 2007.

As had been the case in the fight for FAP in 1969 and 1970, partisan bitterness and ideological warfare enveloped the lengthy struggle for welfare reform that followed in 1995 and 1996. The issue remained, as Joseph Califano had said, the Middle East of U.S. domestic politics. Many of the actors who engaged in the haggling observed—as earlier—that Moynihan in 1965 had first focused public attention on black family problems and on welfare issues. As had frequently been the case during the previous thirty years, newspaper accounts and headlines also featured the continuing relevance of his report. In 1995 and 1996, however, a sign of the times was that the report was more often praised for its prescience—especially by conservatives—than it was maligned for its passages about pathology. The times had surely changed.

As always, Moynihan rejected charges that his report had blamed welfare for breaking up families—in fact, he maintained correctly, it had said the reverse—that poverty and unemployment forced people to go on the rolls. He remained adamant that government had a duty to help people, especially children, who could not help themselves. Indeed, thinking about the miseries of life on welfare seemed to upset him. After telling an interviewer in 1994 that his mother had received aid before remarrying, he added he did not like to talk about the trials of trying to survive on the dole.

Moynihan had displayed especially strong feelings about broken families during a finance committee hearing on welfare in July 1994. Musing about dire predictions that one-half of all U.S. children within the next decade would be born out of wedlock, he went on to speculate about the reasons for the development of such a trend. As was his wont, he drew upon scholarly sources, this time from the field of evolutionary biology. "If you were a biologist," he remarked, "you could find yourself talking about speciation here." By speciation, he meant that the spread of broken homes and fatherless families could yield the creation of a new species that could not breed with the one from which it had evolved. The Rev. Al Sharpton, the feisty black minister challenging him for his Senate seat, was quick to retort that Moynihan's comments had demonized single mothers. Sharpton explained that his own mother, a wonderful parent, had done a fine job of raising him. "Moynihan," he exclaimed, "rose to fame talking about the black family, while I'm a broken family product." Battered by criticism of his statement, Moynihan soon apologized.[2]

Moynihan had good reason, however, for being even more alarmed than in earlier years about trends in family life. Aided by Paul Barton and others, he had kept up with social developments in other nations. Well before 1995, he had become painfully aware of statistics showing that the proportions of nonmarital births were increasing rapidly throughout most of the industrialized world.[3] Citing such trends in 1995, he professed to be staggered and unsure of how to respond. In the past, he said, policymakers had learned how to deal with social problems of the industrial age. But the world was now in a new and relatively uncharted postindustrial era. Regarding the rise of nonmarital childbearing, he said, "We know desperately little about this great transformation, save that it is happening in all the industrial nations of the North Atlantic."[4]

Despite Moynihan's informed reflections and long experience, he did not fare well during the acerbic battle over welfare reform that ensued. Bad blood continued to poison his relations with the president. During struggles over the issue that led Clinton to veto two conservative bills, Moynihan did little to mobilize Democrats behind efforts to forge a compromise. Instead, as one observer put it, he mainly contented himself with rising up on the Senate floor to embark on "eloquent, learned, entertaining, and wholly ineffective" orations. As the fighting grew nasty, moreover, he became furious. "Just how many millions of infants will be put to the sword is not clear," he said of the welfare bill as it was worded in late 1995. "Those involved," he added in reference to supporters of the bill, "will take this disgrace to their graves. The children alone are innocent." The hot-tempered Clinton deeply resented such statements. On one occasion, during an Air Force One trip to New York, the president angrily accused the senator from New York of firing off gratuitous attacks, whereupon Moynihan, incensed, shot back that Clinton was wavering on long-standing Democratic Party principles.[5]

The bill that finally passed in August 1996 enjoyed the backing of Republicans as well as twenty-five of forty-six Democrats in the Senate. Many Democrats who voted for it feared retribution from conservative voters at the polls if they did not. In abolishing AFDC, the act ended a federal entitlement that many liberals, and of course beneficiaries, had valued for sixty-one years. Nearly 70 percent of its long-term recipients at the time were African Americans. Many, suffering not only from poverty but also from drug addiction or other severe health problems, could not help themselves.

Having ignored Clinton's appeals, the legislators who passed the new program did not provide for public jobs in community service. These, opponents argued, would not only be expensive to set up; they would also result in "make work" of little benefit either to recipients or to the economy. Instead, Congress replaced AFDC with a program titled Temporary Assistance to Needy Families (TANF). This was to be run by states, which would receive federal block grants. Unlike federal money that had gone to states under AFDC, the block grants would not automatically increase if the number of recipients grew. When and if the economy ran into trouble, many liberals predicted, federal support would become inadequate, states (faced with budget deficits) would cut benefits, and women and children would suffer.

Under the new program, states were required to move adult welfare recipients off cash assistance and into job training, education programs, and then, within two years, into jobs. The law further specified that adults (save for particularly "worthy" cases) would not be allowed to receive federal cash assistance for more than five years in their lifetimes. (States, permitted to shorten this limit, generally did.) By 1998, states were expected to be able to show that at least 30 percent of adult recipients were working. This was supposed to rise to 50 percent by 2002.

Critics, notably liberals (among them many black leaders), complained that the act in no way attacked the deep-rooted sources of poverty in the United States. First among the sources, which Moynihan had highlighted in 1965, was the shortage of employment opportunities for low-skilled men or women. A second source closely associated with the first was the tangle of problems—ever higher numbers of nonmarital births and of female-headed families—that had led to the feminization of poverty and to a range of behavioral family ills. TANF, liberal opponents complained, had far less ambitious goals—namely to curb welfare dependency.

Four cabinet secretaries urged Clinton to veto the bill that reached his desk. Moynihan exclaimed that children would be sleeping on grates. "I don't want to sound apocalyptic," he added, "but the effect on New York City could be something approaching an Apocalypse." Marian Wright Edelman, who headed the Children's Defense Fund—and was a personal friend of Bill and Hillary Clinton—was one of many black leaders who opposed the bill. When Clinton signed it into law, their friendship collapsed. Her husband, Peter Edelman, a white man who had previously worked in the Clinton administration on welfare issues, resigned his post. That the president, who had enjoyed especially good relations with blacks, nonetheless signed the law showed that he, like many moderates who voted for it, figured that voters favored it.

Were liberals' fears about the law justified? In part because the legislation contained no provision for thorough governmental evaluation of the outcomes, those who tried to answer this question differed sharply in later years. Going into effect as it did in the late 1990s, when the economy was booming, the act initially did not seem to do any harm. The official poverty rate plummeted, from 11.2 percent in 1995 to 9.5 percent in 2000. Child poverty, at 20.2 percent in 1995, dropped to a low of 15.6 percent in 2000. Among African

American children, it fell during these years from 41.5 percent to 30.9 percent—a tremendously heartening decline that followed decades of discouraging statistics.

Because most states vigorously enforced work requirements, the act led to a dramatic fall in the welfare rolls. The number of people (more than two-thirds of them children) receiving cash assistance plummeted between 1997 and 2004 from roughly 12.1 million to 4.1 million. This was the first sustained decrease in the rolls (and, of course, in federal expenditures for cash assistance) since the old system had been established in 1935. Supporters of the new law proclaimed that it had changed the "welfare culture," which, they said, had featured the mindless handing out of checks. Many women who were helped to find stable employment, no longer stigmatized as members of the undeserving poor, reported feeling better about themselves.

Encouraging numbers such as these led many people to conclude that opponents like Moynihan had underestimated the adaptability of the poor on welfare—and (perhaps) the sheer perversity of the old system of AFDC. His friend James Q. Wilson, a supporter of the act, concluded Moynihan had been uncharacteristically mistaken in predicting the act would exacerbate child poverty. Moynihan had been in error, Wilson believed, because in his concern for fatherless children he had accepted a flawed scholarly analysis foreseeing such a result—and in so doing had failed to observe his own often-stated view that social science could not always predict the outcome of legislation.[6]

Whether the new system had an effect on the incidence of out-of-wedlock pregnancy, however, is surely doubtful. Supporters of the law, clearly hoping it would do so, had included a provision that offered $100 million per year to the five states with the largest decreases in the proportion of nonmarital births. This proportion, having risen considerably to 32.6 percent in 1994, briefly stabilized thereafter. But toward the turn of the century, it started to creep up again, reaching an all-time high of 34 percent by 2002. Moreover, it is evident in retrospect that the primary reason for the temporary stabilization of the proportions of out-of-wedlock births during the late 1990s was not the carrot of $100-million rewards but the economic boom.[7]

The advancing economy was also the reason poverty declined at that time. Many poor people in these unusually prosperous years benefited not only from the boom but also from other programs: EITC, which Clinton and Congress managed to expand substantially after 1993; higher appropriations for Food Stamps; and a hike in the minimum wage that Congress approved in 1996. TANF, in fact, was only the sixth largest means-tested federal program, with a budget as of 2004 of only $14.1 billion, or a little less than $3,000 per recipient.[8]

Even during the good years of the late 1990s, moreover, it was estimated that between 30 and 50 percent of the women who had to leave welfare were unable to find steady jobs. When the economy slumped between 2001 and 2003, poverty rates rose again. Many states, as liberals had feared, began scaling back their funding of educational and job training programs and became ever more insistent that women on welfare find work. This was not easy for many of the women to do, for job training had prepared few of them for anything beyond unskilled, low-wage labor. Most women who secured living-wage employment were those who had before 1996 already acquired some job skills.

Though TANF increased funding for child care, women who found work incurred significant new expenses, notably for transportation and clothing. Other working mothers hit by the slump took pay cuts or lost their jobs. Still other women, as before, could not find work and were worse off under the new regime than under the entitlement of AFDC. If one looked beyond statistics to understand the struggles of many individual recipients, one could see that the new system, though helping many women, was in some places as harsh—especially for black women in southern states—as critics had predicted it would be.

In all these ways, passage of the new law was a turning point in the history of American welfare policies. Even as economic conditions became unstable in the early 2000s, few Americans demanded that states or the federal government step in to restore something like the guarantees of the earlier system. On the contrary, the issues of poverty and welfare, which had provoked heated political warfare since the late 1960s, all but vanished from the U.S. political agenda until the recession of 2008—at which time state budget cuts deepened the plight of many thousands of female-headed families. The virtual absence of visible controversy, at least until then, revealed an important legacy of the welfare law of 1996: it had established an approach to public aid for dependent women and children more in accord than the old system had been with powerful values in the United States—that is, with primarily conservative values—about sexuality, family organization, and the importance of work effort.

Thanks to welfare "reform," people thought, the nasty old system would no longer be around to magnify perverse incentives. It would not reward the promiscuous, pamper the dependent, or support the indolent. Taxpayers would no longer have to take care of the "undeserving."

In all these ways, Ellwood was right when he said that "everyone hated welfare." Having "fixed" the system in 1996, many Americans could put the whole business, including the still-serious situation of lower-class black families, out of mind.

In 1987, Toni Morrison published a novel that dramatized the horrors of slavery. The main character of her book *Beloved* was a runaway slave woman captured during her effort to escape. Rather than see her baby daughter sold into bondage, she cut the girl's throat. *Beloved* received rave reviews, helping catapult Morrison, already an accomplished novelist, to a Nobel Prize in literature.

Beloved was of course fiction, and it had little to do with contemporary scholarly debates about the cultural inheritances of slavery. In writing her novel, Morrison was not trying to challenge the relatively benign depictions of slave family patterns that revisionist historians such as Herbert Gutman had been publishing throughout the 1970s. Nor did *Beloved* prevent social scientists in the 1990s from continuing to endorse such depictions, which had described the creativity and resourcefulness of African Americans, thereby downplaying to an extent the long-range impact of slavery on black family life and culture. A leading advocate of such scholarship, Andrew Billingsley, reiterated in 1997 arguments he had been making for thirty years, again singling out Moynihan for criticism. Moynihan's *The Negro Family*, he wrote, had "ignored the variety and complexity of the internal and external forces shaping African American family life." As earlier, Billingsley hailed the resiliency of blacks both under slavery and thereafter.

A number of scholars, however, were already starting in the early 1990s to revise the revisionists—and in so doing to look again at slavery as Morrison (and Moynihan, less dramatically) had viewed it. In 1992 and 1993, Samuel Preston and coauthors looked carefully at recently published early twentieth-century census data on black families, most of whom lived in the South. These data indicated that many unmarried black women with children had most likely misrepresented themselves by reporting to census takers that they were widows, perhaps in an attempt to account for births outside of marriage. These misrepresentations had led the census to undercount the number of unmarried women who had children. Moreover, "marital turnover was faster than could be expected by active widowhood or formal divorce."[9]

Preston and his coauthors determined that E. Franklin Frazier had taken note of Census Bureau warnings at the time about these "seriously flawed" marital status reports. But later historians, notably Gutman, had ignored the warnings, thereby counting many women with children as widows when in fact they had never been married. Evidence suggested, moreover, that "patterns of marital instability among blacks show greater historical continuity than is suggested by some current discussions." In a conclusion that directly challenged revisionist histories of slavery, Preston concluded, "Gutman's portrait of stable black marriages in the South before the mass migrations to northern cities is overdrawn."

Preston and his collaborators did not claim to know for sure why this historical continuity had occurred. This was, after all, a highly complicated and controversial area of research over which social scientists and historians had fought for years. Still, noting studies that revealed the survival of African linguistic and religious practices among blacks, they observed that sub-Saharan, West African family networks (which featured extended kin supports) were "more fluid than European models." They then offered a hypothesis for social scientists to ponder. "Apparently," they wrote, "the role of slavery and its aftermath, and perhaps also the legacy of West African family trends, deserve more than a footnote in the evolution of the black family."

It normally takes a good deal of time for the findings in scholarly publications to reach the larger public. So it was with these articles, which included many mathematical equations and correlations. But word of Preston's conclusions quickly reached scholars, notably Orlando Patterson, who had long studied the historical legacy of cultural forces. In *Rituals of Blood: Consequences of Slavery in Two American Centuries*, published in 1998, he praised Preston's findings (and those of earlier demographers) in the course of criticizing revisionists such as Gutman. Patterson's horrific depiction of slavery, indeed, resembled that of earlier scholars such as W. E. B. Du Bois and Frazier. It would surely have rung true with Moynihan, whose savaging from ethnic chauvinists Patterson had long deplored.[10]

Patterson's argument relied in part on the research and writing of Du Bois, Frazier, and the evidence of Preston and his collaborators to highlight the lasting impact of slavery on the behavior of African American families in the present. Slavery, Patterson emphasized, had launched an "ethnocidal assault on gender relations." Slave women, he added, had strong "uterine ties" with their children. Indeed, the relationships these black women formed with their children—and with each other—were much stronger than those they developed with enslaved men; similarly strong ties also persisted as a significant characteristic of African American society up to the present. By contrast, male slaves had "no legitimate ties to, or rights in, their female partners." They experienced "utter insecurity about the biological parentage of their children," and they could not prevent whites from abusing their women. In short, "the roles of father and husband [were] very weakly institutionalized, possibly the worst heritage of the slave past."

The deep-seated insecurities of enslaved men, Patterson emphasized, had long-range consequences. "Ex-slaves," he wrote, "emerged after emancipation with chronic gender and familial problems." To document the persistence of these ills in the years of "neo-slavery and Jim Crow," Patterson cited Preston's findings about the instability of black families in the early 1900s as well as the work of John Dollard, who had done field research among southern blacks in the 1930s. Dollard had discovered a great deal of "anger and self-loathing" among the black men. The aggressive and "disproportionate" sexuality of lower-class blacks, Dollard wrote, was "a feature of [their] permissive slave culture."

Patterson agreed with Dollard's emphasis on the historical continuity of gender and family issues among black people tracing back to enslavement. In the present, he wrote, one finds among black men "the vicious desire to impregnate and abandon black women, as if Afro-American men were unable to shake off the one gender role of value (to the master) thrust upon them during slavery, that of progenitors." Disputing the view of scholars who had argued in the 1970s that extended kin relationships had done a great deal to hold black families together, he also maintained that blacks had fewer personal contacts and friendships than whites.[11] As he put it, blacks are "the most unpartnered and isolated group of people in America and possibly in the world." Some 60 percent of black children in the United States, moreover, were "being brought up without the emotional support of a father."

In his arguments, Patterson was explicit that scholars should look for "internal" as well as "external" causes of people's behavior. By "internal" causes, he meant long-range cultural-historical forces that directly and/or indirectly affect the behavior of subsequent generations of individuals. "External" causes—the socioeconomic environment, racism, and so forth—mattered, too. These two kinds of forces are "closely linked not so much in a causal chain as in a layered net." Scholars who insist that their explanations must concentrate upon one or the other are "playing tiresome and obfuscating games."

Patterson clearly understood the power of oppressive socioeconomic conditions on the lives of Americans, both in the past and in the present day. Though he believed that white racism had decreased in the United States, he agreed with the obvious: it had held black people down, and serious racist encumbrances persisted. Still, the thrust of his argument was unmistakable: historical-cultural forces had especially powerful long-range consequences. "*Current* socioeconomic conditions," he argued, "are no longer the proximate causes of Afro-American marital and familial problems."[12] "The nation as a whole" and "Afro-Americans in particular are still paying the ethnocidal price of slavery and the . . . Jim Crow system." He added, "The cultural damage already done, today these [socioeconomic] factors make no difference."

Finally, Patterson could not rest without chastising revisionist historians—writers who had underplayed (as he saw it) the catastrophic impact of slavery and who had emphasized instead the force of relatively recent (and more remediable) economic burdens as causes of the dysfunctional behavior of many black men. As if referring to the fate that had befallen Moynihan, he charged that "a whole generation of historians" had wrongly maintained that cultural explanations of historical change blamed the victim. In so doing these scholars had "downplayed the role of cultural factors explaining Afro-American life."

Because the difficulties facing black families had cultural roots, as reflected most disastrously in the behavior of many low-income black men, solutions to contemporary problems, according to Patterson, lay in part in getting the men to "radically alter their ways." (Thanks to TANF, he thought, black women were doing a little better than before.) Like other observers of ghetto behaviors at the time, he cited the "cool pose culture" (or the "code of the street") of irresponsible black men as something that had to be attacked both from without—via a range of public policies, especially early childhood interventions—and from within, that is, by blacks themselves.

By no means have all who concern themselves with racial issues accepted Patterson's arguments about the long-range impact of slavery (or about the possible virtues of TANF). Indeed, because the intergenerational transmission of this impact remains extremely hard to document, debates over the reasons for the woes of families in the ghettos continue to exist. Many civil rights activists and liberal scholars still insist that the roots of inner-city black problems do not for the most part lie in slavery and Jim Crow but instead—as Gutman and others had maintained—mainly in relatively recent external forces such as mass urbanization and deindustrialization.

Scholars also continue to debate the role of culture in explaining the depth and persistence of black poverty. In 2009, William Julius Wilson observed that it is "not helpful to speak of an African-American culture that differs from an Asian culture or Anglo-American culture in the study of racial differences in poverty." "Cultural frames," he points out, "are necessary but not sufficient explanations for behavior. . . . The relative importance of the combination of cultural continuity and contemporary socio-economic factors in accounting for black family patterns remains an open question that can best be answered through careful empirical research."[13] Other scholars, too, have questioned interpretations that highlight long-range historical forces. If cultural legacies from slavery are the prime villains, why have the most rapid increases in black out-of-wedlock births occurred in the relatively recent past?

William Julius Wilson is nonetheless among many scholars who agree today that cultural sources of black family ills, inextricably intertwined as they have been with contemporary structural obstacles, cannot be omitted from explanations of ghetto behavior. He has also distanced himself from Gutman's interpretation of the legacy of slavery. Cultural matters, he has insisted, mediate the impact of economic forces and create an "interplay" that resembles a "chain of cumulative causation."

Moreover, there is no doubting Patterson's point that bitter gender relations dividing African American men and women have a considerable history. Michele Wallace, a black feminist, has argued, "There was between the black man and the black woman a misunderstanding as old as slavery. . . . For perhaps the last fifty years there has been a growing distrust, even hatred between black men and black women."[14]

Finally, it is clear that the *memories* many African Americans have had of slavery, as handed down from generation to generation, continue to affect understandings of it and to shape the worldviews and burden the ambitions of many black people in the present. For all these reasons, Patterson's arguments, which have helped to inform contemporary views of African American culture, are useful reminders of the complexity of the forces that have combined to affect the behavior of African American families and that have sustained the magnitude of black family issues that continue to confound reformers.

Do these scholarly debates make a great deal of difference? After all, they never seem to end. At first glance, they may not, for as Moynihan ruefully concluded on many occasions, policymakers rarely pay serious attention to what scholars say, and they have difficulty coming up with workable solutions to the problems they do claim to understand. Moreover, as he discovered to his great regret, what scholars say can be badly misunderstood or misrepresented. Messengers must beware.

Scholars being scholars, however, the research will continue. There is always a chance that some of their findings—over time—will promote greater public understanding and reform. The stakes are large. No social issues in the United States are more pressing than the family-based problems that have long burdened and continue to trouble sizable numbers of lower-class, mostly inner-city black people.

Jeremiads about family life in the United States—regarding whites as well as blacks—peaked in the late 1990s and thereafter and reached far more people than did the debates among scholars. Many of these incantations, delivered in print and over the air, came close to prophesying that the disintegration of families threatened civilization itself in the United States.

Some of the writers who studied family trends, to be sure, urged Americans not to worry too much about them. One was Stephanie Coontz, a prolific writer about marriage and the family. Many people, she wrote, have wrongly tended to imagine that almost all Americans in earlier years had lived in a Norman Rockwell sort of world in which two loving parents had watched over a nest of contented children. Sharply rejecting such an idyllic understanding of the past, Coontz maintained that the rise of out-of-wedlock childbearing in modern times is not a terribly serious matter—just an alternative lifestyle. A "large proportion of non-marital births," she pointed out, "are to parents in stable, cohabiting relationships."[15]

Coontz was accurate in believing that millions of nostalgic Americans since the 1950s have sided with people—many of them conservative on social issues—who yearn for what they remember as the good old days. Like Moynihan, they also think Americans have "defined deviancy down." Among these writers was James Q. Wilson, who has published many essays about family issues, culminating in his book *The Marriage Problem* in 2002. Moynihan, he observed, had shown in 1965 that nearly 24 percent of black children in 1963 had been born out of wedlock; now, only four decades later, 25 percent of non-Hispanic white children were.[16]

In James Wilson's view, the source of these outcomes was what he called "habituation," a "process whereby people acquire a constant, often unconscious, way of doing something." Incentives that had helped in the past to encourage good behavior—jobs, penalties, and the like—had lost much of their power. In short, culture had changed—and not only in the United States. A worldwide cultural revolution in economically developed nations (except perhaps Japan) had taken place. It had caused large increases in violent crime, drug use, auto theft, burglary, and a host of other social problems. "We have celebrated personal freedom and individual self-expression," he wrote, "in a way that has materially reduced the social stigma attached to unwed pregnancies, drug use, and male idleness."

In this and in some of his other writing, James Wilson focused on social problems afflicting black communities. Hispanic Americans, he argued, have been much more likely than African Americans at the same income levels to search for work and to stay with it, and less likely to look to welfare as a bailout. Culture, he added, lies at the root of these and a number of other differences in the way various groups behave. Wilson reached especially pessimistic conclusions about the situation of children born into female-headed families. Except at relatively decent income levels (more than $50,000 a year), he wrote, children in families headed by never-married mothers were substantially worse off than those at the same levels living in two-parent families. They were far more likely to be suspended or expelled from school, to display emotional problems, and to engage in antisocial behavior. Wilson cited other studies showing that children from female-headed families were considerably more likely to become teenage mothers and to be idle (that is, neither attending school nor working).

Public policies, Wilson observed, had not had much effect on numbers such as these. Federal educational efforts such as compensatory education targeted at the poor or Head Start for preschool children had not done so, or at least (as in the case of Head Start) had not had staying power. Nor had military service. Though good schools were important, they took charge of children only six hours a day and half of the days in a year. Like Coleman thirty-five years earlier, Wilson suspected that only expensive, interventionist programs—perhaps group homes for the most troubled single mothers and their children—might have much of a chance of lessening the perils of the street that damaged the life chances of children in these families.

Insofar as black families were concerned, Wilson's view resembled Patterson's: a key source of their difficulties stemmed from the be-cool behavior of lower-class black *men*, too many of whom fathered children with women they had no intention of marrying. The result, of course, was ever increasing numbers of poor and fatherless families. Trying to enforce child-support payments, Wilson insisted, would not accomplish much—too many of these men were idle or unemployed and had little money. The key, he hypothesized, might lie in trying to socialize the men. Wilson hoped that local, private efforts might improve matters somewhat. He also believed it was best for single mothers with young children to stay in the home. In all, however, his portrait of lower-class black family life was grim about the present and pessimistic about the future.

Wilson's gloomy reflections were by no means the only such forecasts offered in the late 1990s and early 2000s. In 1999, two widely noted books—each by a well-known social conservative—also bewailed trends in U.S. family life. Their titles made it evident all was not well: *One Nation, Two Cultures* (by Gertrude Himmelfarb) and *The Great Disruption: Human Nature and the Reconstitution of Social Order* (by Francis Fukuyama). Both drew upon the work of conservatives such as David Popenoe and David Blankenhorn. Fukuyama, who speculated that the severity of social problems in the United States might have bottomed out in the early 1990s, was a little less pessimistic about contemporary U.S. culture than Himmelfarb. But he, too, focused on declines in family life. Like Wilson, he offered statistical evidence showing that family breakup and single parenting were strongly associated with high rates of domestic violence, crime, and school dropout. Indeed, Fukuyama maintained, family breakdown was not only associated with poverty but was all too often the cause of it. The sexual revolution, he added, had led to liberation *from* marriage. He lamented the fact, as he saw it, that the state had "usurped some of the functions of the family."[17]

It was often observed in the 1990s that the writings of Moynihan had helped to influence conservative argumentation such as this. Indeed they had, though his prescriptions for change had always been very different. In his famous

1965 report, Moynihan had opened a trail that traditionalists were following three decades later. He had maintained, for instance, that children from fatherless homes "seek immediate gratification of their desires far more than children with fathers present," and that "children who hunger for immediate gratification are more prone to delinquency, along with other less social behavior." James Wilson regularly credited Moynihan, his friend, with having drawn public attention to such matters. Fukuyama did, too, stating flatly, "Nearly thirty-five years later, Moynihan has been vindicated."

A black critic of contemporary family life, John McWhorter, also emerged on the scene in the early 2000s. In his pointedly titled *Losing the Race: Self-Sabotage in Black America* (2000), McWhorter elaborated on criticisms of black behavior that black spokespeople such as Eleanor Holmes Norton and Glenn Loury had dared raise in the 1980s. He focused especially on what he considered the excesses of self-appointed African American leaders, some of whom were "sensationalist cultural demagogues." Blacks, he added, "sabotaged" themselves by following racial chauvinists who championed three self-defeating "cults": separatism, victimology (a theme Shelby Steele had emphasized), and anti-intellectualism. These, according to McWhorter, were causing African Americans to "lose the race." He asked, why should blacks honor men like O. J. Simpson or Rodney King instead of truly accomplished representatives of the race such as Louis Armstrong, Paul Robeson, Condoleezza Rice, or W. E. B. Du Bois?

McWhorter then turned to President Johnson's speech at Howard University in 1965. Johnson, he wrote, had been right to say at that time, "You do not take a person who, for years, has been hobbled by chains and liberate him, bring him up to the starting line of a race and then say, 'you are free to compete with all the others,' and still justly believe that you have been completely fair." But, McWhorter added, millions of middle-class blacks had proved since 1965 that they could compete: affirmative action had outlived its usefulness.[18]

The "cult of anti-intellectualism" especially riled McWhorter. The children of various immigrant groups (as Moynihan often had, McWhorter mentioned the Chinese and Jews) had taken advantage of their opportunity to learn. Not so blacks, too many of whom believed that excelling in school was "white." He cited information released by the National Center for Education Statistics that the mean SAT score in 1995 of black students from families earning

$50,000 or more per year was 849 (of a top score of 1,600). At the same time, the mean score for whites from families earning less than $10,000 was 869.

Writing in 2002, James Q. Wilson observed that the changes damaging family life in the United States had been "revolutionary." Like Moynihan, Patterson, and many others, he recognized that cultural damage from slavery and segregation, savage though it had been, had not greatly afflicted all black people: roughly half of African Americans, displaying considerable ambition and talent, had risen into the middle classes. Those who married were especially likely to do well: the income of married black people was nearly as high as it was for married white people of the same age. This was a group of African Americans "for whom the legacy of slavery has been overcome."

But, Wilson continued, only one-third of black men and women aged twenty-five to forty-four were married (compared with two-thirds of white people of that age). Many of the rest, cohabiting or living without partners, were likely to have dropped out of school and/or to exhibit a broad range of deviant behaviors, including domestic violence and crime. Huge numbers of young black men were in prison—many of them because of punitive approaches to drug control—or on parole or probation. The proportion of nonmarital births among blacks, around 70 percent, had remained extraordinarily high.

Wilson then dared answer with a degree of precision a question that had generally seemed largely unanswerable in any quantitative ways: Was poverty the basic cause of serious behavioral problems? In his estimation, poverty by itself accounted for half the difference in how a child behaves. "The rest is explained by living in a one-parent family." This perspective revealed at once a main concern of welfare reformers in 1996 and of contemporary conservative thought, including a great many jeremiads. It was also a logical conclusion to be drawn from research that had followed Moynihan's seminal report of 1965.

CHAPTER 10

Families in the Early 2000s

Following passage of welfare "reform" in 1996, Moynihan continued to concern himself with many of the domestic and international issues, including family matters, that engaged the U.S. Senate. But conservative Republicans maintained control of both houses of Congress, and it was clear to him that the guidelines and provisions of TANF, which he detested, would remain a part of American social welfare policy. In 1999, having served nearly twenty-four years in the Senate, he turned seventy-two, and he chose not to run for reelection in 2000. As his successor, he endorsed Hillary Rodham Clinton.

Bill Clinton, putting aside past differences, awarded him a Presidential Medal of Freedom in 2000 (an honor Moynihan had helped to establish during the Kennedy administration). Pat and Liz, their children grown, sold their property in upstate New York in 2001 and lived in the roomy ninth-floor apartment on Pennsylvania Avenue into which they had moved ten years earlier. Most mornings, he walked along the avenue to his office at the Woodrow Wilson International Center for Scholars, whose research activities and conferences he had long encouraged. In 2002, he received an honorary degree from Harvard—the last of sixty-five during his lifetime. It was a satisfying retirement.

In 2002, Moynihan was also the keynote speaker at a major conference on the subject of family life. Focused on dramatic international developments that were becoming a subject of widening concern to scholars and policymakers alike, the meeting took place in October at the Maxwell School of Citizenship and Public Affairs of Syracuse University. That was where more than forty years earlier he had completed his doctoral thesis and his history of the gubernatorial administration of Averell Harriman of New York, and where he had been named a professor.

Among the well-known scholarly conferees were Lee Rainwater, celebrated for his writing about blacks and family matters, including an incisive evaluation of the Moynihan Report; Timothy Smeeding, a prolific author of papers and books on international aspects of poverty and social policies; Isabel Sawhill, a Brookings Institution researcher on poverty and related concerns; Christopher Jencks, who among other things had studied the underclasses and social policies; David Ellwood, Clinton's aide during the struggle for welfare reform in the mid-1990s; Sara McLanahan, a sociologist who had written studies of single-parent families; and others with expertise concerning families and social programs.[1]

Moynihan's talk set a somber tone for much that followed at the conference. As he had done previously, he lamented that the proportion of children born out of wedlock had been growing rapidly not only in the United States but also in many other nations of the West. Noting the rapid rise of cohabitation, he agreed that statistics on nonmarital births should take into account that many unmarried parents remained in consensual unions at least until their children were born. This was indeed the case: by the 1990s, more than 40 percent of nonmarital births (most of them white) and 14 percent of all births in the United States were to cohabiting couples. But Moynihan was hardly happy about the situation, for he recognized that most of these unions did not last. Roughly half of them dissolved within eighteen months. In the United States, he said, "it seems that cohabitation is neither stable nor long-term."[2]

His talk then dwelt on three points: that the rise in fatherless families had seriously disadvantaged children, that silence about the issue remained pervasive, and that social science seemed inadequate to the task of confronting the problems of black family life.

Moynihan's concern about fatherlessness was hardly controversial. Scholars such as McLanahan, relying on social research accumulated over decades, had carefully documented the fact that most children raised by two biological parents had better childhoods and better chances in life. To support his case, Moynihan cited Coleman, "that giant of his age" who in 1982 had observed, "The process of making human beings human is breaking down in American society." Coleman had then asked if ours could be "the first species to forget how to appropriately raise its young." Moynihan followed by quoting what he called James Q. Wilson's "magisterial summation" of family issues in 2002. "For two nations to become one again," Wilson maintained, "marriage must become more common. Many Americans wish this, but despite some encouraging trends, history is marching in a different direction."

What could the United States or any other nation do about these trends? Moynihan reminded his listeners of what he had written in *Family and Nation* in 1986, in which he had asked what the role of culture was in changing societies. Moynihan explained, "The central conservative truth is that it is culture, not politics, which determines the success of a society. The central liberal truth is that politics can change a culture and save it from itself."

Moynihan's second main point exposed his profound unhappiness about the painful silence regarding black family issues that descended following the Watts Riot and release of his report in 1965. He bemoaned the fact that LBJ's great speech at Howard University, which had "thrilled" everyone at the time, got lost in the recriminations and misrepresentations that followed. The silence had endured. As Moynihan said regretfully, "Academics for a long time have been unwilling to write about the racial dimensions of this issue. In three decades since out-of-wedlock childbearing has exploded, there has not, to my knowledge, been a single book, book review, paper, whatever, that has definitively addressed the racial dimensions of this change."[3]

Moynihan's final point—one that he had often expressed earlier—was at once thoughtful and sad, given his lifelong interest in family issues. He lamented that social science had failed to explain fully the massive changes affecting family life in the Western world. No one, he said, really knew how to arrest these trends. As in the past, he cited what sociologists referred to as Rossi's "Iron Law of Evaluation," as it had been offered by the sociologist Peter Rossi in 1978: "The expected value for any measured effect of a social program is zero."[4]

"We are nowhere near a general theory of family change," Moynihan asserted. "And there we shall leave it," he said, "the question still standing: who indeed can tell us what happened to the American family?"

The picture of family life that other conferees presented elaborated upon views such as Moynihan's. Because it placed his observations in an international perspective, it was also unsettling.

As the presentations revealed, the proportions of births to unmarried women since the 1960s had risen substantially throughout thirty-one nations in the West. Except in Iceland, an outlier where the proportion of such births had been 25 percent in 1960, these numbers had been 10 percent or lower at that time. Statistics also indicated that the proportions of such births by the late 1990s were higher in several Western nations than they were in the United States. Iceland led the developed world in this regard, as it had done throughout the previous forty years. By the late 1990s, more than 60 percent of births there were nonmarital.

The proportions of nonmarital births in Denmark, Sweden, Norway, the former East Germany, and Estonia had increased considerably in recent years. These hovered near 50 percent in the late 1990s. A host of nations had proportions that clustered at a little over 30 percent. These included the United States, Austria, Canada, Finland, France, the United Kingdom, Bulgaria, Latvia, and Slovenia. Slightly lower, in the mid- to high 20 percent range, were the proportions in Ireland, Portugal, Hungary, and the Russian Federation. Increases in out-of-wedlock births in twelve Western nations—Greece, Italy, Luxembourg, the Netherlands, Spain, Switzerland, West Germany, Croatia, the Czech Republic, Lithuania, Poland, and the Slovak Republic— had been relatively slight over the years. All seven had proportions near 15 percent in the late 1990s.

Americans might have derived a few flickers of consolation from looking at these numbers. As the conference summary indicated, "The phenomenon [of out-of-wedlock births] . . . is common among Western countries. By the turn of the twenty-first century, fourteen had rates nearly as high as or considerably higher than the United States, and four others were not far behind." Increases in nonmarital births in the United States, moreover, though considerable over the years (from 5 percent of all births in 1960 to 18 percent in 1980, 28 percent in 1990, and 33.2 percent by 2000), had tapered off as of the mid-1990s, whereas the increases in other nations (excepting Iceland, Denmark, and Sweden) seemed to be continuing.

Still, it was evident Americans had little to brag about. The United States still had the highest divorce rates in the industrialized world. Roughly half of all U.S. marriages ultimately failed. Cohabiting couples in Sweden were more likely to stay together than married couples in the United States. Moreover, vast differences remained between black and white families in the United

States. As of 1995, despite the existence of more effective and more accepted forms of birth control, 45 percent of African American women aged fifteen to forty-four had experienced at least one nonmarital birth—compared with 10 percent among white women and 22 percent among Hispanic women in that age range.

Figures as of 2002 concerning out-of-wedlock births in the United States were indeed discouraging. Though birthrates among teenagers had declined since 1991—a heartening development—they remained higher in the United States than in any other industrial nation. As earlier, the vast majority of these births were out of wedlock. Nonmarital birth ratios among unmarried women in their twenties and thirties, moreover, had continued to increase. More than 70 percent of nonmarital births in the United States in the late 1990s were to women twenty or older. Roughly half of these nonmarital births were second- or higher-order births, and one-quarter of them were third- or higher-order. Statistics such as these made it clear a good deal of out-of-wedlock childbearing in the United States was the result of sexual behavior among people who had already experienced the vicissitudes of childrearing outside of marriage.[5]

Racial differences in the United States in nonmarital childbearing remained glaring. The proportion of out-of-wedlock births among non-Hispanic whites in the United States, having risen steadily over the years (from 2 percent in 1960 to 11 percent in 1980 and to 20 percent in 1990), was still increasing rapidly—it had reached 25 percent in 1995. The much higher proportion among non-Hispanic African Americans (which had jumped from 23.6 percent in 1963—the figure Moynihan cited in 1965—to 70 percent in 1995) had temporarily stabilized between 1995 and 2002 at between 68 and 70 percent, partly (perhaps) because the economy was booming at that time. At any rate, it remained higher than the overall percentage in any other Western country. Demographers, moreover, also estimated that percentages of all nonmarital *first* births in the United States rose between the early 1970s and early 1990s from 15 percent to 33 percent for white women, but from 59 percent to 81 percent for black women. Statistics concerning out-of-wedlock second- and higher-order births were also stunning. These revealed that the proportion of second- or higher-order nonmarital births in these same years rose from 43 percent to 47 percent for white women and from 44 percent to 59 percent for black women.[6]

Consensual unions, moreover, were considerably more common in other developed nations, where more than half of the children born out of marriage were generally living with cohabiting parents, than they were in the United States. Indeed, the United States was the only such nation with more children living in single-mother families than in cohabiting ones. The percentage of U.S. children living with both biological parents was a little below 50 percent. By contrast, two-thirds of fifteen-year-olds in Sweden, France, Austria, and Germany lived with their biological parents. As the conference reported, the United States had "far and away the highest proportion of children who live apart from one or both biological parents before reaching adulthood."

The scholars at the conference added to the force of these numbers by reporting not only that cohabiting relationships tended to be exceptionally fragile in the United States but also that the poverty rate of these cohabiting couples was twice as high as that among married couples. Parents in these unions were less likely than married people to receive help from friends or relatives. It was for these and other reasons that the unions were less enduring in the United States than in other nations and that the percentage of fifteen-year-old U.S. children who lived with one or no biological parent was so high.

Those discussing the issue in 2002, just as Moynihan and many others had in decades past, dwelt on the close relationship between poverty and single parenthood. This connection remained strong—single-parent families were roughly five times more likely to be poor than two-parent families. Ellwood and Jencks reported that in 1964, single mothers had headed 30 percent of poor families with children in the United States, a proportion that jumped by the late 1970s to 60 percent before leveling off. Some 51 percent of children in female-headed families in 2000, they reported, were poor—a percentage that although only slightly higher than those in a few developed nations—Germany, Australia, and Canada—was considerably greater than those in the other nations under study.

Smeeding and Rainwater, who focused on economic matters, emphasized also that the U.S. government definition of poverty differed from those in other developed nations. The United States used absolute income standards ("lines") to measure poverty, whereas other nations used a relative concept. This approach revealed the extent of inequality: to be poor was to live in a family whose income was less than one-half of the median family income for a family of the same size. To be "extremely poor" was to live in a family that had less than 30 percent of median family income. In the United States, they wrote, more than 50 percent of the children living in impoverished single-mother homes were "extremely poor." By contrast, fewer than 5 percent of children in such families in Sweden, Denmark, Finland, Norway, France, and Belgium fit this definition. Smeeding and Rainwater wrote, "The poverty gap of the children of American single mothers is so great that even in countries with much lower 'average' real incomes, their single-mother children fare better in real comparable U.S. dollar terms."

Children in the United States were indeed at risk. Given the greater prevalence of poverty among American children (which conferees placed at 22 percent overall as opposed to an average of 12 percent in other developed nations), it was hardly surprising the researchers were distressed. As in earlier studies, they emphasized that children growing up in impoverished single-parent families were far more likely than those in two-parent families to exhibit high dropout rates, low scores on educational achievement tests, high rates of teen pregnancy, significant problems with personal health and emotional development, high rates of criminal activity, and idleness and unemployment in early adulthood.

In accounting for such trends, Ellwood and Jencks (like many others in the past) stressed the importance of education (and therefore of class)—women with relatively low levels of schooling were much more likely to become single mothers than those who had finished high school. These better-educated young mothers had grown up in what Kay Hymowitz, a knowledgeable authority on family issues, called a "marriage-before-children" culture. Other scholars also continued to report unsettling intergenerational developments. Paul Barton, who was still charting social trends, had recently observed that fourteen- to fifteen-year-olds raised in families receiving public assistance were six times more likely to end up relying upon it in their mid-twenties than were their counterparts who had not been on welfare.[7]

Echoing the conclusions of liberal social scientists in earlier years, the conferees found the United States, though an especially affluent society, remiss in its social safety net. In the 1980s and 1990s, they reported, the nation spent a far smaller percentage of its gross domestic product (GDP) on social welfare for its nonelderly population than did other developed nations. This proportion had then fluctuated between 3 and 4 percent of GDP compared with percentages of between 12 and 15 percent in the most generous Nordic nations of Europe. "Anglo" nations—the United Kingdom, Australia, and Canada—averaged between 5 and 8 percent. The relatively poor nations of southern Europe had set aside funding of around 6 percent during these years. Government transfer payments helped pull an estimated 75 to 90 percent of people out of poverty in the Nordic nations (and in Belgium and Switzerland) compared to 50 percent in Spain, the United Kingdom, and France, but to only 25 percent (the lowest among developed countries) in the United States.

This led to a point Moynihan had harped on for more than forty years: in 2002, most developed nations except the United States offered some form of family allowances. These were generally provided for all families with children, and tended to increase family incomes by around 10 percent. The United States offered refundable tax credits to families with children, but these, of course, went only to parents that earned enough to pay income taxes. Because many low-income American families did not owe income tax, it was estimated that one-third of poor children in the United States lived in families that did not receive these credits.

Yet another difference distinguished low-income female-headed families in the United States from those in most other nations: the availability of work for mothers. A higher percentage of women heading families in many other countries were employed at relatively secure jobs in the social service sector. In the United States, however, the TANF system established in 1996 was still in force. Although many mothers receiving welfare had joined the workforce after 1996, few had found well-paying jobs. As the conference report put it, "Child poverty in the United States is a product of both low wages and a low level of social support."

What were the reasons for the considerable increases in the proportions of nonmarital births, especially of African American births, in the United States? It is hardly surprising that this question, which the Moynihan Report had been important in raising, elicited varied answers.

One explanation, of course, was that economic forces, especially high unemployment among black men, were the key. Moynihan had emphasized the problem of unemployment above all else in 1965, as had many other liberals in later years. In 1987, William Julius Wilson had highlighted the economic burdens that had rendered low-income black men unmarriageable in the eyes of women. As earlier, however, many of those at the meeting in 2002 were not sure the answers stopped there. Ellwood and Jencks reiterated their earlier argument that the deterioration of job opportunities for men had only a modest effect on the decline of marriage and increased single parenthood in the United States. Other conferees, although well aware of the difficulties involved in generalizing about popular values or attitudes, drew special attention to cultural developments. One conferee, pointing to a major trend since the 1960s, attributed increases in nonmarital births to "changes in norms regarding marriage and childbearing," with the rise of the women's movement and female employment playing especially strong roles. Others believed that the availability of the pill, along with newer and effective forms of birth control, and of abortion had weakened the link between marriage and childbearing.

Barton, asked by Moynihan after the conference to submit his thoughts, replied with a list of causal factors, most of which were cultural in nature, that had reduced marriage rates and led to rising numbers of fatherless and poverty-stricken families. These included "decline of religious participation," "growing wealth in general, which permits more choices," "gender equality with its concomitant increase in earnings independence," "the decline of community and neighborhood, where social opinion of marital and family behavior was the enforcer of the social code," "a more compassionate society, with the means and the desire to step in and support children when they are not claimed by the father," and "last but not least, the pill, which cut down on shotgun marriages."

Jencks gave yet another answer to the question of what happened to the family:

> I think this question is the right one, and . . . I obviously don't know the answer, but . . . if I have to answer it I would say the biggest factor was more widespread cultural acceptance of two ideals: "tolerance" and "personal freedom." These ideals made most Americans and Western Europeans less willing to treat sex, childbearing, and marriage as matters of right and wrong. I think that was probably progress, though I sometimes have my doubts. Still, progress is seldom a free lunch.

How, then, should policymakers try to cope with these discouraging aspects of family structure? Dealing with this long-contested question, the experts followed Moynihan in admitting social science did not have all the answers.

After all, the formidable economic obstacles to stable marriage seemed likely to endure, as did the broad-based cultural developments. Because Congress did not normally fund careful evaluations of social programs, policymakers often had to shoot in the dark.

Nevertheless, in looking at strategies to ameliorate harmful economic forces, most of the conferees expressed a preference for work-based approaches to income support over welfare-based ones: a more generous version of the 1996 welfare reform, they believed, would be better than the flawed old system that mainly distributed relief checks to people. Others recommended hikes in the minimum wage as well as further expansion of the EITC program and of child-care tax credits. Isabel Sawhill and Will Marshall, seeking preventive strategies that would help young children, championed creation of a universal system of early learning that would include all four-year-olds and an increasing number of three-year-olds as well as a nationwide system of paid parental leave.

Ellwood and Jencks, however, professed that a policy morass existed, and that they (like Moynihan) were not entirely sure what would help stabilize or reverse long-range trends in family structure. They used the weather as an analogy: "We understand the weather far better than we used to, after all, but while better understanding has produced better forecasts, it has not produced better weather." They added, "For those who want to alter family structure, we can offer only one bit of advice: treat anyone who claims to know how to do this with a high degree of skepticism."

As for the huge racial disparities that sparked endless disagreements among scholars and activists over the decades, the experts at the conference were careful not to blame the victim. But they also avoided singling out white racism as the villain. Instead, they conceded that the reasons for the disparities were complicated and hard to pin down. Ellwood and Jencks admitted they could not "entirely explain why racial differences have grown so large." Ellwood observed that the lack of explanation for changes in family structure is "perhaps the greatest embarrassment of social science in recent times."

Having displayed their modesty, Ellwood and Jencks then suggested a few liberal economic policies that might help. These were familiar; they made no miraculous discoveries. One was for government to improve job opportunities for less skilled men. A second was to do the same for less skilled women, though this, they added, would have "more ambiguous effects." (By this comment they may have intended to say two things—first, that working single mothers would have less time and energy to tend to the needs of their young children and, second, that some of the jobs taken by unskilled women might otherwise have been available for unskilled men.) A third was to offer better support for low-income, two-parent families, such as more generous tax credits, child-care subsidies, and health insurance.

Comments such as these, a little sketchy about specifics, indicated that although most scholars continued to endorse Moynihan's general views concerning the causes and effects of lower-class family problems, further research would be necessary. It was also evident that the forty-year-old struggle to enact significant public policies to help blacks living in poverty would go on.

While this conference was taking place, important field research into the situations and aspirations of 162 low-income single mothers in Camden, New Jersey, and Philadelphia, Pennsylvania, was being done. Building on other studies of inner-city women conducted in the previous few years, the results supplied a level of specificity to theories about the behavior of low-income women that generalizations could not. It thus offered plausible answers to a major question that had bothered many experts over the years: Why were so many low-income women, especially black women, having children out of marriage?

Summarizing the results in a book, *Promises I Can Keep: Why Poor Women Put Motherhood Before Marriage* (2005), the researchers, Kathryn Edin and Maria Kefalas, stated modestly that they did not have all the answers. "The reasons [for the 'growing rarity of marriage among the poor'] remain largely a mystery—perhaps the biggest demographic mystery of the last half of the twentieth century."[8]

Yet, having conceded their bewilderment, Edin and Kefalas went on to supply some provisional answers. They began by outlining three hypotheses that had sought to explain why so many pregnant young women declined to marry. The first was the rise of women's participation in the workforce—more women could now afford to go it alone. The second—Charles Murray's—blamed the tempting but perverse availability of welfare. The third, based on the still-influential work of William Julius Wilson, maintained that structural flaws in the economy—notably deindustrialization since World War II—had increased unemployment among black men and created a shortage of marriageable males.

Neither of the first two hypotheses, they concluded, was persuasive. As their research showed, women who received relatively decent wages from work were more, rather than less, likely to marry. Furthermore, arguments such as Murray's failed to acknowledge that the real value of welfare had declined substantially between the 1970s and early 1990s—years when nonmarital childbirth was rapidly increasing.[9] The authors were partial to Wilson's explanation—the marriageability of men, they agreed, mattered a lot to the women—but went on to say (as others had) that "gigantic" alterations in family structure among the poor had "dwarfed" the economic forces Wilson had emphasized.[10] Other forces must also be at work.

Their ground-level focus on how these other forces affected the thinking and decisions of low-income women—a subject about which Moynihan's report of 1965 had little to say—was most useful in advancing research. To account for what had happened, the authors emphasized the importance of "profound cultural changes" over the decades since 1965. These changes, they wrote, had caused "views about virtually all aspects of family life" to shift "dramatically to the left." As a result, "having sex, establishing a common household, and having children have all become decoupled from marriage." The shift had "weakened the once nearly absolute cultural imperative to marry." In acting as they did, low-income women were not deviant. They were merely adopting the far more liberal "mainstream norms about marriage" that had greatly weakened once-strong stigmas concerning sexual and family life.

In the 1950s, Edin and Kefalas wrote, poor women were likely to marry even if their prospective husbands were working in unstable or low-paying jobs. Since that time, however, women had forged a "new definition of men," and their criteria for marrying had changed. The low-income women they studied regularly rejected marriage even to men who had impregnated them and had stable employment.

This did not mean, however, that the women disparaged the value of marriage as an institution. On the contrary, they strongly embraced middle-class dreams of marriage and upward mobility. As the authors put it, they envisioned living with a husband in a house with a white picket fence. Edin and Kefalas added, "The vast majority of poor, unmarried new parents say they plan to marry each other." Some of the parents cohabited, though usually for only a while.

As the book's subtitle (*Why Poor Mothers Put Motherhood Before Marriage*) indicated, the women in their study desired above all to have children. This finding—that mothering was more important to them than marriage, education, or career—was not new, but it was especially well documented by Edin and Kefalas. It indicated that any approach to dealing with problems caused by out-of-wedlock childbearing had to understand how the women—who were not just pawns swept up in vast impersonal forces—looked at things. Childlessness, the women thought, was "one of the greatest tragedies in life." Having kids was an "absolutely essential part of a young woman's life, the chief source of identity and meaning." The women see an out-of-wedlock birth not as a "mark of personal failure, but instead regard it as an act of valor." A baby "represents an opportunity to prove one's worth. The real tragedy, these women insist, is a woman who's missed her chance to have children."

The single mothers they studied, Edin and Kefalas emphasized, were ill educated. Roughly half of them had not finished high school before becoming pregnant. While being courted, they had generally loved their suitors. But they had become pregnant while experiencing "romantic relationships that proceed at lightning speed—where a man woos a woman with the line, 'I want to have a baby by you,' and she views it as high praise." Believing, however, that marriage should be stable and enduring, they recognized that the men who had impregnated them were likely to be unreliable. Even if a man offered to marry them—which most did not, for the men viewed marriage as tying them down—the mother-to-be was likely to settle for cohabitation (which some of the men were willing to try, though in most cases only for a while) or to go it alone.

The women, moreover, had ample reason for choosing to stay single. Half of the fathers lacked a high school diploma, a quarter did not have a job, and 40 percent ended up in jail or prison by the time the baby was born. As the authors explained, the women "believe it is better to have children outside of marriage than to marry unwisely only to get divorced later." Getting divorced from a man on whom they had become dependent, they thought, would leave them with "nothing."

The women also had great confidence in their ability to handle motherhood alone. They "believe the central tenet of good mothering can be summed up in two words—being there." But just "being there" was sadly shortsighted. As the authors phrased it in a memorable passage, the mothers "take great pride in having enough Pampers to diaper an infant, in potty-training a two-year-old and teaching her to eat with a spoon, in getting a grade-schooler to and from school safely, in satisfying the ravenous appetite of a growing teenager, and in keeping the light on to welcome a prodigal adolescent back home."

Did low-income African American women think and act differently from other low-income women? Not really—a conclusion that suggested (as William Julius Wilson later maintained) the power of color-blind structural forces. The authors, recognizing that the black women were especially doubtful marriage would work, found that they were less likely than the white women to marry or to cohabit. Though the black women were more likely than other women to oppose divorce, they also had higher rates of divorce. Their "*attitudes*" and "*worldviews*," however, were similar.[11] All of the women placed motherhood before marriage.

In their discussion of remedies, the authors began by dismissing as unhelpful the efforts of many conservative activists, and of the George W. Bush administration, to get more people to marry. This was unrealistic. What was needed (and here they returned to Wilson's remarks about marriageable men) were programs that would enable men to develop better skills and to find living-wage jobs.

Edin and Kefalas also highlighted the importance of helping low-income girls early on. Well-designed programs already in existence, they said, had managed in some places to reduce teen pregnancy, mainly by providing girls with meaningful after-school activity. These programs cost between $1,000 and $4,000 per year per teen. It was also necessary, however, to help young women develop the skills that would enable them to find living-wage jobs. A basic problem harming the women, they emphasized, was poverty. Under TANF, they added, roughly half of American women who had left welfare were still poor, and nearly six out of ten had no job. One-seventh of them had no visible means of support.

While Edin and Kefalas were finishing their fieldwork in the early 2000s, the U.S. economy was slowly recovering from an economic downturn that had sharpened social distress. The upturn, though modest, was encouraging. But if a recession were to occur, they prophesied, the already dismal plight of low-income families in the inner cities would become even more wretched.

Their concerns were merited. When an economic crisis of staggering proportions battered the nation in 2008, it devastated low-skilled, low-income people, especially black people, most of all.

Efforts to build on recommendations such as those the conferees at Syracuse—and Edin and Kefalas—developed, however, had to go forward without the assistance of Moynihan. Indeed, his keynote in October 2002 proved his last major public utterance on the subject of family life. Five months afterward he suffered a ruptured appendix. Subsequent complications led to his death fifteen days later, on March 26, at a Washington, D.C., hospital. He was seventy-six years old. At his funeral, in his crowded Catholic church in downtown Washington, a host of friends, former staffers, leaders from both parties, journalists, and scholars convened to pay their respects. An avalanche of admiring obituaries and editorials followed, many of which hailed his lifelong efforts on behalf of the black poor. He was buried at Arlington National Cemetery.

CHAPTER 11

From Cosby to Obama

M ay 17, 2004, was the fiftieth anniversary of the Supreme Court's unan-imous decision, *Brown v. Board of Education*, which ruled against man-dated racial segregation in U.S. public schools. To commemorate that great day, the NAACP invited Bill Cosby to deliver a major address at Constitution Hall in Washington, D.C. Some 3,000 people attended. Many, representing the elite of the black community, dressed formally.

What the celebrants had hoped to hear from Cosby is hard to say. Funny stories, maybe. What they got was an angry enumeration of all manner of misbehaviors by lower-class black people and a stern admonition that black parents and community leaders should assume greater responsibility for im-proving the situation. Too many of the young, Cosby declared, "have done nothing since they dropped out of school other than a little hustling and a little welfare." "Fifty percent drop-out rate," he complained, ". . . and people in jail, and women having children by five, six different men. Under what ex-cuse?" "Pretty soon you're going to have to have DNA cards so you can tell who you're making love to . . . you could have sex with your grandmother . . . you keep these numbers coming, I'm just predicting." He raised his voice, "You can't keep asking that God will find a way. God is tired of you."[1]

Cosby's recitation of black community ills focused on the deterioration of lower-class family life, much of it rooted in the rise of out-of-wedlock child-bearing. "We cannot blame white people," he said. "It's not what they're doing. It's what we are doing. Look, we're raising our own ingrown immigrants. These people are fighting hard to be ignorant. . . . They've grown angry and they have pistols and they do stupid things." Black parents, he said, used to be tough with their kids about crime and sex. But they were not tough anymore because so many fathers had abandoned the mothers and their children. "Parenting works best," he emphasized, "when both a mother and a father participate. Some mothers can do it on their own, but they need help. A house without a father is a challenge. A neighborhood without fathers is a catastrophe, and that's just about what we have today."

By blaming more than explaining, Cosby stunned many of his listeners. At first, they listened nervously. As one later exclaimed, "He hung out our dirty laundry to dry." Roger Wilkins, a historian and black civil rights activist, noted later, "He brought the skunk in." But as Cosby's voice rose, people began to offer up shouts of "Amen" and applause. When he finished, most of the audience gave him a standing ovation. Unlike Moynihan, he was, after all, one of them—a messenger of color. Kweisi Mfumi, executive director of the NAACP, explained the reactions: "A lot of people didn't want him to say what he said because it was an open forum. But if the truth be told, he was on target."[2]

Indeed he was, at least insofar as staggering statistics documenting out-of-wedlock childbearing were concerned. Increases in the proportions of such births, having leveled off between 1998 and 2002, resumed with a vengeance during the next few years. In 2007, 4,317,000 babies were born in the United States. This broke a record set in 1957 at the peak of the baby boom that had followed World War II.[3] A total of 1,714,643 of these, or a record 39.7 percent of all births, were to unmarried women. That was almost 2.6 times the number (665,747) and more than double the proportion (18.4 percent) of nonmarital births reported in 1980. The number in 2007 was an astonishing 26 percent higher than it had been—1,365,966—in 2002. In 2007, the United States ranked seventh highest in the industrialized world in statistics indicating the proportions of babies born out of wedlock. This was eleven places higher than it had stood in 1980.[4]

Key demographic developments that had been powerful since the early 1960s—notably ongoing declines in marriage and higher birthrates among unmarried women—helped explain the increases in nonmarital births.[5] Ascending birthrates among unmarried women rose after 2002 among all ethnic groups and were greatest in 2006 among Hispanics at 106 births per 1,000 unmarried women aged fifteen to forty-four, next highest among blacks at 72 per 1,000, and relatively low among non-Hispanic whites at 32 per 1,000. The overall birthrate among unmarried women in 2007, at 52.9 births per 1,000 unmarried women aged fifteen to forty-four, was 21 percent higher than in 2002 (and 80 percent higher than in 1980).

Birthrates among unmarried teens, having fallen off between 1991 and 2006, were not driving these increases. To be sure, these rates remained high: at 42.5 births per 1,000 teenagers aged fifteen to nineteen in 2007, they were still the highest in the economically developed world. But because they had fallen between 1991 and 2006 (after which they began creeping upward again), births to unmarried teenagers represented only 23 percent of all nonmarital births in the United States in 2007, compared to 50 percent in 1970. The surge in out-of-wedlock childbearing after 2002 accelerated instead because of a trend that had strengthened in recent years: higher birthrates among slightly older unmarried women, many of whom were cohabiting with their lovers. (It was estimated in 2007 that cohabitation preceded 50 percent of all first marriages in the United States and that 40 percent of cohabiting households included children.) Between 2002 and 2007, birthrates rose by 13 percent for unmarried women aged twenty to twenty-four and by 34 percent for unmarried women aged thirty to thirty-four. In 2007, 60 percent of births to women aged twenty to twenty-four and 32.2 percent of births to women aged twenty-five to twenty-nine were nonmarital. Overall, 45 percent of births to women in their twenties in 2007 were to unmarried women.[6]

As earlier, statistics concerning race and ethnicity are arresting. In 2006, the proportions of nonmarital births were 16.5 percent for Asian and Pacific Islanders, 26.6 percent for non-Hispanic whites, 49.9 percent for Hispanics (62.4 percent for Puerto Ricans), 64.6 percent for American Indians and Alaska Natives, and 70.7 percent for non-Hispanic blacks. In that year, only 35 percent of black children lived with two married parents—compared to 76 percent of non-Hispanic white children, 66 percent of Hispanic American children, and 87 percent of Asian American children. Nine percent of black children lived with neither parent.[7]

With media accounts featuring numbers such as these, it was hardly surprising that other African Americans echoed Cosby's complaints (as did Cosby himself, in prisons and in packed town hall forums). One prominent supporter was John McWhorter, whose book *Losing the Race* had made similar points in 2000. In 2006 he wrote another book, this one titled *Winning the Race*, in which he presented a somewhat sunnier view of race relations than he had expressed six years earlier. Still, McWhorter again chastised African Americans who damaged themselves, notably young men who made no effort to find work and students—disdaining to act "white"—who deliberately failed in school. All too many young black men, he complained, cared only for basketball, rap music, and sex. Rap, McWhorter wrote, was "the most overtly and consistently misogynistic music ever produced in human history." Hip-hop culture was "anti-family, anti-education, anti-civilization, anti-decay, anti-everything else except the glorification of street life, violence, and the denigration of women."[8]

Juan Williams, an African American journalist, author, and radio and TV commentator, also bolstered the slowly growing chorus of black people who, breaking with the silences of old, were singing Cosby's praises. In 2006, he published *Enough: The Phony Leaders, Dead-End Movements, and Culture of Failure That Are Undermining Black America—and What We Can Do About It*. After citing Cosby's speech as his inspiration, Williams denounced the "deafening batch of shrill voices . . . shouting excuses for why the poor remained poor." It had become nearly impossible, he added, to improve the status of African Americans when "smart, successful black people, under the banner of racial solidarity, refuse to hold poor black people responsible for their own failures."[9]

In 2007, Cosby again made himself heard, this time more temperately than in his speech three years earlier to the NAACP. With Alvin Poussaint, a long-time collaborator active in the civil rights movement during the 1960s, he wrote a book titled *Come on, People: On the Path from Victims to Victors*, offering guidance for black parents and community leaders. Imperative headings interspersed with inspirational comments from successful black people spelled out the ways to get ahead: "give fatherhood a second chance," "claim your children," "role models, please apply," "take back the community," "keep those kids in school," "turn off the TV," "back off the rap," "chill the sex," "reinforce standard English," "reject victimhood," "take any legitimate job," "stop the violence," "lose the guns and the rage," "sister, seize the day," and "walk the walk."

Cosby and Poussaint stressed the persistence of a problem Daniel Patrick Moynihan, Orlando Patterson, and others had highlighted over the decades— the antisocial behavior of many young black males in the inner cities. Their opening chapter, "What's Going On with Black Men?" deplored their "be cool" style, which led far too many to abandon responsibility for the children they fathered. The chapter featured statistics showing that fewer than two out of six black children at that time were born into two-parent homes—as contrasted with five of six in 1950.

As their subtitle indicated, Cosby and Poussaint argued that white racism, while important, had declined and that African Americans must stop acting like victims. Government alone, they wrote, could not change dysfunctional families. In order to succeed, young people needed above all to follow simple steps: stay in school, get further training or go to college, find a job and hold it, only then marry, and don't have children unless married and over twenty-one. "The most important thing," they wrote," was "within reach of just about everyone"—"to make sure that every black child has two active parents in his or her life." If no father was present, some other male—a stepfather, godfather, uncle, or grandfather—must step in and help. They closed, *"No more excuses, no more delays. Come on, people!"*

Hectoring such as this hardly convinced everyone. Some who heard of these admonitions pointed to the heavy economic and educational burdens holding low-income blacks down—or to the desperation and confusion of many young and unskilled black parents—and continued to opine that challenges such as those of Cosby and Poussaint would accomplish little or nothing. After all, 50 percent of black students (and 57 percent of black males), heedless of repeated warnings, were dropping out of high school.

It was hardly surprising, therefore, that a number of black activists challenged Cosby's general approach, which had always been a hard sell among civil rights leaders. Some had confronted him following his animated lecture at Constitution Hall. Theodore Shaw, head of the NAACP Legal Defense and Educational Fund, Inc., complained at the time that Cosby had ignored "systemic issues of race and racism." Maya Angelou (Cosby said later) told him, "You know, Bill, you're a very nice man, but you have a big mouth." Michael Eric Dyson, a prolific author and activist, published another book, *Is Cosby Right? Or Has the Black Middle Class Lost Its Mind?* specifically to criticize

Cosby for many of his assertions. Predictable rejoinders such as these made it plain that intramural debates would persist.

Given such debates, it is hard to say if advocates like Cosby and Poussaint have made a difference for inner-city black people. While the economy was moving slowly ahead between 2004 and 2007, some evidence suggested that blacks were managing a little better than in the past. As Moynihan and others had often noted, young, married black people were fairing roughly as well as young, married white people. Census data, moreover, show that poverty rates among African Americans have declined over time—from 32.5 percent in 1980 to 29.3 percent in 1995 and to 24.7 percent in 2008.

But at any given time in 2007, some 50 percent of black children and 52 percent of Hispanic children in female-headed households were poor. And racial inequality remains sharp. The poverty rate among blacks, as earlier, is roughly three times that of non-Hispanic whites (8.6 percent in 2008) and twice that of the nation as a whole (12.5 percent). When the economy collapsed in 2008, it threw many low-income minorities out of work and raised the likelihood that more pregnant young women would not marry and that more existing partnerships would fall apart.

A host of behavioral ills, including violent crime and domestic violence, also continue to plague the black poor. In 2007, infant mortality was still more than twice as high among blacks as among whites.[10] The Centers for Disease Control reported in 2008 that one-half of African American girls between the ages of fourteen and eighteen were infected with at least one of four common sexually transmitted diseases. A study of African American high school dropouts aged sixteen to twenty-four in 2008 revealed that 69 percent were unemployed and 25 percent were in jail, prison, or juvenile detention. Female dropouts were nine times more likely than girls who had stayed in school and gone to college in 2006 or 2007 to become single mothers. During the 2008–2009 school year in Chicago, 290 shootings affected public school students, most of whom lived in heavily black neighborhoods.[11]

Arrests and convictions of young black men, especially for possession or abuse of drugs, continue to increase. Glenn Loury, having shed his conservative image, has cited U.S. Department of Justice figures showing that black children in 2008 were nine times more likely than white children to have a parent in prison. If current trends continue, he predicted, one of every three black male babies born in 2008 would see the inside of a prison cell during his lifetime. This was a percentage more than five times higher than that of white male babies.[12]

In figuring out what to do about these problems, most reformers today recognize that the powerful demographic, economic, and cultural trends that since the mid-1960s have caused the decline of marriage—and increases in the numbers and percentages of out-of-wedlock children and fatherless households—are unlikely to be reversed. Nor is it probable that the relatively high birthrates among unmarried black women will soon fall to the levels of whites. Better sex education, though desirable, is unlikely to make a large difference. Instead, most reformers hope to pursue three key strategies, none of which is either new or a magic bullet.

The first, favored in particular by conservatives (but also by people like Cosby), focuses on moderating the disruptive impulses of many low-income young black men. This effort, as Moynihan realized, is far easier said than done, for a relatively small but highly antisocial group of black men has long spread havoc in U.S. inner cities. As if shut off inside, these men seem all but immune to both carrots and sticks. Still, community activists fight the good fight, hoping that better-targeted efforts by parents and local leaders, assisted by greater public as well as private funding, will improve the life chances of those who are willing to be helped.

A second strategy—one Moynihan always favored—features pressure for liberal public social policies. One that is politically imaginable involves earned income tax credits (EITCs). Benefits under federal and state programs, which aid "deserving" low-income working families with children, have for that reason grown since the federal initiative was first approved in 1975. Congress might consider further expanding EITCs to aid more working people without children, part-time workers, or even some of the unemployed poor. Broadening of this sort would presumably increase the numbers of "marriageable" low-income men.

Many public options, however, still remain off the table. Significant liberalization of welfare, which many Americans continue to perceive as aiding the "undeserving," seems today, as since 1965, highly unlikely. Now, as earlier, low-income mothers with out-of-wedlock children, especially single black mothers, receive relatively little public sympathy. Given the federal government's monumental budget deficits, passage of anything so broad as a guaranteed annual income plan like the Family Assistance Plan (FAP)—or of large-scale public employment programs targeted at the unskilled and the jobless—also seems as remote as ever. So do major changes in the way the criminal justice system deals with the issue of drugs. And efforts to combat racial segregation in housing continue to face formidable barriers—notably the refusal of many whites (and a good many middle-class blacks) to live in proximity to the African American lower classes.

The third strategy, seeking to reach young people before it is too late, singles out education as the key to equalizing opportunity in the future. Lyndon Johnson had believed deeply in it, proclaiming in 1965 that education was the "only valid passport from poverty." So does President Barack Obama, who told the NAACP in 2009 on the occasion of its hundredth anniversary, "There is no stronger weapon against inequality and no better path to opportunity than an education that can unlock a child's God-given potential."[13]

Sharing this faith, many reformers still struggle to extend school desegregation, which when advanced in the 1970s appeared to shrink black-white test-score gaps. This is a campaign, however, that confronts opposition in predominantly white communities, much of it aided by decisions of the Supreme Court, and that therefore has dim political prospects. Reformers of U.S. education, including many black community leaders, understandably concentrate instead today on waging more practical campaigns: getting good teachers assigned to schools in minority neighborhoods, seeking better funding for curricular enrichment at all levels of schooling, establishing summer and after-school programs trying to improve child health and social development, and raising academic standards.

Promising initiatives to strengthen inner-city schools have expanded in recent years. The Teach for America program, begun in 1990, has grown steadily. For the 2009–2010 school year, it enlisted a total of 7,300 recent college graduates who teach low-income students in 35 different areas. The Knowledge Is Power Program (KIPP), started in 1994, caters especially to poor and minority students, and has helped to establish and oversee academically rigorous schools. In 2009–2010, these were serving some 20,000 children. Its advocates argue that dedicated teachers, a broad curriculum, and demanding standards (KIPP schools run from 7:30 A.M. to 5 P.M. and half days every other Saturday in a school year that is three weeks longer than the norm) enhance both the social and academic development of inner-city minority children.

In quest of model programs, several observers have identified the Harlem Children's Zone Project, founded in 1997. In 2008, this ambitious effort was reaching 8,000 children over a 100-block area in Harlem. Described as "perhaps the most intensive set of youth programs of our time," it then had a budget of $58 million—most of it from private funding. Its goal is to "contaminate" the culture of Harlem with inspirational values, self-improvement, and better cognitive skills.[14]

This project concentrates its efforts not only on children but also on parents. It operates a Baby College that consists of a nine-week parenting program, all-day kindergarten classes, and two K–12 charter schools. Other offerings, such as family counseling, a health clinic, after-school tutoring, and summer school, are also available. Parents are expected to read a great deal more to their children (sixth-graders in the area had been reading on the average at third-grade levels)—that is, to do far more to energize their children than just being there. Some critics worry that the project is a venture aimed at making blacks act white—it is "racial imperialism." It costs a lot of money per child. And its effect on helping middle school students seems to be relatively slight. But early reports on its impact among elementary school children have been positive. In 2008, Obama promised to help replicate it in twenty cities.[15]

Yet the political, bureaucratic, and financial hurdles impeding the establishment of such schools and projects are formidable, and the number of children covered remains tiny. In 2008, roughly 45 percent of all American children aged six and under—some 4.2 million of them black and 6.1 million of them Hispanic—were members of minority groups. Large gaps, moreover, continue to exist between the scores of black and white students on the well-regarded National Assessment of Educational Progress (NAEP) tests. Though black as well as white children in the 1990s did a little better on average on these tests than earlier, scores leveled off in the early 2000s. In 2009, fourth-grade and eighth-grade black students still lagged around three grade levels behind white children on tests such as these. Many of the gaps widen in the high school years, and they appear in northern and western as well as southern school districts.[16]

Raising black test scores involves far more than getting black children into better schools. The gaps continue to be wide well before kindergarten: as Coleman had shown in 1966, a major source of cognitive development lies in the homes and the neighborhoods. SAT scores, moreover, reflect family wealth. Many low-income black parents, themselves ill educated, scramble to earn a living and cope day and night with chaotic surroundings. Low-income single mothers in particular are unlikely to have the experience or the time to focus on the academic needs of their children. Even to make a start at lowering the gaps, the mothers have to be there to turn off the TV, to read more often to their children, and to be strict in ensuring that their kids go regularly to school.[17]

It is evident, moreover, that many Americans today continue to blame "black culture" for black problems and therefore oppose large-scale public programs intended to aid the "undeserving" poor. Some throw up their hands in anger or in despair, perceiving badly behaving and low-achieving black people as suffering from what some have called "poverty of inner resources." In addition, social scientists concede there is still a good deal to learn about policies to help minorities and the poor. More needs to be done to evaluate experiments that have been tried. As Rebecca Blank, a leading researcher in the field, has noted, "Policy evaluation is one of the least appreciated tests of long-term policy design."

Moynihan could not have said this better. Indeed, this is one of his many re-flections about social policy that still receives respectful attention. Many people, citing especially his focus on the travails of black men, call him a "prophet." McWhorter wrote in 2006 that the Moynihan Report in 1965 had "raised a sin-cere alarm, his purpose being to call for public policy to improve the quality of life for poor blacks." Like Michael Harrington's rediscovery of poverty, McWhorter added, Moynihan's contribution was to emphasize that low-income black family problems did not stem from "laziness or bad luck." Rather, they followed from "self-perpetuating aspects of the capitalist system."[18]

In *The Audacity of Hope* (2006), Obama, too, made a point of reminding people of Moynihan's prescient warnings about the rise of out-of-wedlock pregnancy among the black poor. Deploring what he called "the casualness toward sex and child-rearing among black men that renders black children more vulnerable—and for which there is no excuse," Obama insisted that blacks have "responsibilities as well" for improving their situations. He also complained that Moynihan had been wrongly accused of racism and of blam-ing the victim. Echoing Moynihan's oft-expressed complaints about the low quality of public discussion, he added, "Liberal policy makers and civil rights leaders didn't help; in their urgency to avoid blaming the victims of historical racism, they tended to downplay or ignore evidence that entrenched behavioral patterns among the black poor really were contributing to intergenerational poverty."[19]

In September 2007, scholars at Harvard University, also recognizing the continuing relevance of the Moynihan Report, hosted a scholarly conference to revisit it. Most of the attendees agreed that Moynihan had been prophetic and that his emphasis on the structural causes of low-income black family difficulties was sound. Robert Sampson, a Harvard sociologist and coeditor of the book of articles from the proceedings, credited Moynihan with having cast a "no-holds-barred, unflinching eye" on the neighborhood roots of lower-class black problems. Harry Holzer, writing about employment issues, opined that Moynihan had been "insightful and stunningly prescient." Ron Haskins, a senior fellow at the Brookings Institution, remarked, "Subsequent events have proven him correct."[20]

Not all the scholars were quite so supportive. Demographer Frank Furstenberg wrote that the report had underplayed the role of class and of economic forces. Indeed, the conferees at Harvard, highlighting the damage to black families caused by economic developments, had less to say about the role of cultural changes than those who had spoken at Syracuse in 2002. William Julius Wilson, however, argued again that various manifestations of lower-class black culture, having been shaped (and in some ways damaged) by a long history of living under oppressive conditions, had to be considered if one were to fully understand the varying responses and behaviors of African Americans. Wilson concluded, Moynihan's "presentation certainly lacked elegance, but it was an attempt to synthesize structural and cultural analyses to understand the dynamics of poor black families and the plight of low-skilled black males."[21]

Wilson elaborated on these views in 2009 in a new book aptly titled *More Than Just Race*, in which he endeavored to disentangle and weigh the role of cultural and economic forces afflicting black people. He urged readers to avoid sweeping generalizations about dysfunctional black behaviors and to recognize that people are not trapped in a puncture-proof culture. How individual African Americans behave depends on a number of things: among these, how they "frame" and "narrate" their situations; how they deal with them—that is, how they use their "tool kits" of habits, skills, and styles; and how much "cultural capital" they may have inherited.

Although this approach to understanding lower-class black behavior may seem commonsensical—and it is in many ways an updated version of arguments Wilson had expressed earlier—it is nonetheless more nuanced (as was the Moynihan Report, in its less academic way) than many explanations offered over the decades by agitators on the left as well as the right.[22]

During his campaign in 2008, Obama generally avoided racial issues, but he nonetheless seized occasions to talk about the responsibilities of black parents. He made a special point of doing so on Father's Day in June. Addressing a packed congregation in one of Chicago's largest black churches, he invoked his own absent father—and the travails of his abandoned mother—in the course of speaking frankly and at length to black men. "More than half of all black children," he said, "live in single-parent households"—a number, he added, that had "doubled—doubled—since we were children." "Too many fathers," he added, "are M.I.A., too many fathers are AWOL, missing from too many lives and too many homes." "They have abandoned their responsibilities, acting like boys instead of men. And the foundations of our families are weaker because of it." Fathers, he emphasized, "need to realize that responsibility does not end at conception."[23]

As Cosby had done in Washington, Obama seemed to strike a chord with his audience. At one point he told his listeners not to "just sit in the house watching *SportsCenter*" or to praise themselves for mediocre accomplishments. He added, "Don't get carried away with that eighth-grade graduation. You're supposed to graduate from eighth grade." Hearing this admonition, many of his listeners jumped to their feet and applauded.

Obama's comments made headlines. Nationally syndicated columnist E. J. Dionne wrote, "Government simply cannot replace absent fathers. Government cannot do all the things that parents ought to do. The reason Obama's speech is important beyond all of the short-term calculations and analysis is that it reflects a hard-won consensus that family structure matters." As if to cinch his case, Dionne reminded his readers that Daniel Patrick Moynihan way back in 1965 had written about the "deterioration of the Negro family," whereupon he had been denounced for blaming the victim. Moynihan's view, Dionne wrote, "was vindicated years later when many of the most important

African American advocates of equality came to see strengthening the black family as essential to the civil rights agenda."[24]

The speech did not please everyone. Here and there, it resurrected rancor that had greeted the Moynihan Report and that had often reappeared over the years. The Rev. Jesse Jackson, caught in a sotto voce aside on a *Fox News* tape, complained that Obama was "talking down to black people." "I want to cut his nuts off," he snapped. But the Rev. Al Sharpton was more politic, indicating that even militant black leaders are now willing to do more than blame institutional racism. Obama's address, he said, was "courageous and important." Issuing a caution, he added, "There are a lot of those who will say that he should not be airing dirty laundry, those that will say he's beating up on the victim." He concluded, however, "This will not be something that will be unanimously applauded, but I think that not discussing it is not going to make it go away."[25]

Obama, moreover, has continued to raise the issue. In his talk to the NAACP in 2009, he reiterated his tough-love approach. "No one has written your destiny for you," he lectured his listeners. "Your destiny is in your hands, and don't you forget that." He has backed legislation to hike funding for early education programs such as Head Start, Early Head Start, and other prekindergarten initiatives, and Congress has set aside $4.4 billion—the most that the federal government has ever provided—to support states that participate in a Race to the Top initiative aimed at reforming public schools. And he is obviously a role model for many young black people. As Michelle, his wife, remarked during the 2008 campaign, "Barack and I will cut an unfamiliar figure to most of America, a loving, opinionated upper-middle-class black couple with children."[26]

So far, however, Obama has not acted decisively to address the black family issues of which he is clearly aware. Urgent concerns—economic recession, struggles to enact health care legislation, wars in Iraq and Afghanistan, ongoing terrorist threats, the Middle East—have preoccupied him as president and absorbed his energies. Dealing with these matters has cost trillions of dollars and vastly increased public deficits. Relatively few political leaders, moreover, have jumped in to demand action on black family issues. Coping with the distress of black families in the ghettos—as ever a very complicated matter to address—continues to be a relatively low priority among politicians.

As the tortuous trail of the Moynihan Report has shown, a lot of misunderstandings and misrepresentations, most of them rooted in abiding racial antagonisms, also hamper efforts to talk forthrightly and productively about black family problems. These misunderstandings and distortions continue to impede the search for effective public policies.

Still, the efforts of well-intentioned policymakers, combined with those of parents and community leaders, must continue. If and when these efforts secure substantial political support, Lyndon Johnson's springtime dream at Howard University, as scripted for him long ago by Moynihan, might become possible: larger numbers of Americans might recognize that "freedom is not enough" and agree that black Americans should be helped to enjoy "not just equality as a right and a theory but equality as a fact and a result."

ACKNOWLEDGMENTS

I thank the following people for their encouragement and for their willingness to criticize parts of earlier drafts of my book: Marnie Cochran, my daughter (and an editor, Ballantine Books); Robert Self, historian, Brown University; Timothy Smeeding, economist, University of Wisconsin; Luther Spoehr, historian, Brown University; and John Wright, my agent, New York City.

Brandon Proia, associate editor, Basic Books, and Lara Heimert, editorial director of the press, offered very helpful criticism of a final draft of the book. I also benefited greatly from careful criticism by Paul Barton, Labor Department adviser to Moynihan, and by the following friends, all of whom took time to read an entire draft of the book: Gareth Davies, historian, Oxford University; John Dittmer, historian, DePauw University; and Steven Gillon, historian, History Channel and University of Oklahoma.

A NOTE ON THE SOURCES

Although my text and endnotes indicate key sources, many readers will wish for a better guide to these in one place. Hence this brief note.

ARCHIVES

I rely often on the extraordinarily rich Moynihan papers (Part 1) at the Library of Congress in Washington, D.C., as well as on the (less illuminating) papers of Kenneth Clark (also there). I thank archivist Jeff Flannery and others for their excellent guidance at the library. Helpful sources at the National Archives in College Park, Maryland, include the papers of W. Willard Wirtz, Moynihan's boss at the Department of Labor (Record Group 174) as well as letters and memos in the President's Handwriting Files of the Nixon Project. Among the most useful papers for me at the Lyndon Johnson Presidential Library in Austin, Texas, are those of Harry McPherson, Lee White, and those concerning the White House conferences of 1965 and 1966. Relevant oral history accounts at the Johnson library are those of Morris Abram, Clifford Alexander, Patricia Harris, Ben Heineman, Harry McPherson, and Bayard Rustin. Allan Fisher and Laura Eggert, archivists at the Johnson library, went out of their way to help me.

MOYNIHAN

Two useful biographies are Godfrey Hodgson, *The Gentleman from New York: Daniel Patrick Moynihan: A Biography* (Boston: Houghton Mifflin, 2000); and Douglas Schoen, *Pat: A Biography of Daniel Patrick Moynihan* (New York: Harper & Row, 1979). Books that evaluate his ideas include Robert Katzmann, ed., *Daniel Patrick Moynihan: The Intellectual in Public Life* (Washington, DC: Woodrow Wilson Center Press, and Baltimore: Johns Hopkins University Press, 2004), which includes articles as well as an annotated bibliography of many of Moynihan's writings; Peter Steinfels, *The Neoconservatives: The Men Who Are Changing America's Politics*

(New York: Simon and Schuster, 1979); and a chapter (on the Moynihan Report) in Steve Estes, *I AM A MAN! Race, Manhood, and the Civil Rights Movement* (Chapel Hill: University of North Carolina Press, 2005). For descriptions of Moynihan and his activities, see Chester Finn, *Troublemaker: A Personal History of School Reform Since Sputnik* (Princeton: Princeton University Press, 2008); Harry McPherson, *A Political Education* (Boston: Little, Brown, 1972); Allen Matusow, *The Unraveling of America: A History of Liberalism in the 1960s* (New York: Harper & Row, 1984); and Roger Wilkins, *A Man's Life: An Autobiography* (New York: Simon and Schuster, 1982).

THE MOYNIHAN REPORT

Moynihan's *The Negro Family: The Case for National Action* did not carry his name. It was first printed by the Office of Policy Planning and Research (headed by Moynihan) of the United States Labor Department in March 1965. When demand for it developed that summer, it was published and sold (for 45 cents) by the United States Government Printing Office (Washington, D.C.). Greenwood Press, in Westport, Connecticut, republished it in 1981.

Three sources focusing on the report deserve special mention. First, Lee Rainwater and William Yancey, *The Moynihan Report and the Politics of Controversy* (Cambridge, MA: MIT Press, 1967). This excellent volume includes the text of the report, Lyndon Johnson's address at Howard University in 1965, analysis of the report by Rainwater and Yancey, and considerable contemporary commentary by others about it. Second, Paul E. Barton (a key Moynihan adviser and researcher at the Labor Department in 1965), "The Unknown Moynihan Report: What Else It Said, What Happened, What Now?" (unpublished, October 2007), copy in my possession. Third, Douglas Massey and Robert Sampson, eds., *The Moynihan Report Revisited: Lessons and Reflections After Four Decades* (Thousand Oaks, CA: Sage Publications, 2009). This is a collection of scholarly essays by participants in a conference at Harvard University in 2007.

WRITINGS BY MOYNIHAN

Among Moynihan's many writings, the following are especially relevant to an understanding of his ideas about family life. In chronological order, they are *Beyond the Melting Pot: The Negroes, Puerto Ricans, Jews, Italians and Irish of New York City* (with Nathan Glazer) (Cambridge, MA: MIT Press, 1963); *Maximum Feasible Misunderstanding: Community Action in the War on Poverty* (New York: Free Press, 1969); *The Politics of a Guaranteed Income: The Nixon Administration and the Family*

Assistance Plan (New York: Random House, 1973); *Coping: Essays on the Practice of Government* (New York: Random House, 1973); *Family and Nation* (San Diego: Harcourt Brace Jovanovich, 1986); and *Miles to Go: A Personal History of Social Policy* (Cambridge, MA: Harvard University Press, 1996).

STUDIES OF SLAVERY, BLACK HISTORY, AND BLACK FAMILY LIFE PUBLISHED AS OF EARLY 1965

In chronological order, key sources on the subject of black family life, most of which Moynihan relied on to write his report, include W. E. B. Du Bois, *The Philadelphia Negro: A Social Study* (Philadelphia: University of Pennsylvania Press, 1899); Du Bois, ed., *The Negro American Family* (Atlanta: Atlanta University Press, 1908); E. Franklin Frazier, *The Negro Family in the United States* (Chicago: University of Chicago Press, 1939); Gunnar Myrdal, *An American Dilemma: The Negro Problem and American Democracy* (New York: Harper and Brothers, 1944); Stanley Elkins, *Slavery: A Problem in American Institutional and Intellectual Life* (Chicago: University of Chicago Press, 1959); Whitney Young, *To Be Equal* (New York: McGraw-Hill, 1964); Charles Silberman, *Crisis in Black and White* (New York: Random House, 1964); and Kenneth Clark, *Dark Ghetto: Dilemmas of Social Power* (New York: Harper & Row, 1965).

STUDIES OF SLAVERY, BLACK HISTORY, AND FAMILY LIFE (WHITE AS WELL AS BLACK) PUBLISHED POST-1965

All of these (listed chronologically) reflect on issues raised by the report: Talcott Parsons and Kenneth Clark, eds., *The Negro American* (contains an essay by Moynihan) (Boston: Houghton Mifflin, 1966); Andrew Billingsley, *Black Families in White America* (Englewood Cliffs, NJ: Prentice Hall, 1968); Lee Rainwater, *Behind Ghetto Walls: Black Families in a Federal Slum* (Chicago: Aldine Publishing, 1970); Joyce Ladner, *Tomorrow's Tomorrow: The Black Woman* (Garden City, NY: Doubleday, 1971); Carol Stack, *All Our Kin: Strategies for Survival in a Black Community* (New York: Harper & Row, 1974); Herbert Gutman, *The Black Family in Slavery and Freedom, 1750–1925* (New York: Pantheon Books, 1976); Walter Jackson, *Gunnar Myrdal and the American Conscience: Social Engineering and Racial Liberalism, 1938– 1987* (Chapel Hill: University of North Carolina Press, 1990); and Nicholas Lemann, *The Promised Land: The Great Black Migration and How It Changed America* (New York: Alfred A. Knopf, 1991).

Also Shelby Steele, *The Content of Our Character: A New Vision of Race in America* (New York: St. Martin's Press, 1990); Thomas Sugrue, *The Origins of the Urban*

Crisis: Race and Inequality in Postwar Detroit (Princeton: Princeton University Press, 1996); Daryl Michael Scott, *Contempt and Pity: Social Policy and the Image of the Damaged Black Psyche, 1880–1896* (Chapel Hill: University of North Carolina Press, 1997); Orlando Patterson, *Rituals of Blood: Consequences of Slavery in Two American Centuries* (Washington, DC: Civitas/Counterpoint, 1998); John McWhorter, *Losing the Race: Self-Sabotage in Black America* (New York: Free Press, 2000); James Q. Wilson, *The Marriage Problem: How Our Culture Has Weakened Families* (New York: HarperCollins, 2002); Moynihan, Timothy Smeeding, and Lee Rainwater, eds., *The Future of the Family* (New York: Russell Sage Foundation, 2004); Kathryn Edin and Maria Kefalas, *Promises I Can Keep: Why Poor Women Put Motherhood Before Marriage* (Berkeley: University of California Press, 2005); Kay Hymowitz, *Marriage and Caste in America: Separate and Unequal Families in a Post-Marital Age* (Chicago: Ivan R. Dee Publisher, 2006); and Bill Cosby and Alvin Poussaint, *Come on, People: On the Path from Victims to Victors* (Nashville: Thomas Nelson, 2007).

A useful collection of essays concerning demographic trends is Lawrence Wu and Barbara Wolfe, eds., *Out of Wedlock: Causes and Consequences of Nonmarital Fertility* (New York: Russell Sage Foundation, 2001).

STUDIES OF WELFARE, RACE RELATIONS, CIVIL RIGHTS, AND POVERTY

Vincent and Vee Burke, *Nixon's Good Deed: Welfare Reform* (New York: Columbia University Press, 1974); Orlando Patterson, *Ethnic Chauvinism: The Reactionary Impulse* (New York: Stein and Day, 1977); Charles Murray, *Losing Ground: American Social Policy, 1950–1980* (New York: Basic Books, 1984); William Julius Wilson, *The Truly Disadvantaged: The Inner City, the Underclass, and Public Policy* (Chicago: University of Chicago Press, 1987); Christopher Jencks and Paul Peterson, eds., *The Urban Underclass* (Washington, DC: Brookings Institution, 1991); Christopher Jencks, *Rethinking Social Policy: Race, Poverty, and the Underclass* (Cambridge, MA: Harvard University Press, 1992); Gareth Davies, *From Opportunity to Entitlement: The Transformation and Decline of Great Society Liberalism* (Lawrence: University Press of Kansas, 1996); and Orlando Patterson, *The Ordeal of Integration: Progress and Resentment in America's "Racial" Crisis* (Washington, DC: Civitas/Counterpoint, 1997).

Also Francis Fukuyama, *The Great Disruption: Human Nature and the Reconstitution of Social Order* (New York: Free Press, 1999); Alice O'Connor, *Poverty Knowledge, Social Science, Social Policy, and the Poor in Twentieth-Century U.S. History* (Princeton: Princeton University Press, 2000); Jason DeParle, *American Dream:*

Three Women, Ten Kids, and a Nation's Drive to End Welfare (New York: Viking, 2004); Frank Stricker, *Why America Lost the War on Poverty—and How to Win It* (Chapel Hill: University of North Carolina Press, 2007); Brian Steensland, *The Failed Welfare Revolution: America's Struggle over Guaranteed Income Policy* (Princeton: Princeton University Press, 2008); David Carter, *The Music Has Gone out of the Movement: Civil Rights and the Johnson Administration, 1965–1968* (Chapel Hill: University of North Carolina Press, 2009); and William Julius Wilson, *More Than Just Race: Being Black and Poor in the Inner City* (New York: W. W. Norton, 2009).

INTERVIEWS

The following people (in alphabetical order) graciously talked to me about Moynihan and issues relating to black families and social policies: Paul Barton, top Moynihan aide in the Department of Labor; E. J. Dionne, syndicated columnist; Vicki Bear Dodson, Moynihan's personal secretary; John Ehrman, independent scholar and historian of neoconservatism; Steve Estes, historian, Sonoma State University; Chester Finn, Moynihan senatorial staffer and authority on U.S. education; Nathan Glazer, sociologist (retired), Harvard University, and friend and coauthor with Moynihan; Kay Hymowitz, scholar of American family life; Glenn Loury, economist, Brown University, and activist on racial issues; and Harry McPherson, LBJ counsel and friend of Moynihan.

Also Elizabeth B. Moynihan, widow of Daniel P. Moynihan; Orlando Patterson, sociologist, Harvard University; Charles Peters, founding editor, *Washington Monthly*; Alvin Poussaint, civil rights activist, psychiatrist, and coauthor with Bill Cosby; Lee Rainwater, sociologist (retired), Harvard University, friend of Moynihan, and coauthor of a major study of the report; Donald Ritchie, historian of the U.S. Senate; Wendy Schiller, Moynihan senatorial staffer and political scientist, Brown University; Samuel Wells, associate director (retired), Woodrow Wilson Center; George Will, syndicated columnist and friend of Moynihan; Roger Wilkins, civil rights activist, JFK-LBJ official, and historian; William Julius Wilson, sociologist, Harvard University; and W. Willard Wirtz, LBJ's secretary of labor.

Of the above, Paul Barton, Steve Estes, Elizabeth B. Moynihan, Donald Ritchie, George Will, and William Julius Wilson were especially helpful, corresponding with me and sending me documents, manuscripts, and/or guides to sources. Bill Moyers (top LBJ aide) and Ira Berlin (historian of slavery, University of Maryland) also corresponded with me.

NOTES

PREFACE

1. For the text of this speech, see Lee Rainwater and William Yancey, *The Moynihan Report and the Politics of Controversy* (Cambridge, MA: MIT University Press, 1967), hereafter referred to in notes as *Moynihan Report*). Drafts of the speech are in Part 1, box 28 of the Moynihan papers (henceforth referred to as DPM papers), Library of Congress, Washington, DC. This is a rich collection that until recently was not available to scholars. All my citations are from the boxes in Part 1. My notes will mostly cite archival sources. "A Note on the Sources" at the end of the book offers a guide to these and to major secondary accounts.

2. These drafts can be found in the papers (boxes 220, 290) of Moynihan's boss, Secretary of Labor W. Willard Wirtz, Record Group 174, National Archives, College Park, Maryland.

3. Moynihan's top researcher for the report, Paul E. Barton (letter to me, December 18, 2008), later estimated that some 100,000 copies of the report had been sold as of the early 1970s.

4. Christopher Foreman, "The Rough Road to Racial Uplift," in Foreman, ed., *The African American Predicament* (Washington, DC: Brookings Institution, 1999), 5; Rainwater and Yancey, *Moynihan Report*, 410.

CHAPTER ONE

1. For biographical data here and in later chapters, see Douglas Schoen, *Pat: A Biography of Daniel Patrick Moynihan* (New York: Harper & Row, 1979); and Godfrey Hodgson, *The Gentleman from New York: Daniel Patrick Moynihan: A Biography* (Boston and New York: Houghton Mifflin, 2000).

2. Thomas Meehan, "Moynihan of the Moynihan Report," *New York Times Sunday Magazine* (July 31, 1966).

3. Moynihan in later life rarely spoke of his father, who died in 1955. Letter from Elizabeth Moynihan to me, April 12, 2009.

4. Jason DeParle, *American Dream: Three Women, Ten Kids, and a Nation's Drive to End Welfare* (New York: Viking, 2004), 137–139, 371.

5. For information concerning his appointment, see box 52, DPM papers.

6. For Moynihan's varied tasks at the Labor Department, see boxes 33 and 77, DPM papers.

7. Nicholas Lemann, *The Promised Land: The Great Black Migration and How It Changed America* (New York: Alfred A. Knopf, 1991), 154.

8. See box 77, DPM papers for DPM memos to Wirtz regarding selective service from 1963 to 1965. Also, an unpublished manuscript by Paul E. Barton (in my possession), "The Unknown Moynihan Report: What Else It Said, What Happened, What Now?" (October 2007). Then and later Moynihan often consulted Barton, an analyst of social and educational issues.

9. For information about this report, subtitled "A Report on Young Men Found Unqualified for Military Service," see files of U.S. Department of Labor, Documentary Supplement, box 5, Lyndon Baines Johnson Presidential Library, Austin, Texas (henceforth referred to in notes as Johnson library).

10. DPM to McPherson, July 16, 1965, box 21, McPherson papers, Johnson library (emphases in original). In October 1966, Defense Secretary Robert McNamara, following up on Moynihan's ideas, announced Project 100,000, which lowered requirements for young men seeking to enlist in the military so as to enlist some 100,000 additional men per year. Within the next year and a half, some 150,000 men (40 percent of them black) had been admitted under the auspices of the program. A disproportionate number of them, however, were killed in Vietnam. Evaluation of Project 100,000 indicated that those who survived and reentered civilian life suffered from high unemployment and other ills. Judged a failure, the experiment was discontinued.

11. Moynihan, "The Professionalization of Reform," *The Public Interest* (Fall 1965): 6–16.

12. See Chapter 6 of this volume.

13. Moynihan, who strongly favored birth control, was not a devout Catholic—and his children did not attend Catholic schools. But throughout his life he attended services, read Catholic publications, and published in Catholic magazines. He wrote President Nixon in 1970, "I am indeed a *practicing Catholic*, and have been involved in Church work more or less regularly over the years." DPM to Nixon, December 7, 1970, President's Handwriting File, box 8, Nixon Project, National Archives, College Park, Maryland.

14. For example, DPM to Wirtz, January 12, 1965, box 290, Wirtz papers.

15. DPM to Wirtz, April 20, 1964, box 77, DPM papers,

16. DPM to Wirtz, May 6, 1964, box 190, Wirtz papers. See also DPM to Wirtz memos, 1964, box 290, Wirtz papers. Also Rainwater and Yancey, *Moynihan Report*, 22–25.

17. Moynihan's critical retrospective on planning for the War on Poverty is *Maximum Feasible Misunderstanding: Community Action in the War on Poverty* (New York: Free Press, 1969). See also Gareth Davies, *From Opportunity to Entitlement: The Transformation and*

Decline of Great Society Liberalism (Lawrence: University Press of Kansas, 1996), 10–74; Lemann, *The Promised Land*, 144–158, 154–155, 167–179, 202–218; and James Patterson, *America's Struggle Against Poverty in the Twentieth Century* (Cambridge, MA: Harvard University Press, 2000), 122–149.

CHAPTER TWO

1. DPM to Wirtz, November 9, 1964, box 27, DPM papers, and DPM to Harry McPherson, September 22, 1965, box 21, McPherson papers, Johnson library. Key sources concerning the origins and importance of the Moynihan Report include Paul Barton, "The Unknown Moynihan Report"; Steve Estes, *I AM A MAN! Race, Manhood, and the Civil Rights Movement* (Chapel Hill: University of North Carolina Press, 2005), 197–229; Rainwater and Yancey, *Moynihan Report*; David Carter, *The Music Has Gone out of the Movement: Civil Rights and the Johnson Administration, 1965–1968* (Chapel Hill: University of North Carolina Press, 2009); and Douglas Massey and Robert Sampson, eds., *The Moynihan Report Revisited: Lessons and Reflections After Four Decades* (Thousand Oaks, CA: Sage Publications, 2009).

2. Lemann, *The Promised Land*, 172–179.

3. Allen Matusow, *The Unraveling of America: A History of Liberalism in the 1960s* (New York: Harper & Row, 1984), 194–195; Harry McPherson, *A Political Education* (Boston: Little, Brown, 1972), 334–339; interview with McPherson, January 2009; McPherson oral history, Johnson library.

4. Barton, "The Unknown Moynihan Report." For Barton's research, see boxes 66 and 92, DPM papers.

5. All emphases in this chapter—by Barton, Wirtz, or Moynihan—are theirs, not mine.

6. DPM to Bill Moyers, box 92, and to Arthur Goldberg, box 28, DPM papers.

7. Memo to Willard Wirtz, February 9, 1965, box 77, DPM papers.

8. Lemann, *The Promised Land*, 174.

9. W. E. B. Du Bois, *The Philadelphia Negro: A Social Study* (Philadelphia: University of Pennsylvania Press, 1899).

10. W. E. B. Du Bois, ed., *The Negro American Family* (Atlanta: Atlanta University Press, 1908).

11. Quote in E. Franklin Frazier, *The Negro Family in the United States* (Chicago: University of Chicago Press, 1939), 487.

12. Gunnar Myrdal, *An American Dilemma: The Negro Problem and American Democracy* (New York: Harper and Brothers, 1944).

13. See Walter Jackson, *Gunnar Myrdal and America's Conscience: Social Engineering and Racial Liberalism, 1938–1987* (Chapel Hill: University of North Carolina Press, 1990).

14. Nathan Glazer and Daniel Patrick Moynihan, *Beyond the Melting Pot: The Negroes, Puerto Ricans, Jews, Italians, and Irish of New York City* (Cambridge, MA: MIT Press, 1963), 53–78.

15. Stanley Elkins, *Slavery: A Problem in American Institutional and Intellectual Life* (Chicago: University of Chicago Press, 1959), 52–56, 88–92, 104–122.

16. Kenneth Clark, *Dark Ghetto: Dilemmas of Social Power* (New York: Harper & Row, 1965), xviii–xxii, 47–50, 70–74, 81–110, 221–222.

17. Peter Novick, *That Noble Dream: The "Objectivity Question" and the American Historical Profession* (Cambridge: Cambridge University Press, 1988), 480–481.

18. James Baldwin, *Notes of a Native Son* (New York: Dial Press, 1963).

19. Here and throughout, I rely for many official statistics on various annual editions of the U.S. Census Bureau's *Statistical Abstract of the United States* (Washington, DC: U.S. Government Printing Office).

20. Letter to DPM, September 15, 1967, box 442, DPM papers.

21. Whitney Young, *To Be Equal* (New York: McGraw-Hill, 1964), 23–33, 168–175.

22. Charles Silberman, *Crisis in Black and White* (New York: Random House, 1964), 94–95, 235.

23. Barton, "The Unknown Moynihan Report." Drafts of the report, printings of it, and related material may be found in box 66, DPM papers.

24. Wirtz to Moyers, March 23, 1965, box 290, Wirtz papers.

25. Box 220, Wirtz Papers.

26. DPM to Wirtz, box 28, DPM papers; DPM to McPherson, box 290, Wirtz papers.

27. For DPM comments on writing the speech, see memos to Wirtz, June 1, 1965, box 290, Wirtz papers, and June 4, 1965, boxes 28 and 104, DPM papers. For Richard Goodwin's drafts, see Statements of Lyndon Baines Johnson, June 4–8, 1965, box 149, Johnson library. For Goodwin's recollections, see his book, *Remembering America: A Voice from the Sixties* (Boston: Little, Brown, 1988), 343–348.

28. Barton, "The Unknown Moynihan Report."

CHAPTER THREE

1. Here and henceforth in this chapter, italics, capital letters, and boldfaces in quotes are Moynihan's.

2. Moynihan did not estimate the number of lower-class black Americans who would have belonged to the subset he described. Then, as later, it was hard to be precise about these numbers. The report of the National Advisory Commission on Civil Disorders (Washington, DC: U.S. Government Printing Office, 1968) estimated that in 1966 between 2 and 2.5 million impoverished blacks—or roughly 10 to 12 percent of the total black population of 21.4 million—resided in "disadvantaged neighborhoods" of inner cities. The number of these blacks who also exhibited one or more dysfunctional behaviors—people often labeled in later years as members of the "underclass"—was generally agreed to be very much smaller (though their disruptive behavior often created serious trouble for many more people in their neighborhoods). See also Chapter 8 of this volume.

3. The "illegitimacy ratio" (a term widely used by demographers and others at the time) measures the percentage of births that are out of wedlock. The "illegitimacy rate"—sometimes confused with the illegitimacy ratio—measures the proportion of unmarried women of childbearing age (normally understood to be ages fifteen to forty-four) giving birth to children out of wedlock.

4. Moynihan's chapter on the Irish in that book included a section describing the "wild Irish" of the mid-nineteenth century who "poured into the city to drink and dance and fight in the streets."

5. Harris oral history, Johnson library, 27.

6. Frank Stricker, *Why America Lost the War on Poverty—and How to Win It* (Chapel Hill: University of North Carolina Press, 2007), 89.

CHAPTER FOUR

1. Moynihan, "The President and the Negro: The Moment Lost," *Commentary* (February 1967): 31–45.

2. For information about these and other planning meetings later in 1965, see Lee White papers, box 5, Johnson library, as well as Harry McPherson oral history, Johnson library.

3. For information on how the report became public, and on DPM's assistance to Rainwater and Yancey, see box 442, DPM papers; and Rainwater and Yancey, *Moynihan Report*, esp. 133–193.

4. Daryl Michael Scott, "The Politics of Pathology: The Ideological Origins of the Moynihan Controversy," *Journal of Policy History* 8 (Winter 1996): 81–105.

5. Rainwater and Yancey, *Moynihan Report*, 193; Rustin oral history, Johnson library.

6. For quotes in the preceding paragraphs, see Nick Kotz, *Judgment Days: Lyndon Baines Johnson, Martin Luther King Jr., and the Laws That Changed America* (Boston: Houghton Mifflin, 2005), 338–345; and Joseph Califano, *The Triumph and Tragedy of Lyndon Johnson: The White House Years* (New York: Simon & Schuster, 1991), 59–64.

7. Leslie to Frank Ervin, July 30, 1965, and Lee White to Bill Moyers, August 8, 1965, box 6, White papers, Johnson library.

8. Estes, *I AM A MAN!* 107–129; Jackson, *Gunnar Myrdal and America's Conscience*, 302–305.

9. In a book of scholarly essays reflecting on the report, Massey and Sampson, eds., *The Moynihan Report Revisited*, 6.

10. Rainwater and Yancey, *Moynihan Report*, 147.

11. *Daedalus* 94 (Fall 1965): 745–770.

12. For Moynihan's comments on this article, see DPM to Hyman Rodman, March 3, 1967, box 192, DPM papers.

13. For DPM's activities at Wesleyan and correspondence concerning the book, see boxes 148, 149, 430, and 460, DPM papers.

14. For commentaries, including many that follow in this section, see Rainwater and Yancey, *Moynihan Report*, esp. 233–291.

15. Ibid., 402–408.

16. DPM to McPherson, September 22, 1965, box 22, McPherson papers, Johnson library.

17. For the Wirtz-Moynihan relationship, see McPherson to the president, June 24, 1965, box 52, McPherson papers, Johnson library.

18. Interview with William Wirtz, Washington, DC, January 2009; oral histories of Harry McPherson, Berl Bernhard, and Morris Abram, Johnson library. LBJ named Bernhard chief organizer of the conference. McPherson later prepared a letter of appreciation to Moynihan for Johnson to send, and urged him to sign it. There is no evidence that Johnson did (letter of October 7, 1965, Moynihan file, Johnson library).

19. Lemann, *The Promised Land*, 182.

20. DPM to McPherson, September 22, 1965, box 22, McPherson papers, Johnson library.

21. Ibid.

22. Bernhard oral history, Johnson library.

23. Young, *To Be Equal*, 16.

24. For Bayard Rustin, Martin Luther King Jr., and Whitney Young, see Rainwater and Yancey, *Moynihan Report*, 200–202, 402–408, 413–426.

25. For Christopher Jencks and Herbert Gans, see Rainwater and Yancey, *Moynihan Report*, 218–220, 442–456. Later discussions of responses to the report include Peter Steinfels, *The Neoconservatives: The Men Who Are Changing America's Politics* (New York: Simon and Schuster, 1979), 130–145; Alice O'Connor, *Poverty Knowledge: Social Science, Social Policy, and the Poor in Twentieth-Century U.S. History* (Princeton: Princeton University Press, 2000), 207–210; and Michael Katz, *The Undeserving Poor: From the War on Poverty to the War on Welfare* (New York: Pantheon Books, 1989), 45–47.

26. Richard Goodwin to Herbert Gans, September 17, 1965, box 5, White papers, Johnson library.

27. McPherson, *A Political Education*, 342–343.

28. For Payton, see Rainwater and Yancey, *Moynihan Report*, 233–244, 395–411. Payton later became president of Tuskegee Institute.

29. For controversy over Ryan, see Rainwater and Yancey, *Moynihan Report*, 220–232, 457–465.

30. Monroe Price to Willard Wirtz, December 20, 1965, box 240, Wirtz papers. For an account of the conference, see Carter, *The Music Has Gone out of the Movement*, 77–83.

31. Hylan Lewis, "The Family: Resources for Change," box 435, DPM papers. For many documents relating to the conference, see White House conference, boxes 23, 49, 67, 72, Johnson library.

32. Rainwater and Yancey, *Moynihan Report*, 409–412.

33. Reïnhold Niebuhr to DPM, November 27, 1965, box 466, DPM papers.

34. DPM to Lee Rainwater, December 1, 1965, and transcript of *Meet the Press* interview, December 20, 1965, both in box 464, DPM papers.

35. DPM to Kenneth Clark, December 20, 1965, box 25, Clark papers, Library of Congress.

CHAPTER FIVE

1. Oral history accounts of Ben Heineman, 18, and Clifford Alexander, Tape II, 31, Johnson library; Carter, *The Music Has Gone out of the Movement*, 84–97.

2. DPM to Abe Raskin, September 12, 1966, box 184, DPM papers.

3. *New York Times*, July 31, 1966; Dewey Eckes to DPM, August 5, 1966, box 187, DPM papers.

4. Jackie Boudreaux to DPM, September 15, 1966, box 184, DPM papers.

5. This was widely known as the Kerner Report, after Governor Otto Kerner of Illinois, head of the commission. Moynihan's name appeared (among 200-odd others) at the end of the report in a listing of "Consultants, Contractors, and Advisers," but he, like LBJ, sharply dismissed what he regarded as the report's one-sided emphasis on white racism.

6. Subsequent chapters offer more detailed figures for later years. This measure of proportions was termed the "illegitimacy ratio." What were then called "illegitimacy rates" tracked the number of live births per 1,000 unmarried women of childbearing age (fifteen to forty-four). Reflecting the rapidly changing times, use of the word "illegitimate" (referring to births) went out of favor in the United States in the 1970s, often (but not always) replaced by relatively nonjudgmental terms such as "out of wedlock" and "nonmarital."

7. Key sources for these demographic developments are Lawrence Wu et al., "Historical and Life Course Trajectories of Nonmarital Childbearing," in Wu and Barbara Wolfe, eds., *Out of Wedlock: Causes and Consequences of Nonmarital Fertility* (New York: Russell Sage Foundation, 2001), 3–48; Stephanie Ventura and Christine Bachrach, "Nonmarital Childrearing in the United States, 1940–1999," *National Vital Statistics Reports* 48, no. 16 (2000); and Robert Rector, "Understanding the Rise in Illegitimacy," Welfare Reform Academy, June 5, 1998, www.welfareacademy.org/conf/papers/rector_p.shtml.

8. The proportion of premarital conceptions in the United States that led to marriage before birth stood at 52 percent between 1960 and 1969, but then declined to 45 percent between 1970 and 1974 and to 27 percent between 1985 and 1989.

9. For statistics concerning other nations, see especially Chapter 10 of this volume.

10. See Kay Hymowitz, *Marriage and Caste in America: Separate and Unequal Families in a Post-Marital Age* (Chicago: Ivan R. Dee Publisher, 2006).

11. Great increases also took place in the 1970s and early 1980s. See Chapter 7 of this volume.

12. See Chapter 6 of this volume.

13. Vincent Burke and Vee Burke, *Nixon's Good Deed: Welfare Reform* (New York: Columbia University Press, 1974), 204–205.

14. For this "reform," which Moynihan, then a senator, opposed bitterly, see Chapter 9 of this volume.

15. DPM to Hyman Rodman, March 8, 1967, box 192, DPM papers.

16. Later, Tim Moynihan attended Exeter and Tufts (dropping out after his first year to study art for two years in Paris, then returning to live in New York City). Maura Moynihan was graduated from the U.S. International School in New Delhi and from Harvard, and John Moynihan was graduated from Andover and Wesleyan. Tim became a cartoonist and sculptor, Maura an author, artist, singer, and human rights organizer (she spent four years in Nepal running Radio Free Asia's operation in Tibet from there), and John a journalist and animator.

17. "Urbanologist Pat Moynihan," *Time*, July 28, 1967, 10–15.

18. For some of these, see his appropriately titled collection, *Coping: Essays on the Practice of Government* (New York: Random House, 1973). During these years, his most creative as a social critic, Moynihan also edited a collection of essays, including one of his own, stemming from a seminar he helped to organize at Harvard, *On Understanding Poverty: Perspectives from the Social Sciences* (New York: Basic Books, 1969).

19. His friends Irving Kristol and Daniel Bell (a professor at Harvard) were coeditors of the journal.

20. See Moynihan, "The Politics of Stability," *New Leader* 50 (October 9, 1967): 6–10.

21. DPM comment lauded by his good friend and syndicated columnist, George Will, *Washington Post*, April 15, 1993.

22. The Office of Education, as mandated by the 1964 Civil Rights Act, had commissioned the report. For background information concerning the conference, see Theodore Sizer to Kenneth Clark, November 21, 1966, box 36, Clark papers. Sizer was dean of the Harvard Education School, which helped sponsor the conference.

23. James Coleman, "Equal Schools or Equal Students?" *The Public Interest* 4 (Summer 1966): 70–75. Emphasis his.

24. James Coleman to DPM, March 20, 1967, box 422, DPM papers.

25. According to Moynihan, the friend who told him "it's all family" (thereby distorting Coleman's more nuanced conclusions) was the sociologist Seymour Martin Lipset, *New York Times*, December 31, 1995.

26. Moynihan collected his complaints about community action in *Maximum Feasible Misunderstanding* (1969).

27. For Moynihan and AFDC, see his "The Crises in Welfare," *The Public Interest* 10 (Winter 1968): 3–19.

28. Moynihan reiterated his faith in "family policy"—and his lament that the United States had not followed "Catholic social doctrine" concerning family welfare or the social democratic path of Sweden, Denmark, Holland, and Britain—in an introduction he wrote in 1968 for a new edition of the book *Nation and Family: The Swedish Experiment in Democratic Family and Population Policy* (Cambridge, MA: MIT Press, 1941) by Alva Myrdal (Gunnar Myrdal's wife). He continued, however, to dissent from official Catholic teaching about birth control.

CHAPTER SIX

1. Moynihan, "The Politics of Stability," 6–10.

2. Harry McPherson to DPM, September 30, 1968, and DPM to McPherson, October 3, 1968, box 180, President's Handwriting File, Nixon Project, National Archives, College Park, Maryland. Unless otherwise indicated, this file will henceforth be the source for letters and memos by Moynihan, Nixon, and others cited in this chapter. See also Lemann, *The Promised Land*, 201–217, for discussion of Moynihan's relationship with Nixon from 1969 to 1970.

3. DPM letter to Nixon, October 24, 1968, box 192.

4. The scholar was Gilbert Steiner, cited in Davies, *From Opportunity to Entitlement*, 215. This is an important source for what follows in this chapter. See also Brian Steensland, *The Failed Welfare Revolution: America's Struggle over Guaranteed Income Policy* (Princeton: Princeton University Press, 2008). For Moynihan's recommended books, see DPM memo to Nixon, January 3, 1969, box 248.

5. DPM memo to Nixon, February 20, 1969, box 1. Congress, following President Ronald Reagan, did away with the CSA in 1981.

6. Nixon to DPM, June 20, 1969, box 2. For DPM's opposition to Nixon's policies in Vietnam, see DPM to Nixon, November 25, 1969, box 3, and DPM to H. R. Haldeman, October 1, 1969, box 249. See also Stephen Ambrose, *Nixon: The Triumph of a Politician, 1962–1972* (New York: Simon and Schuster, 1989), 236–237.

7. See DPM, "The Crises in Welfare," *The Public Interest* 10 (Winter 1968): 3–19.

8. Benefits varied in part because attitudes toward support of the poor varied. In the South, for instance, racist views of blacks (many of whom were members of impoverished, female-headed families) helped depress benefit levels. Higher levels, moreover, were thought to encourage poor people to stay on welfare instead of working at low-wage jobs. Furthermore, the total amount of federal-state AFDC aid per recipient in any given state depended upon the amount per recipient first approved by that state. The federal government, following a congressionally established formula, then added a predetermined standard percentage of its own. (The percentage varied over time, increasing slowly after 1935.) Some municipalities—New York, for example—also pitched in to help.

9. Steensland, *The Failed Welfare Revolution*, 85–94.

10. Lemann, *The Promised Land*, 212.

11. Ibid.

12. Steensland, *The Failed Welfare Revolution*, 91.

13. Nixon's views, in Ambrose, *Nixon*, 268; Moynihan cited in Burke and Burke, *Nixon's Good Deed*, 45.

14. DPM speech, July 1, 1970, box 6; Steensland, *The Failed Welfare Revolution*, 124.

15. Moynihan, *The Politics of a Guaranteed Income: The Nixon Administration and the Family Assistance Plan* (New York: Random House, 1973), 255; Gary Burtless, "Inequality, Economic Mobility, and Social Policy," in Peter Schuck and James Q. Wilson, eds., *Understanding America: The Anatomy of an Exceptional Nation* (New York: Public Affairs Press, 2008), 532.

16. Emphasis mine. See also Davies, *From Opportunity to Entitlement*, 211–232.

17. Patterson, *America's Struggle*, 188.

18. Burke and Burke, *Nixon's Good Deed*, 157.

19. Michele Wallace, *Black Macho and the Myth of the Superwoman* (New York: Dial Press, 1979), 11.

20. Patterson, *America's Struggle*, 188–189. See also Johnnie Tillmon, "Women on Welfare," [originally published in 1972] in Susan Ware, ed., *Modern American Women: A Documentary History* (Boston: McGraw-Hill, 2002), 286–290. Tillmon, a black woman and the mother of six children, was the first chair of the NWRO.

21. DPM, memo of July 24, 1970, box 6.

22. See Chapter 9 of this volume.

23. See Glen Cain and Harold Watts, *Income Maintenance and Labor Supply: Econometric Studies* (New York: Academic Press, 1973).

24. Steensland, *The Failed Welfare Revolution*, 215.

25. The original of the memo is in box 5 of the President's Handwriting file, Nixon Project. Copies can be found in box 255 of the DPM papers.

26. *New York Times*, March 11, 1970.

27. DPM complaint to *Newsweek* cited in Hodgson, *The Gentleman from New York*, 192; DPM in *New York Times Magazine* (June 27, 1971): 54.

28. David Broder, *Washington Post*, July 7, 1970.

29. DPM to Nixon, May 9, 1970, box 6.

30. *New York Times*, January 3, 1971; *Washington Post*, December 28, 1970.

31. Moynihan, *The Politics of a Guaranteed Income*.

32. Ambrose, *Nixon*, 425; *Life* article cited by Steinfels in *The Neoconservatives*, 116–117.

33. Because this book focuses on family issues, it does not concern itself with Moynihan's political campaigns. Suffice it to say here that he narrowly won a Democratic primary in 1976—over the liberal feminist Bella Abzug and others—before triumphing in November over the incumbent conservative, James Buckley. Though black leaders in New York continued to denounce his report of 1965, Moynihan swept to one-sided victories in his three later senatorial contests, all of them directed by Liz, his politically savvy wife.

CHAPTER SEVEN

1. Moynihan, "The Schism in Black America," *The Public Interest* 27 (Spring 1972): 3–24, and retitled "The Deepening Schism" in Moynihan, *Coping: Essays on the Practice of Government* (1973). The book jacket informed readers that Moynihan had by then written or cowritten three books, edited or coedited four, and received twenty honorary degrees. (He received forty-five more during his lifetime and one more posthumously.)

2. Orlando Patterson, "Rethinking Black History," *Harvard Educational Review* 41, no. 3 (1971): 297–315, and "On Guilt, Relativism, and Black-White Relations," *The American Scholar* 43 (Winter 1973–1974): 122–132. In his *Ethnic Chauvinism* (New York: Stein and Day, 1977), Patterson offered a fuller statement of these ideas.

3. Elliott Liebow, *Tally's Corner: A Study of Negro Streetcorner Men* (Boston: Little, Brown, 1967); Lee Rainwater, *Behind Ghetto Walls: Black Families in a Federal Slum* (Chicago: Aldine Publishing, 1970).

4. Still another book by a black scholar making such arguments was Robert Hill, *The Strengths of Black Families* (New York: Emerson Hall Publishers, 1972).

5. William Styron, a white novelist, had published *The Confessions of Nat Turner* (New York: Random House) in 1967. His depiction of the sexual urges of Turner, who had led a famed slave revolt in Virginia in 1831, aroused widespread criticism—indeed rage—among black scholars.

6. Joyce Ladner, *Tomorrow's Tomorrow: The Black Woman* (Garden City, NY: Doubleday, 1971). In 1994, Ladner became interim president of Howard University, the first black person to head that institution.

7. Carol Stack, *All Our Kin: Strategies for Survival in a Black Community* (New York: Harper and Row, 1974).

8. Gilbert Osofsky, *Harlem: The Making of a Ghetto: Negro New York, 1890–1930* (New York: Harper and Row, 1966); Allan Spear, *Black Chicago: The Making of a Negro Ghetto, 1890–1920* (Chicago: University of Chicago Press, 1967); Kenneth Kusmer, *A Ghetto Takes Shape: Black Cleveland, 1870–1930* (Urbana: University of Illinois Press, 1976); Arnold Hirsch, *Making the Second Ghetto: Race and Housing in Chicago, 1940–1960* (Cambridge: Cambridge University Press, 1983); and Joe William Trotter, *Black Milwaukee: The Making of an Industrial Proletariat, 1915–1945* (Urbana: University of Illinois Press, 1985).

9. Robert Fogel and Stanley Engerman, *Time on the Cross: The Economics of American Negro Slavery* (Boston: Little, Brown, 1974).

10. Herbert Gutman, *The Black Family in Slavery and Freedom, 1750–1925* (New York: Pantheon Books, 1976). See Chapter 9 of this volume for critiques of Gutman in the 1990s.

11. Douglas Massey and Robert Simpson in 1995, cited in Massey and Sampson, eds., *The Moynihan Report Revisited*, 12.

12. Thanks to the rise of no-fault divorce laws—and to the rising power of rights consciousness—divorce rates mushroomed in the United States during the 1970s. In 1965, the rate (as measured by the number of divorces per 1,000 population) had been 2.5 percent. It reached 3.5 percent by 1970, whereupon it jumped to 5.3 percent—an all-time high in the United States—in 1981. The rate inched down slowly but steadily in later years, to 3.5 percent in 2009. The number of divorces, 479,000 in 1965, leapt to 1,213,000 in 1981.

13. Moynihan, *Family and Nation* (San Diego: Harcourt Brace Jovanovich, 1986), 151.

CHAPTER EIGHT

1. Ken Auletta, *The Underclass* (New York: Random House, 1982). Excerpts from the book appeared earlier in *The New Yorker* and aroused considerable interest.

2. Glenn Loury, "A New American Dilemma," *New Republic* (December 31, 1984): 14–18. Loury's political views later moved well to the left. See Chapter 11 of this volume.

3. Glenn Loury, "The Moral Quandary of the Black Community," *The Public Interest* 79 (Spring 1985): 9–11.

4. Samuel Preston, "Children and the Elderly: Divergent Paths for America's Dependents," *Demography* 21 (November 1984): 453–457.

5. For material in this and following paragraphs, see Moynihan, *Family and Nation*.

6. Glenn Loury, "The Family, the Nation, and Senator Moynihan," *Commentary* 81 (June 1986): 21–26.

7. Eleanor Holmes Norton, "Restoring the Traditional Black Family," *New York Times Magazine* (June 2, 1985). In 1991, Norton began serving as a delegate from the District of Columbia to the U.S. House of Representatives.

8. William Julius Wilson, *The Truly Disadvantaged: The Inner City, the Underclass, and Public Policy* (Chicago: University of Chicago Press, 1987).

9. Wilson's emphasis.

10. Orlando Patterson, *The Ordeal of Integration: Progress and Resentment in America's "Racial" Crisis* (Washington, DC: Civitas/Counterpoint, 1997), 31–35.

11. Christopher Jencks, "Is the American Underclass Growing?" in Christopher Jencks and Paul Peterson, eds., *The Urban Underclass* (Washington, DC: Brookings Institution, 1991), 28–100.

12. Todd Purdum, "The Newest Moynihan," *New York Times Magazine* (August 8, 1974): 24–29. Most close observers believe that Moynihan's drinking, though heavy in those years, did not seriously hamper his work as a senator.

13. Chester Finn, *Troublemaker: A Personal History of School Reform Since Sputnik* (Boston: Little, Brown, 2008), 77–81, 93.

14. The government's official poverty lines, established in the early 1960s, took into account family size and were adjusted annually for inflation. But they rested on a formula for aid that in effect determined the size of a family's cash benefit by multiplying by three the cost of basic foods deemed necessary for the family. Over time, the cost of foods included in the formula rose less rapidly than did other costs—notably housing—thereby resulting in cash benefits per family that became smaller in real dollars. Well before the 1980s (and afterward), liberal critics called in vain for revising the formula.

15. Many deeply pessimistic books about race appeared in these years: for instance, Douglas Massey and Nancy Denton, *American Apartheid: Segregation and the Making of the Underclass* (Cambridge, MA: Harvard University Press, 1993); John Hope Franklin, *The Color Line: Legacy for the Twenty-First Century* (Columbia: University of Missouri Press, 1993); Tom Wicker, *Tragic Failure: Racial Integration in America* (New York: William Morrow, 1996); and Carl Rowan, *The Coming Race War in America: A Wake-up Call* (Boston: Little, Brown, 1996).

16. Quoted in Herbert Hill and James Jones, eds., *Race in America: The Struggle for Equality* (Madison: University of Wisconsin Press, 1993), 18.

17. Shelby Steele, *The Content of Our Character: A New Vision of Race in America* (New York: St. Martin's Press, 1990).

18. Moynihan, "Defining Deviancy Down," *The American Scholar* (Winter 1993): 17–30. A subtitle read, "How We've Become Accustomed to Alarming Levels of Crime and Destructive Behavior."

CHAPTER NINE

1. For the influence of James Coleman's report on Moynihan, see Chapter 5 of this volume.

2. See Foreman, "The Rough Road to Racial Uplift," in Foreman, ed., *The African American Predicament*, 163.

3. For these developments, see Chapter 10 of this volume.

4. Moynihan, "America at Midnight," in *Miles to Go: A Personal History of Social Policy* (Cambridge, MA: Harvard University Press, 1996), 45.

5. Moynihan speech cited in George Will, *Suddenly: The American Idea Abroad and at Home, 1986–1990* (New York: Free Press, 1990), 252.

6. James Q. Wilson, "Pat Moynihan Thinks About Families," in Massey and Sampson, eds., *The Moynihan Report Revisited*, 28–33.

7. See Lawrence Wu et al., "Historical and Life Course Trajectories of Nonmarital Childbearing," in Wu and Wolfe, eds., *Out of Wedlock*, 3–48.

8. The largest means-tested programs (total federal-state expenditures) in fiscal 2004 were Medicaid ($300 billion), SSI ($39.8 billion), EITC (refundable portion) ($30.9 billion), and subsidized housing ($29.8 billion). Except for SSI, all included low-income mothers and children among their beneficiaries. Ranking in size below TANF were child care ($11.9 billion), Head Start ($8.5 billion), and jobs and training ($7 billion). See Robert Moffitt, "A Primer on U.S. Welfare Reform," *Focus* (Institute for Research on Poverty, Madison, Wisconsin) 26 (Summer–Fall 2008): 18–25.

9. Samuel Preston, Suet Lim, and S. Philip Morgan, "African-American Marriage in 1910: Beneath the Surface of Census Data," *Demography* 29 (February 1992): 1–15; and S. Philip Morgan et al., "Racial Differences in Household and Family Structure at the Turn of the Century," *American Journal of Sociology* 98 (January 1993): 798–828.

10. Orlando Patterson, *Rituals of Blood: Consequences of Slavery in Two American Centuries* (Washington, DC: Civitas/Counterpoint, 1998).

11. Orlando Patterson used the terms "Afro-American" and "Euro-American" as stand-ins for "black" and "white."

12. Emphasis is Patterson's.

13. William Julius Wilson, "Foreword: The Moynihan Report and Research on the Black Community," in Massey and Sampson, eds., *The Moynihan Report Revisited*, 34–46; and William Julius Wilson, *More Than Just Race: Being Black and Poor in the Inner City* (New York: W. W. Norton, 2009).

14. Michele Wallace, excerpt from *Black Macho and the Myth of the Superwoman* (ed. 1990), cited in Miriam Schneir, ed., *Feminism in Our Time: The Essential Writings, World War II to the Present* (New York: Vintage Books, 1994), 301.

15. Stephanie Coontz, *The Way We Never Were: American Families and the Nostalgia Trap* (New York: Basic Books, 1992).

16. James Q. Wilson, *The Marriage Problem: How Our Culture Has Weakened Families* (New York: HarperCollins, 2002).

17. Frâncis Fukuyama, *The Great Disruption: Human Nature and the Reconstitution of Social Order* (New York: Free Press, 1999); and Gertrude Himmelfarb, *One Nation, Two Cultures* (New York: Alfred A. Knopf, 1999). See also David Blankenhorn, *Fatherless America: Confronting Our Most Urgent Social Problem* (New York: Basic Books, 1995); and David Popenoe, *Life Without Father* (New York: Martin Kessler Books, Free Press, 1996).

18. John McWhorter, *Losing the Race: Self-Sabotage in Black America* (New York: Free Press, 2000), 257.

CHAPTER TEN

1. Daniel Patrick Moynihan, Timothy Smeeding, and Lee Rainwater, eds., *The Future of the Family* (New York: Russell Sage Foundation, 2004), is a primary source for many of the data in this chapter.

2. For statistics on these and other matters, see also Shelly Lundberg, "Nonmarital Fertility: Lessons for Family Economics," and Andrew Cherlin, "New Developments in the Study of Nonmarital Childbearing," in Wu and Wolfe, eds., *Out of Wedlock*, 383–389 and 390–402, respectively.

3. Given the publication of books such as William Julius Wilson's *The Truly Disadvantaged* (1987), this was an odd statement. How it would have been received would have depended on one's understanding of the word "definitively."

4. Moynihan's wording of this "law" at the conference in 2002 was slightly different from that in Rossi's original, but the meaning was the same.

5. Lawrence Wu et al., "Historical and Life Course Trajectories of Nonmarital Childbearing," in Wu and Wolfe, eds., *Out of Wedlock*, 38.

6. Ibid.

7. Paul Barton, *Welfare: Indicators of Dependency* (Princeton, NJ: Educational Testing Service, 1998). This report carried a foreword by Moynihan.

8. Berkeley: University of California Press.

9. Some scholars, however, continue to believe that the U.S. welfare system both before and after 1996 has had a small but discernible negative impact on marriage rates.

10. William Julius Wilson later wrote favorable comments about their book.

11. Emphases of the authors.

CHAPTER ELEVEN

1. See Juan Williams, *Enough: The Phony Leaders, Dead-End Movements, and Culture of Failure That Are Undermining Black America—and What We Can Do About It* (New York: Crown Publishing Group, Random House, 2006), for extensive coverage of Cosby's talk.

2. Interview with Roger Wilkins, February 2009.

3. These increases did not stem from a new baby boom. Birthrates in the United States, stable since the mid-1970s, did not increase in the early 2000s. They stemmed, rather, from overall population increases, especially from immigration.

4. Iceland continued to lead the developed world in this respect, with 66 percent of its babies born out of wedlock in 2007. Next in order, with proportions between 55 and 44 percent, were Sweden, Norway, France, Denmark, and the United Kingdom. Some industrialized countries—Germany, Spain, Canada, and Italy—had proportions of 30 percent or less, and Japan had one of 2 percent.

5. See Chapter 5 of this volume for the varied causes of these long-range developments.

6. Stephanie Ventura, "Changing Patterns of Nonmarital Childbearing in the United States," Division of Vital Statistics, Centers for Disease Control and Prevention, Data Brief 18 (May 2009). In 2008, a year of economic decline, the total number of births in the United States decreased by 68,000.

7. See *New York Times*, February 21, 2008, and March 13, 2009; Paul Barton and Richard Coley, *The Family: America's Smallest School* (Princeton, NJ: Educational Testing Service, 2007); U.S. Department of Health and Human Services, *Indicators of Welfare Dependence* (Washington, DC: Government Printing Office, 2007), pt. 3, p. 43; and Brady Hamilton et al., *National Vital Statistics Report* 57, no. 12 (March 18, 2009).

8. John McWhorter, *Winning the Race: Beyond the Crisis in Black America* (New York: Gotham Books, 2006), 379.

9. Williams, *Enough*.

10. *New York Times*, November 27, 2009. Nationwide, infant mortality in 2007 was 13 per 1,000 births among blacks and 6 per 1,000 births among whites.

11. *New York Times*, October 7 and 9, 2009.

12. Ibid., July 26, 2009.

13. Ibid., July 17, 2009.

14. See Paul Tough, *Whatever It Takes: Geoffrey Canada's Quest to Change Harlem and America* (Boston: Houghton Mifflin, 2008).

15. Ibid.

16. *New York Times*, April 2 and 29, July 15, and October 15, 2009. Demographic data are relevant to a full understanding of many of these discouraging scores. Considerably higher percentages of minority students—many of them from low-income families whose parents do not have extensive educational backgrounds—have taken these tests in recent years than was the case in the early 1970s. Experts agree that their participation has weighed down the average test scores of students over the years. The percentage of white students who take the tests has risen more slowly. Still, the gaps are real.

17. Barton and Coley, *The Family*, estimate that two-thirds of the large differences among the states in eighth-grade National Association of Educational Progress (NAEP) reading test results can be explained by four factors: single-parent families, parents reading to their children, time spent by children watching TV, and frequency of school absences.

18. McWhorter, *Winning the Race*, 118.

19. Barack Obama, *The Audacity of Hope: Thoughts on Reclaiming the American Dream* (New York: Crown Publishers, 2006), 295–304.

20. Massey and Sampson, eds., *The Moynihan Report Revisited*.

21. William Julius Wilson, "Foreword: The Moynihan Report and Research on the Black Community," in Massey and Sampson, eds., *The Moynihan Report Revisited*, 44.

22. A major source for Wilson is Michele Lamont and Mario Luis Small, "How Culture Matters: Enriching Our Understanding of Poverty," in Ann Lin and David Harris, eds., *The Colors of Poverty: Why Racial and Ethnic Disparities Exist* (New York: Russell Sage Foundation, 2008).

23. Barack Obama, quoted in *New York Times*, June 16, 2008.

24. Barack Obama, quoted in *Washington Post*, June 18, 2008. Interview with E. J. Dionne, February 2009.

25. Rev. Al Sharpton, quoted by *Fox News*, July 5, 2008; Barack Obama, quoted in *New York Times*, June 16, 2008.

26. Michelle Obama, quoted in *Providence Journal*, June 18, 2008.

INDEX

Abrams, Elliott, 143
After Freedom (Powdermaker), 28
Agnew, Spiro, 124, 126
Aid to Families with Dependent Children
    (AFDC)
    and breakdown of Negro family
        (Moynihan), 52
    cost of benefits 1990–1993, 168
    critics of, 96–97
    as flawed (Moynihan), 60
    as flawed (Preston), 148
    Johnson, Lyndon B., on, 14–15
    Moynihan in Nixon administration
        trying to overhaul, 113
    Moynihan on, 15
    nonwhite male unemployment rates
        and, 25
    Personal Responsibility and Work
        Opportunity Reconciliation Act
        (PRWORA) and, 167
    rates (1960–1975)/cost of, 96
    recession of 1990–1991 and, 160
    relationship with unemployment,
        57–58
    replaced by TANF, 172–173
    Wilson, William Julius on, 154–155
Alcohol. *See* Substance abuse
Alexander, Clifford, and "To Fulfill These
    Rights," 88
All Our Kin (Stack), 131–132
Almanac of American Politics (Barone), 101

Ambrose, Stephen, as biographer of
    Nixon, 112
America, "A Family Policy for the Nation"
    (Moynihan), 72–73, 86
American Academy of Arts and Sciences
    Daedalus, 34
    and "unequal treatment for the
        Negro," 16
An American Dilemma (Myrdal), 29, 31, 34
The American Scholar, Moynihan's essays
    in, 100
American Sociological Association (ASA),
    29
American Sociological Society, 29
Americans for Democratic Action,
    Moynihan as member of, 7
Amsterdam News, Farmer in, 84–85
Angelou, Maya, 207
Anisfield Prize, 30
Architectural Forum, Moynihan's essays in,
    100
Arlington National Cemetery, 201
Armed forces
    as induction of black males into
        American society, 13, 44
    Moynihan in ROTC, 2
    One-Third of a Nation (Moynihan)
        and, 12–13, 24, 56
Atlantic Monthly, Moynihan's essays in,
    100
The Audacity of Hope (Obama), 212

Auletta, Ken, 146
Automobile industry, Moynihan on safety
    of, 8

Baby boom, 92, 96
Baldwin, James
    and resiliency of black people to
        slavery, 132
    on slavery, 36
Barone, Michael, 101
Barton, Paul, 12, 24, 26
    Howard University commencement
        address (1965) and, 45
    on marriage reduction rates, 195
    and Moynihan as part of Nixon
        administration, 111
    on speed of writing Moynihan Report,
        42
    on trends of family life (1995), 171
To Be Equal (Young), 40, 82
Bell, Daniel
    on family issues, 150
    and "unequal treatment for the
        Negro," 16
Beloved (Morrison), 176
Benign neglect memo of Moynihan,
    124–126
Benjamin Franklin High School, 2–3
Bergen, Candice, 162
Bernhard, Berl, 83
Berry, Mary Frances, 152
Bettelheim, Bruno, 33
Beyond the Melting Pot (Glazer and
    Moynihan), 9–10, 19, 32, 56
Bigger Thomas, 152
Billingsley, Andrew, 131, 176
Birth control information
    illegitimacy and, 44
    Ryan on, 82
Birth rates among unmarried women of
    childbearing age, 91

*The Black Family in Slavery and Freedom,
    1750–1925* (Gutman), 133–134
The Black Family in the United States
    (Frazier), 30
Black Muslims, 56–57
Black Panthers, 124, 126
Blackstone Rangers, 18
Blaming the Victim (Ryan), 81
Blank, Rebecca, 212
Blankenhorn, David, 162, 183
Blassingame, John, 132
Board of Education, Brown v.
    as civil rights milestone, 34
    Cosby speaking on fiftieth anniversary
        of, 203
    in preface of Moynihan Report, 47
Brennan, Elizabeth "Liz," 98, 111
    introduction to Moynihan, 7–8
    and Senate elections, 234n33
Broder, David, and Moynihan's memo
        concerning silent black majority,
        125–126
Broderick, Ellen, 24
Brotherhood of Sleeping Car Porters,
        Randolph, A Philip and, xi
Brown, Edmund "Pat," 67
Brown, Murphy, 162
Brown v. Board of Education
    as civil rights milestone, 34
    Cosby speaking on fiftieth anniversary
        of, 203
    in preface of Moynihan Report, 47
Buckley, William, 101
Bureau of Labor Statistics, Moynihan and,
        12
Burgess, E. W., 28–29
Burns, Arthur, as Counselor to Nixon, 111
Burtless, Gary, 117
Bush, George H. W.
    election of, 161
    FAP and, 117

Califano, Joseph, 118, 170
Cambridge, Massachusetts, 97–98
    and threat to burn Moynihan's home
        by SDS, 126
Carter administration, guaranteed income
    plan and, 123–124
Carter, Jimmy, social programs and, 142
"The Case for National Action" (fifth
    chapter), 57–58
Cater, Douglas, 9
Catholic Home, Moynihan's essays in, 100
Cayton, Horace, 28
CBS, "The Vanishing Family—Crisis in
    Black America" and, 151
Center for Advanced Studies (Wesleyan
    University), 74
Centers for Disease Control (CDC), 208
Challenge to Affluence (Myrdal), 39
Child care, TANF and, 175
Child-support. *See also* Welfare
    Family Support Act (FSA) and, 160
Children of Bondage (Dollard and Davis), 28
The Children of Sanchez (Lewis), 18–19
Children's Defense Fund, 173
Chisholm, Shirley, 118–119
City College of New York (CCNY), 2
Civil Rights Act
    as hope for equality, 88
    Moynihan on, 21, 42
Civil rights movement
    Brown v. Board of Education and, 34,
        47, 203
    impact of Watts Riot on, 69
    Johnson's civil rights speech (1965)
        and, ix–xi
    and LBJ's State of the Union address
        (1966), 85
    and negative feelings toward
        Moynihan Report, 76–77
    "The Negro American Revolution"
        (first chapter) and, 49–50

Clark, Kenneth
    on civil rights (1993), 164
    and *Daedalus* essays after publication
        of Report, 73
    Dark Ghetto, 24, 34, 49, 156–157
    defense of Moynihan, 86
    on ghettos, 63
    having received Report privately, 67
    losing hope for equality, 89
    Moynihan seeking advice from, 24
    and Moynihan's memo concerning
        silent black majority, 125
    on pathology, 149
    portrayal of black Americans by, 34–35
    as respected psychologist, 36
    on "tangle of pathology," 129
Clinton administration, health care reform
    instead of welfare reform, 169
Clinton, Bill
    Personal Responsibility and Work
        Opportunity Reconciliation Act
        (PRWORA) and, 167
    welfare reform and, 165–170, 172–173
Clinton, Hillary Rodham, 187
Cognitive difficulties of blacks, "The
    Tangle of Pathology" (fourth
    chapter) and, 57
Coleman, James, 103–105, 188
Coleman Report, 170
College of the City of New York
    (CCNY), Clark and, 34
*Come on, People: On the Path from Victims
    to Victors* (Poussaint and Cosby),
    206–207
Commentary
    and Moynihan as neoconservative,
        101–102
    Moynihan's essays in, 100, 149
    Rustin and, 40, 50
Committee on Juvenile Delinquency and
    Youth Crime, 34

Commonweal
    and equality to blacks, 74
    Gans' summary of Report, 78
    Moynihan's essays in, 100
Community Action Programs (CAPs)
    birth of, 17
    "The Negro American Revolution"
        (first chapter) and, 50
Community Services Administration
    (CSA), OEO and, 112
Concerned Women for American (CWA),
    139
Conference. *See* "To Fulfill These
    Rights"
Conference (2002) at Syracuse University,
    187–197
Congress on Racial Equality (CORE)
    Farmer of, 84–85
    on Moynihan Report, xv
    Ryan of, 81
    Watts Riot and, 69
*The Content of Our Character: A New
    Vision of Race in America* (Steele),
    164
Coontz, Stephanie, 181
Cosby, Bill, 146–147, 203–204, 206–208
The Cosby Show, 146–147, 164
Crime rates. *See also* Violence
    black children (2008) and, 208–209
    prison, 185
    "The Tangle of Pathology" (fourth
        chapter) and, 55
    underclass and, 146
Crisis in Black and White (Silberman), 40
Crisis, "The New Genteel Racism," 81
Criticisms of Moynihan Report
    during Clinton administration, 171
    gender emphasis on men, 60
    from liberal whites, 74–75
    need for more educational/economic
        controlled comparisons, 61
    no specific solutions, 59–60

oversimplification/overdramatization,
    61–62
    welfare for abetting illegitimacy, 60–61
Cultural attachments
    armed forces as induction of black
        males into American society, 13
    Coleman on, 103–104
    contraception/abortion and, 92
    criticism of Moynihan and War on
        Poverty, 18–19
    and decline of marriage, 209
    Dobson, James and, 139
    formation of black folk culture, 30
    Frazier on urban migration and, 30–31
    hip-hop as misogynistic, 206
    housing as, 38
    importance according to Moynihan, 6
    Ladner on, 131
    marriage in 1980s, 138
    More Than Just Race (Wilson) and, 213
    Patterson on, 178–179
    and the "undeserving" poor, 212
    Wilson, James Q. on, 182
    Wilson, William Julius on, 154, 180
Cultural factors
    Moynihan emphasizing, 59
    and structural dislocations as self-
        perpetuating, 58

Daedalus, 34, 55
    essays after publication of Report, 73
    "The Negro American"
        (Clark/Bayard/Moynihan), 66
Daley, Richard, 18
Dark Ghetto (Clark), 24, 34–35, 49,
    156–157
Davies, Joseph, 10
Davis, Allison, 28
Day-care centers during Nixon
    administration, 121
de Tocqueville, Alexis, 101
"The Decline of Marriage," 92

"Defining Deviancy Down" (Moynihan), 165

Deindustrialization, 156

Delinquency. *See also* Crime rates
"The Tangle of Pathology" (fourth chapter) and, 55

Democrats. *See also* Clinton, Bill
Moynihan as (1950s–early 1960s), 7
Moynihan as (late 1960s–early 1970s), 102
and Moynihan as part of Nixon administration, 112

Demographics
and 2002 conference at Syracuse University, 188–192
and 2002 conference at Syracuse University and poverty, 192–193
and decline of marriage, 209
family issues and, 91–92
illegitimacy and, 204–205
National Assessment of Educational Progress (NAEP) tests and, 211–212
poverty (2007) and, 208
Preston and, 147–148
underclass and, 146

Demography, 148

Department of Health, Education, and Welfare (HEW)
Califano and, 118
criticism of Report by, 75
estimate of AFDC, 52

Department of Housing and Urban Development, creation of, xii

Department of Labor
Keyserling of, 84
Moynihan as assistant secretary of labor for policy planning and research, 11–12
on title page of Moynihan Report, 47

Dionne, E. J., 214–215

Disraeli, Benjamin, 101, 112

Disturbing the Nest: Family Change and Decline in Modern Societies (Popenoe), 163

Dobson, James, 139

Dollard, John, 28–29, 178

Drake, St. Clair, 28

Dropout rates
2008, 208
Cosby, Bill on, 203, 207
McWhorter on, 206
underclass and, 146
Wilson, James Q. on, 182
Wilson, William Julius on, 154
Young on, 40

Drug trade, noninclusion in Moynihan Report of, 63

Du Bois, W. E. B., 26–28
The Philadelphia Negro, 156
Preston and, 177–178
as respected academe, 36
"The Schism in Black America" and, 129

Dukakis, Michael, 161

Durkheim, Émile, 165

Dyson, Michael Eric, 207–208

Early Head Start, 216

Earned Income Tax Credit (EITC), 121, 169, 209

Economic condition
and 2002 conference at Syracuse University, 192–193, 196–197, 196–198
Bush, George H. W. and welfare, 161–162
as criticism of Moynihan, 130–131
and decline of marriage, 209
education and, 212
Family Assistance Plan (FAP) (1969) and, 115–118
influencing sexual mores, 27–28
Lewis on, 83–84

Economic condition *(continued)*
 as major factor in black family
  problems, 37
 matriarchy and, 60
 More Than Just Race (Wilson) and, 213
 Novak and Evans failure to
  emphasize, 71
 Patterson on, 179
 political influence of low-income
  families, 122
 poverty and, 136–137
 and poverty during Clinton
  administration, 174–175
 and poverty of cohabiting couples, 192
 and prosperity masking
  unemployment rates for blacks, 72
 and recovery of 2000, 200–201
 SAT of students (1995) and, 184–185
 as self-perpetuating, 143–144
 Silberman on, 40–41
 and structural dislocations as self-
  perpetuating, 58
 Watts Riot and, 67
 Wilson, William Julius on, 155–156
Edelman, Marian Wright, 173
Edelman, Peter, 173
Edin, Kathyrn, 197–201
Education
 Coleman on, 103–104
 Coleman Report and, 170
 Early Head Start, 216
 Ellwood and Jencks on importance of,
  193
 gender in black children and excelling
  in, 49
 Harlem Children's Zone Project, 211
 Head Start, 17, 122, 182, 216
 as key to equality, 210
 memo regarding testing of blacks, 13
 of Moynihan, 2, 4–5, 8
 Moynihan's honorary degree from
  Harvard, 187

 Moynihan's move to Middletown,
  Connecticut for Wesleyan
  teaching position, 74
 National Assessment of Educational
  Progress (NAEP) tests and,
  211–212
 need for sex education, 209
 One-Third of a Nation and, 12–13
 SAT as reflection of wealth, 212
 SAT of students (1995), 184–185
 Teach for America program, 210
 "The U.S. and the International Labor
  Organization, 1889–1934" (thesis),
  5
 Young on dropout rates, 40
"Education and Urban Politics" (Harvard
 class), 98
Ehrlichman, John, as Nixon's advisor, 111
Elementary and Secondary Education Act,
 passing of, xi
Eliot, T. S., 101
Elkins, Stanley, 33
 critics of, 36
 on racism/economic discrimination, 62
 and resiliency of black people due to
  slavery, 132
 "The Roots of the Problem" (third
  chapter), 52
Ellison, Ralph, 65, 134
Ellwood, David
 at 2002 conference at Syracuse
  University, 188
 on economic policies, 196–197
 on education, 193
 on welfare, 167, 176
Employment
 of black women (1970–1980s), 137
 Concerned Women for American
  (CWA) and, 139
 labor unions and, 29
 Moynihan and black GIs from
  Vietnam, 98–99

overemployment of black women, 84
TANF and, 194
for the uneducated, 156
and unemployment rate for
blacks/whites (1964), 15
women leaving welfare (1990s) for,
175
Engerman, Stanley, 133
*Enough: The Phony Leaders, Dead-End
Movements, and Culture of Failure
That Are Undermining Black
America—and What We Can Do
About It* (Williams), 206
"Epidemic on the Highways" (Moynihan),
8
Equal Employment Opportunity
Commission (EEOC), Norton on,
150
Equal Rights Amendment, Concerned
Women for American (CWA)
and, 139
Equality as goal, 44–45
armed forces and, 56
Civil Rights Act/Voting Rights Act
as, 88
as continuing outcome, 217
and disillusionment of Report, 80
at end of Moynihan Report, 58–59
importance according to Moynihan,
106
importance of education, 210
in preface of Moynihan Report, 47–48
via preferential treatment to Negroes,
71
and voting down of FAP, 122
welfare reform and, 117
Equality of Educational Opportunity
(Coleman), 103
Erikson, Erik, and "unequal treatment for
the Negro," 16
"Errors and No Facts," 71
Estes, Steve, 71

Ethnic chauvinism (Patterson), 130
Evans, Rowland, 71

Family and Nation (Moynihan), 149, 189
Family Assistance Plan (FAP) (1969)
birth of, 115
defeat of, 120
economic policies of, 115–118
Family issues
and 2002 conference at Syracuse
University, 187–197
"A Family Policy for the Nation"
(Moynihan), 72–73, 72–73, 86
AFDC (1970s–1980s), 140
as continuing low political priority,
216–217
Coontz on, 181–182
Cosby, Bill on, 203–204
Dobson, James and, 139
Himmelfarb and Fukuyama on, 183
and illegitimacy in 1980s, 92
impact of decline of marriage, 92
instability as positive adaptation, 78
Jencks on, 195
jeremiads in 1990s about, 181
King, Martin Luther, Jr., and, 74
Ladner on, 131
as legacy of slavery, 27–29
Lewis and, 83
Moynihan on family allowances,
99–100, 194
Moynihan's focus on, 21–22, 41–44
National Marriage Project and, 163
"The Negro American Family"
(second chapter) and, 50–52
as nonexistent in black family
structure, 88–89
noninclusion in Moynihan Report of
changing, 63
Obama on, 214–215
political influence of low-income, 122
and preface of Moynihan Report, 48

Family issues *(continued)*
    and resiliency of black people to
        slavery, 132–133
    "Restoring the Traditional Black
        Family" (Norton), 150
    riot commission report and, 90–91
    "The Roots of the Problem" (third
        chapter), 53
    as self-perpetuating, 143–144
    Stack on, 131–132
    "The Tangle of Pathology" (fourth
        chapter) and, 54–55
    and thesis of Moynihan Report, 24
    welfare reform and, 114–118
    Wilson, James Q., on, 185
"A Family Policy for the Nation"
        (Moynihan), 72–73, 86
Family Research council, 139
Family Support Act (FSA)
    Clinton and, 168
    Reagan and, 160
Family values, Quayle and, 162
Farmer, James
    Amsterdam News, 84–85
    Congress on Racial Equality (CORE)
        and, xv
    on impact of Watts Riot, 69
Finn, Chester, 143, 159
Fisk University, Frazier and, 29
Fletcher School of Law and Diplomacy, 4
Focus on the Family, 139
Fogel, Robert, 133
Food Stamps
    1970s–1980s and, 140
    during Clinton administration, 174–175
    during Democratic control of
        Congress, 120
Ford, Gerald
    Moynihan as ambassador to United
        Nations, 127
    OEO transferred to CSA, 112
    social programs and, 141–142

Foreman, Christopher, xiv, xvi
Fortune, Silberman and, 40
Franklin, John Hope, and *Daedalus* essays
        after publication of Report, 73
Frazier, E. Franklin, 29–31
    Preston on, 177
    as respected academe, 36
    "The Roots of the Problem" (third
        chapter), 52–53
    on slavery, 130
    Stack on, 131–132
Friedman, Milton, 114
Fukuyama, Francis, 183–184
Fulbright award, 4
Furstenberg, Frank, 213

Gans, Herbert, 78–79
Geertz, Clifford, and "unequal treatment
        for the Negro," 16
Genovese, Eugene, 101, 132–133
GI Bill. *See also* Government programs
    Moynihan on, 2
    and Moynihan's thesis on ILO, 4
Gilder, George, 138–139
Gimbels Department Store, 2
Glazer, Nathan, 9, 23
    on matriarchy, 33
    and Moynihan at Harvard, 98
    "The Negro American Revolution"
        (first chapter) and, 50
    and psychological theories to
        historical study, 33
    as respected sociologist, 36
    "The Roots of the Problem" (third
        chapter), 52
Goals 2000, 170
Goldberg, Arthur, 10
    Supreme Court and, 11
Goodwin, Richard, 22, xiii
    Gans and, 79
    Howard University commencement
        address (1965), 44–45

Government Printing Office (GPO),
    printing/selling of Moynihan
    Report, 66–67
Government programs. *See also* specific
    program
    and 2002 conference at Syracuse
        University, 187–197
    to blame for broken black families, 106
    Earned Income Tax Credit (EITC)
        and, 121, 169, 209
    Family Assistance Plan (FAP) (1969)
        and, 210
    Ford/Carter/Reagan and, 141–142
    hastily assembled, 6
    and liberalization of welfare, 209–210
    Moynihan on family allowances, 99–100
    Murray on, 140
    negative income tax, 114
    Obama administration and, 216
    Race to the Top initiative, 216
    Supplementary Security Income (SSI),
        120
    Wilson, James Q., on, 183
*The Great Disruption: Human Nature and
    the Reconstitution of Social Order*
    (Fukuyama), 183
Great Society liberals, 141
    on Nixon's election, 90
Greenfield, Meg, 9–10
Gross domestic product (GDP), 193–194
Guaranteed income plan, 114, 123–124
Gutman, Herbert, 133–135, 153, 176–177

Habituation, 182
Hacker, Andrew, 164
Haldeman, H. R., and Moynihan's memo
    concerning silent black majority,
    125
Handlin, Oscar, 67
Harlem Children's Zone Project, 211
Harlem Youth Opportunities Unlimited
    (HARYOU), 34, 36

Harriman, Averell, 7–8, 188
Harrington, Michael
    in defense of the Report, 74
    on intergenerational culture of
        poverty, 62
    The Other America, 19
    on *The Truly Disadvantaged*, 153
    Young, Whitney and, 40
Harris, Patricia, 61
Harvard, 4
    Moynihan's honorary degree from,
        187
Harvard-MIT Joint Center for Urban
        Studies
    and Moynihan as ambassador to
        United Nations, 128
    Moynihan as head of, 97–98
    and Moynihan's resignation from
        Nixon administration, 126
Haskins, Ron, 213
Head Start
    birth of, 17
    equality and, 122
    ineffectiveness of, 182
    Obama and, 215
Heineman, Ben, as chair of "To Fulfill
        These Rights," 86
Hell's Kitchen, 2
Herbers, John, 86
Hershey, Lewis, 12
Hill, Herbert, Moynihan seeking advice
        from, 24
Hilton Hotel conference, 83–84
Himmelfarb, Gertrude, 183
Hip-hop culture, as misogynistic, 206
Hodgson, Godfrey, 75
Hofstadter, Richard, 101
Holzer, Harry, 213
Hooks, Benjamin, 146
Horgan, Paul, 74
Housing and Urban Development,
        establishment of, 70

Housing, as source of change in cultural
     trait, 38
Howard University commencement
     address (1965), 189
Humphrey, Hubert, 90, 110

"I Have a Dream" speech (King), 39
"Idea Broker in the Race Crisis," 99–100
Illegitimacy ratios. *See also* Demographics
     1946–1964, 86
     1950–1960, 91
     1960, 37
     1963 compared to 2007, xvi
     1964, 43–44
     1965/1970/1980s, 136–137
     1970, 58
     1970–1990s, 91
     1980s–1990s, 145–146
     1991, 168
     1994–2002, 174
     1998–2002, 204
     and 2002 conference at Syracuse
          University, 188–191
     2006–2007, 208
     2007, 204–205
     The Audacity of Hope (Obama) and,
          212
     Beyond the Melting Pot (Moynihan and
          Glazer) and, 9
     birth control information and, 44
     and birth rates among unmarried
          women of childbearing age, 91
     Clark on, 35
     Cosby, Bill, on, 203
     and criticisms of Moynihan Report, 60
     and *Daedalus* essays after publication
          of Report, 73
     Dollard and Davis on, 28
     Du Bois on, 28
     Frazier on slavery and, 30
     Gutman on, 134–135

     and initial public appearance of
          Moynihan Report, 67
     instability as positive adaptation, 78
     Loury on, 147
     Moynihan Report and, xiv
     and Moynihan's memo concerning
          silent black majority, 124
     "The Negro American Family"
          (second chapter) and, 51
     Obama on, 214–215
     Patterson on, 158
     relationship with unemployment,
          53–54
     "Restoring the Traditional Black
          Family" (Norton), 150
     Ryan on, 81–82
     and stigma of 1960's, 92
     Wilson, James Q., on, 182, 185
Immediate gratification, 55
Income tax. *See* Earned Income Tax Credit
     (EITC)
Incomes strategy, 114
Industrial proletariat, Frazier on, 29–30
"Inside Report" (Novak and Evans), 70–71
Institute for American Values, 162
Intelligence, "The Tangle of Pathology"
     (fourth chapter) and, 55
International Labour Organisation (ILO),
     4
International Rescue Committee, 7
Invisible Man (Ellison), 134
Iron Law of Evaluation, 189
*Is Cosby Right? Or Has the Black Middle
     Class Lost Its Mind?* (Dyson),
     207–208

Jackson, Jesse
     on Obama, xvi
     on Obama's 2008 speech, 216
     "The Vanishing Family—Crisis in
          Black America" and, 151

Jackson, Walter, 71
Jencks, Christopher
    at 2002 conference at Syracuse
        University, 188
    on complexity of underclass, 157
    on economic policies, 196–197
    on education, 193
    endorsement of public programs by,
        169
    on factors of declining marriage, 156
    on family issues, 195
    on family stability, 139–140
    on Moynihan's Report, 78
Jim Crow, 52–53, 178–180
Job Corps
    initiation of, 13
    as training/education program, 17
Job Training, 50
"Jobless Negroes and the Boom"
    (Moynihan), 72
Jobs. *See* Employment
John F. Kennedy School of Government
        (Harvard), Moynihan's lectures at,
        148–150
Johnson administration
    authorizing aid to blacks, 69–70
    and burgeoning civil rights movement,
        22–23
    Freedom Budget and, 39–40
    immediately after JFK assassination,
        11
    negative feelings toward Moynihan
        Report, 76
    Vietnam War and, 89
Johnson, Charles, 28–29
Johnson, Lyndon B.
    and antiwar sentiments regarding
        Vietnam, 66, 76
    and *Daedalus* essays after publication
        of Report, 73
    on education, 210

    on first reading of Moynihan Report,
        43–44
    Great Society and, 141
    Howard University commencement
        address (1965) and, 44–45, 65, 189,
        ix–xi, xiii
    negative feelings toward Moynihan,
        75–76
    "The President and the Negro: The
        Moment Lost" (Moynihan), 65
    State of the Union address (1966), 85
    and "To Fulfill These Rights," 86
Joyce, James, 101

Kefalas, Maria, 197–201
Kennedy administration
    Committee on Juvenile Delinquency
        and Youth Crime, 34
    economic policies of, 14
    poverty and, 13–14, xi
    Task Force on Manpower
        Conservation, 12
Kennedy, John F.
    assassination of, 11
    on civil rights legislation, 38
    election of, 10
Kennedy, Robert F., 75
    assassination of, 90
    Moynihan campaigning for, 22
Kent State University, 126
Keynesian economics, and Moynihan's
        observations of social change, 14
Keyserling, Mary, criticism of Moynihan
        Report, 84
King, Martin Luther, Jr.
    assassination of, 90
    in defense of the Report, 74
    on Howard University
        commencement address (1965),
        65
    as influence on Moynihan, 38–39

King, Martin Luther, Jr. *(continued)*
  on Johnson's civil rights speech
    (1965), xi
  and negative feelings toward
    Moynihan Report, 77
  and "unequal treatment for the
    Negro," 16
  Watts Riot and, 69
King, Rodney, 163–164
Kissinger, Henry, 109, 124, 127–128
Kristol, Irving, 8–9, 102

Labor unions, Frazier on interracial, 29
Ladner, Joyce, 131
LaHaye, Beverly, 139
Lemann, Nicholas
  on Moynihan as intellectual, 22
  on Moynihan's style, 12
  The Promised Land, 163
  suggesting Moynihan leaked initial
    Report information, 67
Leslie, John, on reception to Report, 70
Lewis, Hylan
  as expert on family issues, 83–84
  Moynihan seeking advice from, 24
Lewis, Oscar, 18–19
Liberal legislation, Johnson administration
    and, xi–xii
Liberal organizations, Americans for
    Democratic Action, 7
Liberal thoughts, and preface of Moynihan
    Report, 49
Liberals. *See also* Democrats
  to blame for broken black families,
    105–106
  on Carter, 142
  and critics of AFDC, 97
  disillusionment of, 79
  Family Support Act (FSA) and,
    160–161
  and Moynihan as neoconservative,
    102–103

treating Moynihan as racist, 100, 107
  voting down FAP by, 120
  wanting overhaul of AFDC, 113–114
  Wilson, William Julius, as, 155
Life
  "Idea Broker in the Race Crisis,"
    99–100
  and Moynihan on equality, 102
  Moynihan's defense of Report, 85–86
  and Moynihan's resignation from
    Nixon administration, 127
Lindsay, John, 112
London School of Economics and Political
    Science (LSE), 4
Long, Russell, 117–118
Los Angeles. *See* Violence
*Losing Ground: American Social Policy,
    1950–1980* (Murray), 140
*Losing the Race: Self-Sabotage in Black
    America* (McWhorter), 184, 206
Loury, Glenn
  "A New American Dilemma," 147
  on blacks in prison, 208–209
  as critic of black behavior, 184
Lumpenproletariat, 151. *See also*
    Underclass

MacLeish, Archibald, 101
Malcolm X
  as influence on Moynihan, 39
  and resiliency of black people due to
    slavery, 132
Manpower Development Training
    Program
  initiation of, 13
  "The Negro American Revolution"
    (first chapter) and, 49–50
March on Washington (1963), Bayard and,
    39
Marcuse, Herbert, 101
Marriage. *See also* Illegitimacy ratios;
    Matriarchy

and 2002 conference at Syracuse
University, 190, 192, 197–200
birth rates of married women, 92
decrease among women of
childbearing age who are, 92
Du Bois on, 28
employment and, 194
factors for decline of, 209
rates of black women versus white
women, 94–95
reasons for reduction rates for, 195
white versus black percentages, 92
of women (1970–1980s), 137–138
The Marriage Problem (Wilson), 182
Marshall, Thurgood, and "To Fulfill
These Rights," 87
Marshall, Will, 196
Massey, Douglas
on impact of Report in social science
studies, 136
on importance/obscurity of Report,
72
Matriarchy
1860–1880, 135
1950–1970, 94
and 2002 conference at Syracuse
University, 188, 192
adaptiveness of, 61
as being at disadvantage in America,
60
Beyond the Melting Pot (Moynihan and
Glazer) and, 9
consequences of illegitimacy, 94
as feminization of poverty, 173
Frazier on slavery and, 30
Glazer on, 33
and immediate gratification of
children, 55
and initial public appearance of
Moynihan Report, 67
instability as positive adaptation, 78
Lewis on, 83

marriage in 1980s and, 138–139
Moynihan on, 41–42
Moynihan Report and, xiv
"The Negro American Family"
(second chapter) and, 51
as outcome of illegitimate births, 82
overemployment of black women, 84
Patterson on, 158
poverty and, 136–137, 192
Powdermaker on, 28–29
religion and, 56–57
"The Roots of the Problem" (third
chapter), 52–54
"The Tangle of Pathology" (fourth
chapter) and, 54–57
Wilson, James Q., on, 182
Matusow, Allen, 23
Maxwell Graduate School of Citizenship
and Public Affairs, 8, 187–189
McCarthy, Eugene, NWRO and, 120
McCarthy, Joseph, Nixon supporting, 109
McCarthyism, Ryan's criticism as, 82
McGovern, George, NWRO and, 120
McGrory, Mary, 10–11
McLanahan, Sara, at 2002 conference at
Syracuse University, 188
McPherson, Harry
disillusionment of, 79–80
and memo regarding equality for
blacks, 44–45
and memo regarding testing of blacks,
13
on Moynihan as part of Nixon
administration, 110
and Moynihan responding to
HEW/OEO criticism, 75
as promoter of Moynihan, 23
McWhorter, John, 184, 206
Medicaid
1970s–1980s and, 140
during Democratic control of
Congress, 120

Medicare
    during Democratic control of
        Congress, 120
    Reagan and, 142
Meet the Press
    Moynihan's defense of Report, 85–86
    Russert as chair of, 143
Merton, Robert, and "unequal treatment
    for the Negro," 16
Mfumi, Kweisi, 204
Middlebury College (Vermont), 2
Migration to urban areas. *See also* Urban
    ghettos
    Frazier on, 30–31
Minimum wage
    and 2002 conference at Syracuse
        University, 196
    during Clinton administration,
        174–175
Mogul architecture, Brennan, Elizabeth
    "Liz" and, 8
"The Moment Lost" (Moynihan), 149
"The Moral Quandary of the Black
    Community" (Loury), 147
More Than Just Race (Wilson), 213
Morrison, Toni, 176
Moyers, Bill
    on first reading of Moynihan Report,
        42–43
    on LBJ's attitude toward Moynihan,
        76
    Moynihan seeking advice from, 24–25
    "The Vanishing Family—Crisis in
        Black America," 151
Moynihan, Daniel Patrick "Pat"
    at 2002 conference at Syracuse
        University, 187–189
    "A Family Policy for the Nation,"
        72–73, 86
    academic regard for, 23, 98
    agreement with Coleman, 103–105
    as ambassador to United Nations, 127

Americans for Democratic Action
    and, 7
as assistant secretary of labor for
    policy planning and research,
    11–12
Beyond the Melting Pot, 9–10, 19
career moves of, xv
as chair of Senate Finance Committee,
    169
childhood of, 1–3, 86
on Clinton, Bill, 169–170
comparing Japanese/Chinese
    Americans with blacks, 43–44
consideration of running for political
    office (1965), 23
critics of, 59–62
and *Daedalus* essays after publication
    of Report, 73
death of, 201
defense of Report, 85–86
"Defining Deviancy Down," 165
denial that he leaked initial Report
    information, 67–68
disillusionment with Democrats of,
    111
Du Bois, W. E. B., and, 26
on economics as factor in black family
    problems, 37
"Education and Urban Politics," 98
education of, 2, 4–5, 8
end of serving in Senate, 187
and fallout from memo concerning
    silent black majority, 124–126
on family allowances, 99–100, 194
Family Support Act (FSA) and, 161
and guaranteed income plan, 114
as head of Harvard-MIT Joint Center
    for Urban Studies, 97–98
hostility toward because of being
    white, 76–77
Howard University commencement
    address (1965) and, 44–45

as "idea broker," 101
"Idea Broker in the Race Crisis"
    (*Life*), 99–100
on impact of Watts Riot, 69
influence of black civil rights leaders
    (King) on, 38–39
influence of black civil rights leaders
    (Malcolm X) on, 39
influence of black civil rights leaders
    (Rustin) on, 39–40
influence of black civil rights leaders
    (Silberman) on, 40–41
influence of black civil rights leaders
    (Young) on, 40
influence of father's absence, 6
influence of
    Frazier/Myrdal/Elkin/Glazer on,
    35–36
introduction/marriage to Brennan,
    7–8
"Jobless Negroes and the Boom," 72
joining Kennedy administration, 10
Kennedy, John F., and, 10–11
lectures at John F. Kennedy School of
    Government, 148–150
matriarchal family according to, 41–42
and memo to Wirtz regarding testing
    of blacks, 13
on more than economic hardship
    damaging families, 25–26
move to Middletown, Connecticut, for
    Wesleyan teaching position, 74
One-Third of a Nation, 12–13
as part of Nixon administration,
    109–111
Presidential Medal of Freedom, 187
Preston, Samuel, and, 148
on problem as self-perpetuating, 58
questioning Payton about
    unemployment, 84
and reiteration of family problems
    arising from poverty, 212

and release of Moynihan Report,
    xii–xiii
Religious Right and, 139
resignation at Labor Department, 66
resignation from Nixon
    administration, 126–127
run for City Council of New York,
    73–74, xiv
"The Schism in Black America," 129
as senator from New York, 128
on TANF, 173
taste in fine living of, 4–5
ten years after Report, 129–130
"Toward Equality as a Fact and as a
    Result: The Dilemma of Negro
    Family Structure," 74
on understanding of statistics, 50–51
"The U.S. and the International Labor
    Organization, 1889–1934" (thesis),
    5
as U.S. senator on subcommittee for
    public assistance, 142–143
on Vietnam War, 126–127
on why no solutions offered in Report,
    59–60
working for Harriman, 7
Moynihan, Elizabeth (wife). *See* Brennan,
    Elizabeth "Liz"
Moynihan, John (father), 1, 3
Moynihan, John McCloskey (son), 8, 98
Moynihan, Margaret (mother), 1–4
Moynihan, Maura Russell (daughter), 8, 98
Moynihan, Mike, 3
Moynihan Report. *See also* War on Poverty
    "The Case for National Action" (fifth
    chapter), 57–58
causal forces as
    poverty/unemployment identified
    in, 61
decision to write, 21
Department of Labor and, 47
first coining of phrase, 71

Moynihan Report *(continued)*
    Harvard's revisiting (2007) of, 213
    initial public appearances of, 66–67
    initial reaction to, 71
    "The Negro American Family"
        (second chapter), 50–52
    "The Negro American Revolution"
        (first chapter), 49–50
    not discussed at "To Fulfill These
        Rights" conference, 86, 88
    preface/contents of, 47
    public interpretation of, 63
    quickness of writing, 42
    release of, xii–xiii
    report published as book, 72
    "The Roots of the Problem" (third
        chapter), 52–54
    "The Tangle of Pathology" (fourth
        chapter), 54–57
    unemployment as instability in poor
        families, 19
    unforeseen developments and, 63
Moynihan, Timothy Patrick (son), 8, 98
Moynihan's Bar, 2, 4
Murphy Brown, 162
Murray, Charles, 140–141, 197
Music, as misogynistic, 206
Myrdal, Gunnar, 28–29, 31–32, 34
    on black inner-city areas, 39
    as respected academe, 36

Nader, Ralph, 8
Nation, Nader, Ralph, and, 8
Nation of Islam, 39
National Advisory Commission on Civil
    Disorders, 90
National Assessment of Educational
    Progress (NAEP) tests, 211–212
National Association for the Advancement
    of Colored People (NAACP)
    Brown v. Board of Education and, 203
    Du Bois, W. E. B., and, 26

    Frazier on, 29
    Hooks, Benjamin of, 146
    Legal Defense and Educational Fund,
        Inc., 207
    Moynihan seeking advice from, 24
    Obama and, 210
    Wilkins on criticism of Moynihan, 82
National Book Critics Circle, 164
National Center for Education Statistics,
    SAT of students (1995), 184–185
National Marriage Project, 163
National Organization for Women
    (NOW), 139
National Review, Novak of, 151
National Urban League
    underclass and, 146
    and "unequal treatment for the
        Negro," 16
    Young and, 40
National Welfare Rights Organization
    (NWRO), 119–120
National Youth Administration (NYA), 14
Native Son (Wright), 151–152
Negative income tax, 114
"The Negro American"
    (Clark/Bayard/Moynihan), 66
The Negro American Family (Du Bois),
    27–28
"The Negro American Family" (second
    chapter), 50–52
"The Negro American Revolution" (first
    chapter), 49–50
The Negro Family in Chicago (Frazier), 29
*The Negro Family: The Case for National
    Action. See* Moynihan Report
Neoconservatives
    birth of, 79
    Moynihan as, 101–103
    Moynihan as (late 1960s–early 1970s),
        6
    and Moynihan as senator, 143–144
    Steinfels on Moynihan, 100–101

"A New American Dilemma" (Loury), 147

"The New Crisis: The Negro Family," 67

New Deal's National Youth Administration (NYA), 14

"The New Genteel Racism," 81

New Leader, Moynihan's essays in, 100

New Republic
  "A New American Dilemma" (Loury), 147
  "Reagan's Revenge," 143

New York City Council, Moynihan campaigning for, 66

New York, Moynihan as senator from, 128

New York Review of Books, Jencks' criticism of Report, 78

New York State Government Research Project, 8

New York Times
  and initial reaction to Report, 72
  on Moynihan, 88–89
  Moynihan on Vietnam War, 126–127
  Moynihan's defense of Report, 85–86
  "Urbanologist Pat Moynihan," 98–99

New York Times Magazine
  and Moynihan's memo concerning silent black majority, 125
  "Restoring the Traditional Black Family" (Norton), 150
  view of Moynihan, 159

New York Times Sunday Magazine, on Moynihan, 1–3

Newark/Detroit (1967) violence, 89–90, 98

Newsweek
  John F. Kennedy School of Government (Harvard) and, 148–150
  Moynihan's defense of Report, 85–86
  and Moynihan's memo concerning silent black majority, 125
  printing/selling of Moynihan Report, 66–68

Niebuhr, Reinhold, 85, 101

Nixon administration
  and fallout from Moynihan's memo concerning silent black majority, 124–126
  Family Assistance Plan (FAP) (1969), 115–118
  government programs during, 120–121
  Moynihan as ambassador to United Nations, 127
  Moynihan in, 109–112
  Moynihan resigning from, 126–127
  and policies for inner-city black families, 107
  services strategy to income strategy, 114
  Vietnam War and, 126

Nixon, Richard M., election of, 90

Nobel Prize, 133

Norton, Eleanor Homes, 150, 184

Notre Dame, 3

Novak, Michael, 151

Novak, Robert, having received Report privately, 70–71

Novick, Peter, 36

Obama administration, Race to the Top initiative and, 216

Obama, Barack
  The Audacity of Hope, 212
  on education, 210
  on fatherless black families, xvi
  on responsibilities of black parents, 214–215

Office of Economic Opportunity (OEO)
  birth of, 17
  criticism of Report by, 75
  CSA and, 112
  Moynihan as critic of, 18
  Rumsfield of, 117

Office of Policy Planning and Research, Moynihan Report and, 47

Office of Religion and Race of the
Protestant Council of the City of
New York, 80
One Nation, Two Cultures (Himmelfarb), 183
One-Third of a Nation (Moynihan), 12–13,
24, 56–57
Organization of Afro-American Unity,
Malcolm X and, 39
Organized crime, 54
Orwell, George, 101
Osofsky, Gilbert, 132
The Other America (Harrington), 19, 40
Out-of-wedlock births. *See* Illegitimacy
ratios

Packwood, Robert, 143
Parsons, Talcott
and *Daedalus* essays after publication
of Report, 73
and "unequal treatment for the
Negro," 16
Partisan politics, Moynihan and, 23–24
Pathology. *See also* Clark, Kenneth
Norton on, 150–151
overemphasis of, 80–81
Wilson, William Julius, on, 153
and Young on white racism, 84–85
Patterson, Orlando
on black unemployment rate, 158
in defense of Moynihan, 130
Rituals of Blood: Consequences of
Slavery in Two American
Centuries, 177–178
on underclass, 156–157
Payton, Benjamin
and criticisms of Moynihan, 80–81
Moynihan questioning, 84
Personal Responsibility and Work
Opportunity Reconciliation Act
(PRWORA), 167, 175
Pettigrew, Thomas
on benefits of warm family home, 55

and *Daedalus* essays after publication
of Report, 73
on Ryan, 82
The Philadelphia Negro: A Social Study
(Du Bois), 26–27, 156
Pindars Corners, purchase of, 10
Political influence of low-income families,
122
Popenoe, David, 163, 183
Population Association of America, 147–148
Postal service, and employment as
Moynihan's answer to poverty, 15
Poussaint, Alvin, 206–207
Poverty
1970–1980s, 136–137
1980–2008, 208
1980s–1990s, 145
1995, 173–174
as basic problem, 200
of cohabiting couples, 192
as condition, not trait, 105–106
Earned Income Tax Credit (EITC)
and, 121, 169, 209
employment as Moynihan's answer to,
15–16
Harrington on, 62
matriarchy and, 192
Moynihan's reiteration of family
problems arising from, 212
Preston on, 147–148
recession of 1990–1991 and, 160
underclass and, 146
and the underclass, 156–157
War on Poverty, 6, xi
Powdermaker, Hortense, 28
"The President and the Negro: The
Moment Lost" (Moynihan), 65
Presidential Medal of Freedom, 187
Preston, Samuel
on black unmarried women
misrepresenting selves in census,
176–177

on crime/nonmarital birth, 165
as critic of AFDC, 148
"The Professionalism of Reform"
    (Moynihan), 14
A Profile of the Negro American
    (Pettigrew), 55
The Promised Land (Lemann), 22, 163
Promises I Can Keep: Why Poor Women Put
    Motherhood Before Marriage (Edin
    and Kefalas), 197
Psychology, "The Tangle of Pathology"
    (fourth chapter) and, 56
The Public Interest
    "The Moral Quandary of the Black
        Community" (Loury), 147
    and Moynihan as neoconservative,
        101–102
    Moynihan's essays in, 100
"The Professionalism of Reform"
    (Moynihan), 14

Quayle, Dan, 162

Racial discrimination. *See also* Slavery
    as criticism of Moynihan, 130–131
    and criticisms of Moynihan, 88–89
    and criticisms of Moynihan Report,
        61
    and critics of AFDC, 96–97
    impact of, 157–158
    and Moynihan as ambassador to
        United Nations, 127
    and Moynihan comparing
        Japanese/Chinese Americans with
        blacks, 43–44
    and Moynihan's memo concerning
        silent black majority, 124
    Obama on Moynahan, 212
    and oppression as self-perpetuating to
        structural dislocation, 58
    Osofsky on, 132
    and preface of Moynihan Report, 48

as self-perpetuating, 136
of sexuality of blacks, 95
white resentment of blacks (1968),
    90–91
Rainwater, Lee
    at 2002 conference at Syracuse
        University, 188, 192–193
    as critic of Report, 59
    on criticism of Moynihan, 83
    and *Daedalus* essays after publication
        of Report, 73
    on difficulty of cultural change, 38
    on leak of Report, 67
    poverty and, 106–107
Randolph, A. Philip
    Freedom Budget and, 39–40
    Johnson administration and, 89
    on Johnson's civil rights speech
        (1965), xi
    and "To Fulfill These Rights," 87
Rap music, as misogynistic, 206
Rashad, Phylicia, 147
Reagan administration
    Family Support Act (FSA), 160
    and Moynihan as senator, 158–160
Reagan, Ronald, government programs
    and, 142–143
"Reagan's Revenge," 143
Rebuilding the Nest: A New Commitment to
    the American Family
    (Blankenhorn), 162
Religion, matriarchy of black, 56–57
Religious Right, Dobson, James and, 139
Reporter
    "Epidemic on the Highways"
        (Moynihan), 8
    Moynihan writing for, 8–9
"Restoring the Traditional Black Family"
    (Norton), 150
Rituals of Blood: Consequences of Slavery in
    Two American Centuries
    (Patterson), 177

Rockefeller, Nelson, 112
  winning over Harriman, 8
*Roll Jordan Roll: The World the Slaves
  Made* (Genovese), 132–133
"The Roots of the Problem" (third
  chapter), 52–54
Rossi, Peter, 189
ROTC, 2
Rousseau, Jean-Jacques, 101
Rumsfield, Donald, 117
Rural folkways, urban migration and,
  30–31
Russert, Tim
  as chair of *Meet the Press*, 143
  on mimicking Moynihan's
    mannerisms, 4
Rustin, Bayard
  and feelings toward Moynihan Report,
    77
  as influence on Moynihan, 39–40
  Johnson administration and, 89
  "The Negro American Revolution"
    (first chapter) and, 50
Rutgers University, National Marriage
  Project, 163
Ryan, William
  and criticisms of Moynihan, 81–83
  "Savage Discovery," 84

Sampson, Robert
  on impact of Report in social science
    studies, 136
  on importance/obscurity of Report,
    72
  on Moynihan's report of urban
    neighborhoods, 213
Saturday Evening Post, Moynihan's essays
  in, 100
"Savage Discovery" (Ryan), 84
Sawhill, Isabel
  at 2002 conference at Syracuse
    University, 188

and early learning programs for
  children, 196
"The Schism in Black America"
  (Moynihan), 129
School desegregation, Nixon
  administration and, 126
Scissors effect, 57, 67
Segregation, inner cities contribution to, 56
Selective Service System, failure of men on
  mental/physical tests of, 12–13
Senate Finance Committee, Moynihan as
  chair, 169
Senate seat
  and Moynihan as senator, 158–160
  Moynihan's winning of, 1
  Senate's view of Moynihan, 158–159
Sensationalism
  in African American cultural
    demagogues, 184
  Gans' summary of Report, 78
  Lewis on, 83–84
  Senate's view of Moynihan, 158–159
  and Steinfels on Moynihan, 101
Services strategy, 114
Sexual Suicide (Gilder), 138
Sexuality
  The Audacity of Hope (Obama) and,
    212
  and CDC (2008) diseases in African
    American girls, 208
  economic condition as influence on,
    27–28
  as healthy in slaves, 133
  impact of decline of marriage on
    families, 92
  need for sex education, 209
  and negative feelings toward
    Moynihan, 77
  noninclusion in Moynihan Report of
    changing mores, 63
  racism and, 95
  Ryan on, 82

Shadow of the Plantation (Johnson), 28
Sharpton, Al, 171, 216
Shaughnessy, Elise, 159
Shaw, Theodore, 207
Sheraton Park Hotel. *See* "To Fulfill These Rights"
Shriver, Sargent, job programs and, 17
Silberman, Charles
  in defense of the Report, 74
  as influence on Moynihan, 40–41
  on Payton's criticism, 81
Slavery
  Beloved (Morrison) and, 176
  Billingsley on, 131
  and decomposition of Negro family (Young), 40
  Elkins on, 33–34, 36
  Frazier on brutality of, 30
  as good/profitable, 133
  impact of memories of, 180–181
  legacy of, 27–29, 33–34, 130
  as major factor in black family problems, 37
  and preface of Moynihan Report, 48–49
  Preston on, 177–178
  and rates of marriage, 94–95
  and resiliency of black people, 132
  Roll Jordan Roll: The World the Slaves Made (Genovese), 132–133
  "The Roots of the Problem" (third chapter), 52–54
  "The Tangle of Pathology" (fourth chapter) and, 55
  Wilson, William Julius, on, 154
Slavery: A Problem in American Institutional and Intellectual Life (Elkins), 33
Smeeding, Timothy, at 2002 conference at Syracuse University, 188, 192–193
Social change
  Billingsley on impact of slavery and, 131

Catholic philosophy of, 15
Coleman on, 103–105
contraception/abortion and, 92
"Defining Deviancy Down" (Moynihan), 165
Du Bois, W. E. B., and, 26
and guaranteed income plan, 114
isolation, 156
marriage in 1980s, 138
and marriage/sex impacts on families, 94
Moynihan's sweeping observations of, 14
Patterson on, 178–179
poverty and, 105–107
Social Security Administration
  inflation indexing and, 120
  poverty and, 136–137
  Reagan and, 142
  welfare reform and, 115
Stack, Carol, 131–132, 153–154
Stagflation, 141
Stapelfield, Henry, 3
Stapelfield, Tommy, 3
Staples, Robert, 133
Steele, Shelby, 164
Steinfels, Peter, 100–101
Structural dislocations, as self-perpetuating, 58
Student Nonviolent Coordinating Committee (SNCC), and "To Fulfill These Rights," 87
Students for a Democratic Society (SDS), threat to burn Moynihan's home by, 126
Styron, William, 131
Substance abuse
  Moynihan, John, and, 3
  underclass and, 146
  Wilson, James Q., on, 185
Supplementary Security Income (SSI), 120
  poverty and, 136–137

Supreme Court, 11, 210
Syracuse University, 8

"The Tangle of Pathology" (fourth
    chapter), 54–57
Task Force on Manpower Conservation,
    12
Teach for America program, 210
Temporary Assistance to Needy Families
    (TANF), 172–174
Tet Offensive, 90
Time
    on life of Moynihan, 1–3
    and Moynihan as ambassador to
        United Nations, 127
    on Moynihan joining Kennedy
        administration, 10
    "Today's Native Son," 151–152
"To Fulfill These Rights"
    convening of, 86
    LBJ calling for conference, 66, x
"Today's Native Son," 151–152
Tomorrow's Tomorrow: The Black Woman
    (Ladner), 131
"Toward Equality as a Fact and as a
    Result: The Dilemma of Negro
    Family Structure" (Moynihan),
    74
Trinity United Church of Christ
    (Chicago), 155
*The Truly Disadvantaged: The Inner City,
    the Underclass, and Public Policy*
    (Wilson), 152–156
Tufts University (Massachusetts), 2, 4
Tuskegee Institute, Frazier and, 29
*Two Nations: Black and White, Separate,
    Hostile, Unequal* (Hacker), 164

Underclass
    according to Auletta, 146
    poverty and, 156–157
The Underclass (Auletta), 146

Unemployment rate. *See also* Employment
    1967, 89
    and AFDC, 25
    armed forces and, 56
    of black males (1969–1970), 137
    blacks/whites (1964), 15
    economic condition masking, 72
    exception of war years to, 95
    and initial public appearance of
        Moynihan Report, 67
    and instability in poor families, 19
    Moynihan questioning Payton about, 84
    "The Negro American Family"
        (second chapter) and, 51
    Patterson on, 158
    relationship with illegitimacy, 53–54
    relationship with welfare, 57–58
    "Restoring the Traditional Black
        Family" (Norton), 150
    underclass and, 146
    Young on, 40
United Nations, Moynihan as ambassador
    to, 127
University of Chicago, 29
Unsafe at Any Speed (Nader), 8
Urban Affairs Council, Moynihan as
    executive secretary of, 110–111
Urban ghettos. *See also* Violence
    isolation in, 62
    and preface of Moynihan Report,
        48–49
    as self-perpetuating, 136
    violence (1967) in, 89
Urban League, 120
Urban migration, Frazier on, 30–31
"Urbanologist Pat Moynihan," 98–99
"The U.S. and the International Labor
    Organization, 1889–1934" (thesis),
    5

Vanishing Family—Crisis in Black
    America" (Moyers), 151

Vanity Fair, Shaughnessy, Elise, in, 159
Vanocur, Sander, 4, 10
Victimization, African Americans and, 164
Vietnam War
    antiwar sentiments regarding, 76, xv
    impact on America of, 88
    Johnson administration and, 89
    LBJ and antiwar activists, 66
    Moynihan and black GIs from, 98–99
    Moynihan on, 126–127
    Nixon administration and, 126
    Tet Offensive, 90
Violence
    1967 rates of, 89
    1980s–1990s, 145
    blamed on "hoodlums and juvenile
        delinquents," 67
    Chicago (2008–2009), 208
    and impulses of low-income young
        black men, 209
    Kent State University, 126
    King, Rodney, and, 163–164
    and Moynihan's memo concerning
        silent black majority, 124
    Newark/Detroit (1967) and, 89–90, 98
    Watts Riot, 67–68, xiii
Volunteers in Training to America
    (VISTA), birth of, 17
Voting Rights Act
    as hope for equality, 88
    LBJ signing of, 66
    Moynihan on, 42

Wagner, Robert, Jr., campaign of, 7
Wallace, Michelle, 180
War on Poverty
    Elementary and Secondary Education
        Act and, xi
    as "hastily assembled," 6
    Johnson administration and, 14
    OEO and, 17–18
Warren, Earl, 34

Washington Post
    and initial reaction to Report, 72
    Moynihan's defense of Report, 85–86
    and Moynihan's memo concerning
        silent black majority, 125–126
Watts Riot. *See also* Violence
    and expectations of black people, 89
    impact on America of, 70, 189
    and initial reaction to Report, 71–72
    and reception to Report, 67–68, 88
    surprise of, xiii
Welfare. *See also* Government programs
    1997–2004, 174
    AFDC explosion, 105
    and breakdown of Negro family
        (Moynihan), 52, 171
    Bush, George H. W., and, 161–162
    Clinton, Bill, and, 165–170, 172–173
    Congress (1987–1988) and, 159–160
    Food Stamps, 120
    and increase of illegitimacy
        (1970s–1990s), 187–197
    liberalization of, 209–210
    Moynihan blaming, 59–60
    Moynihan in Nixon administration
        trying to reform, 113
    Moynihan on (1990s), 6
    Moynihan Report and, xiv
    Murray on, 140–141
    National Welfare Rights Organization
        (NWRO) and, 119–120
    Personal Responsibility and Work
        Opportunity Reconciliation Act
        (PRWORA) and, 167, 175
    rates (1960–1975)/cost of, 96
    Reagan on, 142
    reform, 114–118
    relationship with unemployment, 57–58
    underclass and, 146
    and white resentment of blacks (1968),
        90
    Wilson, William Julius, on, 154–155

Welfare Fighter, 120

Wesleyan University, 74, 85

Westmoreland, William, as Vietnam
    commander, xv

When Work Disappears (Wilson), 169

Whitehead, Barbara Dafoe, 163

Wilkins, Roger, 204

Wilkins, Roy
    as defender of Moynihan, 82
    and "To Fulfill These Rights," 87

Will, George, 151, 159

Williams, John, 118

Williams, Juan, 206

Wills, Garry, 100

Wilson, James Q.
    and *Daedalus* essays after publication
        of Report, 73
    on family issues, 185, 189
    on illegitimacy/matriarchy/dropout
        rates, 181–183, 185
    and Moynihan at Harvard, 98
    "Moynihan's scissors" and, 25–26
    on praise of Moynihan, 184
    and support of Moynihan's tenure at
        Harvard, 97
    as supporter of TANF, 174

Wilson, William Julius
    on cultural frames as explanations for
        behavior, 180
    and Harvard's revisiting (2007) of
        Moynihan Report, 213
    on impact of economy on
        unemployment, 197
    More Than Just Race, 213
    *The Truly Disadvantaged: The Inner
        City, the Underclass, and Public
        Policy*, 152–156
    When Work Disappears, 169

Winning the Race (McWhorter), 206

Wirtz, W. Willard
    asking Moynihan to join Department
        of Labor, 10
    as Department of Labor head, 11
    on first reading of Moynihan Report,
        43
    and memo regarding creation of
        Negro subculture through welfare,
        17
    and memo regarding creation of *The
        Negro Family...*, 21, 25
    and memo regarding testing of blacks,
        13
    and memo regarding "unequal
        treatment for the Negro," 16
    on Moynihan Report, xii–xiii
    negative feelings toward Moynihan,
        75
    and speed of writing Moynihan
        Report, 42–43

Woman's House of Detention, 1

Women of childbearing age. *See also*
    Illegitimacy ratios
    baby boom increase of, 96
    decrease of, 96

Woodrow Wilson International Center for
    Scholars, 187

Wright, Jeremiah, 155

Wright, Richard, 151–152

Yancey, William
    on criticism of Moynihan, 59, 83
    and leak of Report, 67

Yeats, William Butler, 101

Young, Whitney
    To Be Equal, 82
    as executive director of National
        Urban League, 16
    as influence on Moynihan, 40
    and negative feelings toward
        Moynihan Report, 77
    as NWRO's director, 120
    on white racism, 84